# The Democracy of the Dead

# The Democracy of the Dead

*Dewey, Confucius, and the Hope for Democracy in China*

David L. Hall and Roger T. Ames

OPEN COURT

Chicago and Lasalle, Illinois

*ABOUT THE COVER*

The terracotta bust of Dewey represented on the cover is a part of the John Dewey Papers, Special Collections/Morris Library, Southern Illinois University in Carbondale, Illinois. The photograph used in the cover design was taken by Robert Joseph O'Neil. Though the specific origin of the bust is unknown, it is believed to have been presented to Dewey at some time during his visit to Japan and China in 1919–1921. The cover's background is a portrait of Confucius and his seventy-two disciples carved in wood photographed by the China External Cultural Exchange Association.

**To order books from Open Court, call 1-800-815-2280.**

Open Court Publishing Company is a division of Carus Publishing Company.

©1999 by Carus Publishing Company

First printing 1999

Printed and bound in the United States of America.

**Library of Congress Cataloging-in-Publication Data**

Hall, David L.
    The democracy of the dead: Dewey, Confucius, and the hope for democracy in China / David L. Hall and Roger T. Ames.
        p.    cm.
    Includes bibliographical references and index.
    ISBN 0–8126–9394–9 (alk. paper)
    1. Democracy—China. 2. Political culture—China. 3. Confucianism—China.
4. Dewey, John, 1859–1952—Contributions in democracy.  I. Ames, Roger T., 1947–
II. Title.
JQ1516.H34   1998
320.951—dc21

                              98–40756
                                CIP

Tradition means giving votes to the most obscure of all classes, our ancestors. It is the democracy of the dead. Tradition refuses to submit to the small and arrogant oligarchy of those that merely happen to be walking about. All democrats object to men being disqualified by accident of birth; tradition objects to their being disqualified by accident of death.

— G. K. Chesterton, *The Ethics of Elfland*

# CONTENTS

*For Sondra*

On meeting a person of exceptional character, think to stand shoulder to shoulder with her.

*Analects* 4.17

# ACKNOWLEDGMENTS

This book had its origins in an essay written for the 1995 East-West Conference at the University of Hawai'i entitled "China, Dewey, and the Democracy of the Dead." A number of venues in America, China, Europe, and Korea—too numerous to cite in detail—provided the authors the opportunity to air many of the ideas found in this book.

A month-long visit to Western China, principally Xinjiang province, sponsored by the Asian Studies Development Committee of the University of Hawai'i, and the East-West Center, helped to broaden our sense of the importance of minorities in China.

Participation in the 1996 Bangkok Conference sponsored by the Carnegie Foundation provided an important occasion to reflect upon the issue of human rights in China. Some of the ideas that appeared in the Carnegie journal, *Ethics and International Affairs* 1997, vol. 11, in "Continuing the Conversation on Chinese Human Rights" have been reworked here. In addition, the opportunity to give lectures on the topic of "Confucianism and Pragmatism" in a number of Korean locations further sharpened our understanding of the sense of "Asian Democracy." We thank our several hosts at Sogang University, Seoul; Dongeui University and Forum Shinsago, Pusan; Keimyung University and Kyungbuk National University, Taegu and Chonnam National University, Kwangju. We also wish to thank all the USIS (United States Information Service) representatives involved in this project. Special thanks are due to two USIS officers: To John Sullivan, who was always ready at crucial moments with a happy face, and to Hyun-Sun Sohn, whose translations were, by all accounts, a distinct improvement over our original remarks. Thanks, as well, to Chaibong Hahm, of Yonsei University, for soliciting our participation in the ongoing "Liberal, Social, and Confucian Democracy" initiative in Korea.

We are most grateful to Henry Rosemont, Randy Peerenboom, Dru Gladney, and Jim Buchanan for reading our manuscript in a very rough draft and making suggestions that allowed us to improve the text considerably. And, of course, to Daniel Cole, who sailed us through to final pages.

We happily acknowledge the assistance of Karen Dupell Drickamer, Curator of Manuscripts at the John Dewey Papers, Special Collections/ Morris Library, Southern Illinois University for permission to use the representation of the terracotta bust of Dewey appearing on the cover.

Finally, thanks to Sondra Jones who read the penultimate draft of our manuscript with a persistent impatience for convoluted prose. As much as we have benefited from her keen eye, that is the least of the reasons this book has been dedicated to her.

# Introduction
## *A View from the West*

We should, perhaps, apologize for the rather lengthy introduction that follows. Readers opening a book on the topic of democracy in China may reasonably expect a standard political or socioeconomic approach to the subject. But, as those who read on will soon discover, we offer instead a distinctly philosophical discussion which brackets many political and economic issues in favor of a comparison of broad cultural factors and forces relevant to the possible future shape of "Confucian democracy." Since, however, the arguments of this work are directed not only to readers of a philosophical turn of mind, but to the more practical political and socioeconomic theorists as well, we hope in the following paragraphs to persuade any such who have happened upon these pages that our book can indeed serve as a stimulus to those working in more specialized areas who are seeking as broad a range of evidence and stimulation as possible.

## 1. Romanticism, Pragmatism, and Cultural Difference

Alternately comforting and threatening, the realization of China's entrance into the modern world increasingly qualifies the sensibilities of Anglo-European Nations. The thought is comforting to those who feel that the engagements made possible by virtue of a common ground are far more productive than the infrequent and one-sided contacts that, until recently perhaps, have done little to help and much to harm the Chinese people. And China's entrance into the family of nations is threatening to those who recognize the vast potentialities for economic and military growth possessed by an awakening China, and who, as well, sense that China's "enlightenment" may come at the expense of the

West. These contrasting responses, combined in proper proportion, well illustrate the Chinese understanding of "crisis (*weiji* 危機)" as expressive of both "danger (*wei* 危)" and "opportunity (*ji* 機)." For some years to come, this particular sense of crisis will be the healthiest attitude for both the Chinese and we in the West.

But maintaining such a balanced perspective is difficult at best. Viewed from the West, China remains pretty much the exotic land it has always been. As is the case with any one or any thing experienced as strangely "other," two distinct attitudes shape our best efforts to understand that country. It might seem overdrawn to characterize these attitudes by appeal to the *mysterium tremendum et fascinans* which Rudolph Otto used to describe the experience of the radically other. However, there truly are elements of both *fear* and *fascination* in our feelings about China. And when, as so often is the case, the ambiguity becomes too disturbing, we tend to select out of this complex experience the feeling that satisfies us best. Which is to say: We either *demonize* China, or we *romanticize* her.

Presently, we are more inclined toward demonization. Politicians and the media communicate a vision of China as an "oriental despotism" whose government is bent upon denying essential rights to its people. Consider the following report from the *Washington Post*, November 7, 1997:

> The House voted overwhelmingly yesterday to bar Chinese officials from the United States, accusing them of "the worst human rights abuses in the world." Employing heated rhetoric and comparing communist China to the Nazi regime, lawmakers forcefully rejected President Clinton's efforts to work closer with Beijing to promote greater freedom through greater contact.

The malaise that has recently overcome certain segments of American society significantly complicates the demonizing impulse. Now that the United States has inherited the mantle of the world's only superpower, it seems at best tentative, unsure of how to use its power. As the psychology of such circumstances often dictates, there seems an inverse relationship between the senses of power and of purpose among our political and cultural leaders.

The recognition of this malaise has recently been cogently expressed by a coalition of American public figures—Democrats, Republicans, and Independents—in a document entitled, *A Call to Civil Society—Why Democracy Needs Moral Truths*:

> In what direction are we tending? In our present condition are we likely to remain the best hope for a world in which so many human beings still endure neglect and injustice? Are we likely to sustain our commitment to freedom and justice for all, so that those in our midst who are suffering might yet be lifted up by our democratic faith and purpose?[1]

The authors' reply to these questions is that without moral content our principles and practices will inevitably lead American democracy into serious decline. Our sense of moral malaise has led to an unaccustomed feeling of vulnerability. Under these conditions an economically and politically emerging China must be considered a singular threat.

In direct contrast to the demonizers, there are those who consistently romanticize China. Since the inception of contacts between Europe and China, a number of intellectuals—from Leibniz and Voltaire in the seventeenth and eighteenth centuries, down to the present—have been powerfully attracted to the culture of China.

The tendency to romanticize alternative cultures is an occupational hazard of the intellectual, since the "other" of one's own culture may be prized as both a stimulus to one's thinking and a legitimate check upon the temptation to universalize one's parochial sentiments. This vague romanticizing of Chinese culture is shared by perhaps the majority of scholars interested in that country.

Culture critics who would moderate the extremes of individualism in Western societies express this romanticism at a slightly less vague level by appeal to communitarian values. These individuals see in Chinese society, if not the Chinese government, a model for emulation that might stimulate a turning away from the selfishness and greed associated with late industrial capitalism.

Proponents of the superiority of Western values find the intellectuals' tender-minded approach to China all too naïve. There is certainly some basis for this suspicion since China is presently experiencing, in its cities and villages alike, a rush for wealth unlike any ever witnessed in that country. Deng Xiaoping's slogan "To be rich is glorious" seems to have become the motto of the masses.

Even with this acknowledgment, it remains true that the dangers of romanticizing China are certainly less pernicious than are those of demonizing it. In fact, there is little possibility of productive mutual engagement between China and the West without some romantic inclinations on the part of both parties. To gain an understanding of China beyond its strictly governmental presence, it is necessary that one take up the perspective of romantic wonder—albeit a chastened, second-order mode of that sensibility.

Though essential to the entertainment of alternative cultures, this romanticism must be tempered by a distinctly pragmatic attitude. Surprisingly, there is a rather close relationship between pragmatism and romanticism. Along with the romanticist, the pragmatist opposes an overweening rationality that seeks above all the objectivity and generality of the "God's-eye" view. The pragmatist, as well as the romantic, eschews dogmatic, principled approaches in order to ensure openness to alternatives. Unfortunately, this openness is often seen as a casual appreciation of cultural differences merely because they are enticingly "other."

But pragmatic sensibilities are tempered by historicist methodologies that urge one in a concretely realist direction. The same historicism that allows us to appreciate the uniqueness of both Western and Chinese sensibilities prevents us from accepting the inevitability of any particular cultural development. The pragmatic perspective enjoins engagement that opens all participants in the conversation to possibilities for change. Such openness offers one the best chance of avoiding the narrower forms of arrogance associated with a reductionist mentality.

The pragmatist does not ask about the truth of propositions, but is concerned, rather, with the effectiveness of the beliefs that transform such propositions into tools of inquiry and action. Further, a pragmatic perspective does not require the press toward consensus with respect to principles or beliefs. Rather, it urges that the responsible thinker suggest ways of engaging contrasting or conflicting beliefs at the level of social or cultural praxis.

This method enjoins a celebration of the differences between Chinese and Western cultures, and a consideration of what is viable in both sensibilities. To the proponents of the inevitable march of Western enlightenment, such efforts might seem an expression of cultural relativism. But the openness of the pragmatic approach does not entail relativism in any sense that the term is currently bandied about in intellectual circles.

The cultural relativist, if such exists, purports to claim that no set of values, or system of beliefs, may be found superior to any other. To say that no position may be held superior to another by appeal to evidence and argument is one thing. To deny that one position may be more effective or useful than another in specific circumstances, or that one might be required to act upon a principle even if that principle is unproven, is quite another.

The proverbial "atheist in a foxhole" would be easier to find than a relativist in any situation calling for immediate action. Ironically enough, the only relativists around are those who, by virtue of their dogmatic espousal of mutually conflicting dogmas, are unable to demonstrate the superiority of their perspectives, and are fated to flail about in a sea of stubbornly conflicting visions.

Our pragmatic and pluralistic approach to China presumes an attitude recently expressed most cogently by Vaclav Havel. Persuaded that a superficial commonality overlaying world cultures at a popular level belies truly profound differences in ways of living and thinking, Havel insists that these differences must be advertised:

> This new single epidermis of world civilization merely covers or conceals the immense variety of cultures, of peoples, of religious worlds, of historical traditions and historically formed attitudes, all of which in a sense lie "beneath" it. At the same time, even as the veneer of world civilization expands, this "underside" of humanity, this hidden dimension of it, demands more and more clearly to be heard and to be granted a right to life.[2]

The runaway penetration of science and technology, and the unrelenting ingress of capitalist economic forms, exacerbates the danger of the increased exposure by alternative cultures to the universalistic claims of Western culture. This spectral juggernaut makes Havel's cautions particularly timely. In spite of them, there seems to be no consensus in the Western academy as to whether these cultural differences even exist, never mind whether they are of any real importance. At the same time, there is a general agreement that the advances in science, technology, and capitalism are good for all.

With respect to the question of the differences between China and the West, Angus Graham broke with the other doyens of the sinological world by affirming the fundamental importance of cultural differences. In his 1986 *Times Literary Supplement* review of Benjamin Schwartz's *The World of Thought in Ancient China,* Graham noted:

> Some Western explorers of Chinese thought prefer to think of the Chinese as like ourselves, others do not. One tendency is to see in Chinese thought, behind all the divergences, an inquiry into universal problems, through ideas which transcend cultural and linguistic differences; the other is to uncover, behind all the resemblances, distinctions between key words which relate to culture-bound conceptual schemes and to structural differences between Chinese and the Indo-European languages. Benjamin I. Schwartz's *The World of Thought in Ancient China* is a very distinguished representative of the former point of view.[3]

Some scholars are persuaded that the conversation is richest where there is the greatest degree of commensurability. Others believe that beneath "the epidermis of world civilization," there are profound differences that derive from culture-specific ways of thinking and living. Some believe that failing to regard the commonality as most important is to deny the Chinese their humanity; others believe that to assert such an essential commonality is to deny the Chinese their cultural uniqueness.

Graham comes down firmly on the side of difference. We intend to stand with him, and to argue that these differences, at least with respect to China, are both real and fundamental. They can be either an obstacle or a resource, depending on how we engage them. Come what may, they cannot be denied.

Beyond the simple need to report the differences between Chinese and Western cultures with some accuracy, it is essential that these differences be assayed with respect to their potential pragmatic benefit. The mere existence of Chinese culture, with its distinctive institutions and modes of social organization, challenges any smug belief that we in the West have discovered the only viable route to the future. Recognizing this could permit us to avoid an extended period of cultural stagnation born of complacency.

## 2. Modernization, Globalization, and Ethnocentricity

Those most sanguine about the future of Chinese/Western relations presume that modernization is a consequence of dynamics emergent from the European Enlightenment, which is in turn the result of the rationalization of personal, social, economic, and political activities. With but a slight nod to the principle of *mutatis mutandis*, these individuals comport themselves as if China is on the way to becoming "modern" by uncritically embracing liberal democracy, free enterprise capitalism, and increasingly rational technologies. These agencies, it is assumed, will bring with them individual rights and burgeoning freedoms, a high standard of living, and increased control of one's environs as the rewards of entering the modern age.

Though this constitutes heresy to the proponents of universal enlightenment, there is good reason to believe with the authors of this work that the great metanarrative of enlightenment, modernity, and modernization is but one more provincial myth. The principal content of this myth is the belief that being human, and having a correct conception of the human person, means to be and to think pretty much as Anglo-Europeans do.

The irony of this situation is intense: Western ethnocentricity is expressed in a firm belief in the universality of our (provincial) ideals. That is to say: the tacit or explicit belief in universals—Reason, Science, Human Rights—is the mask worn by ethnocentrism in the classical West. We need to face the fact that very few Chinese would hold the same truths as do we to be "self-evident."

Comparing Chinese and Western values involves the comparison of two sets of ethnocentric beliefs. Cultures such as China's that freely acknowledge their ethnocentricity are condemned by Westerners ignorant of the provincial character of their own ideals. Indeed, when the authority of those ideals is called into question by alternative cultural sensibilities, we continue to argue on dogmatic grounds for the "obvious" superiority of our modern values and institutions, and to believe that all the peoples of the world, had they but the opportunity, would live in one of the North Atlantic democracies.

Most of us who occupy a privileged place in a Western democracy consider ourselves autonomous individuals. We possess natural rights. We own a faith in our ability to search out the truth of things, and express some confidence that reason and good will can solve many, if not all of our problems. We are respectful of governmental authority when it serves to nurture freedom and autonomy for its citizens, but are perfectly capable of becoming adversaries of the government if and when it threatens those same values. We identify ourselves with ideas, values, and principles that we believe *reasonable*, and employ our religious, scientific, and political institutions as instruments of their implementation.

Among our intellectual elites there is doubtless a great deal less naive assent to transcendent notions of reason, but the trust in *objectivity*, even in this august population, still lingers. The visions of our natural and social scientists, our theologians and philosophers alike, remain premised upon a belief in an objective order of things. For many of us this faith extends to the idea that human beings have objective natures, identifiable characteristics that make us essentially the same even when moving from one society or culture to another.

There are, of course, rapid changes in these beliefs, especially at the level of philosophic thinking. These changes could eventually lead us to yield the tacit presumptions of objectivity and universality that still ground our central beliefs. But we are far from abandoning our sense of the absoluteness of reason and rationality. This is particularly so with respect to the belief in universal rights and a common human nature— the very ideas Chinese perspectives challenge most directly.

Modernization is a given—at least in the more neutral sense of *globalization*. In its most productive meaning, globalization would constitute a democratic dynamic insuring that the world is "pan-accessible" in both a geographical and cultural sense. That is to say, in a normatively globalized society, all geographical areas and cultural forms constituting the human world would be available to all others. However, globalization has hardly proceeded democratically. Until now, the principal elements of globalization involve those economic, political, and technological dynamics originating in, and sustained by, Anglo-European cultures. Thus, the West is colonizing the rest of the world in accordance with its decidedly parochial values, and the consequential "global" culture looks more and more like the provincial Western world.

Hope for a democratized form of globalization lies largely in the likelihood that Asia, principally China, will be able to provide cultural values and institutions sufficiently attractive to the rest of the World that the Western dominance of the processes of globalization will be mitigated.

In the process of modernization, China will surely establish economic and technological relations with other developed nations. This will occasion internal changes in China. First, some infrastructural and socio-legal changes will be required to accommodate the economic and technological imperatives. Sociopolitical changes may be expected as a result of, for example, any economic growth that raises the average standard of living, and those technologies that alter the manner in which information is acquired and transmitted.

Inevitabilist proponents of Western modernity expect that these changes will lead to increased rights and freedoms for individuals and that soon China will begin to look much like any modern Western nation. For a variety of reasons articulated in the following chapters, we endorse a quite different set of possibilities.

Clearly, the open-minded individual must consider the possibility that globalization may proceed along more democratic lines, and that an increased mutuality of influence may be achieved. This same individual might consider the likelihood that the China that may well come to dominate the twenty-first century world will not be the jerry-rigged, pseudo-Marxist totalitarian society existing principally in the minds of uninformed politicians, and even less informed journalists. One of the greatest defects in the understanding of contemporary China is the failure to grasp the fact that it is Confucius, not Karl Marx, who dominates the culture.

Just as the China of the future is unlikely to be Marxist in character, neither will it be the Netscaped, McDonaldized Theme Park of which inevitablists have begun to dream. China may well maintain more of its traditional character than most now suspect. If so, it may be able to enter the modern world largely on its own terms.

If this scenario is to be taken seriously, we need to reverse polarities and see China as the source as well as the target of globalization. There are two obvious implications of this reversal: First, we must learn more about China in order better to discern the shape of our own future. Second, we need to enter a conversation with China in which the terms are set equally by both parties.

Now that the veneer of Marxism is peeling away from Chinese culture, it is unlikely that China will be speaking the language of Marxist socialism in its conversations with the West. China will come to the table as a "rites"- (not "rights") based society. If this is indeed the case, and if the West insists upon urging the American, rights-based, liberal democracy with its attendant modes of capitalism and technological activities, the parties will be at loggerheads. It is, therefore, incumbent upon us to ask after the potential values of Chinese social and cultural forms before insisting that China become like us. Indeed, we may find that we have something to learn from the Chinese.

# 3. The Argument and Three Fallacies

The rapid growth of the economic and political presence of Asian nations has become an increasingly important topic for discussion around the world. These discussions have as one of their several foci reflections upon the notion of "Asian democracies." This book is a contribution to those discussions specifically with regard to the question of the hope for democracy in China. One of our purposes in writing this work is to defend the value of a distinctly philosophical approach to this issue.

In part 1 of our work we undertake to identify principal features of contemporary China as a distinctive cultural entity. Our argument here is that the image of a uniform and unified China expressed in the characterization "People of the Han" masks an exceedingly complex, highly pluralistic, society currently confronting a series of internal and external forces that threaten to undermine its traditional foundations.

The challenges to the myth of Han cultural unity include external pressures from the non-Chinese world, ethnic conflicts, tensions associated with the increased importance of local identities, economic competition within a growing market economy, class conflict, and a host of competing ideologies concerned with the proper direction of China's modernization.

In part 2, we discuss the narrative strands of interpretation that form the complex concept of "modernity" and argue that modernity, so conceived, is clearly a Western invention whose relevance for the shaping of China's future can by no means be taken for granted.

China and the West are termini of contrasting historical narratives. That fact necessitates some sensitivity to the possible irrelevance of certain dominant elements of Western culture to the realities of Chinese sensibilities. Specifically, Western interpreters of China should make every effort to avoid the imposition of provincially grounded economic or political doctrines under the guise of promoting modernization of the Chinese world.

If we are to benefit from an appreciation of the differences between China and the West, it is important to question the naive assumption that modernization must be solely a Western dynamic. It is likely a great mistake to believe that individualist, rights-based democracy, capitalism, and technological imperatives are inevitable consequences of human development. The tacit assumption that "modernization equals Westernization" must be abandoned. Hopefully, it may be replaced by a belief which allows that globalization may accommodate both *Easternization* as well as Westernization.

The chapters of part 3 argue that China has always been, and will continue to be, a communitarian society and that accommodating the legitimate desires of the Chinese people requires the promotion of a communitarian form of democracy seriously at odds with the liberal democratic model that presently dominates Western democracies. This will best be accomplished, we claim, by appealing to the communitarian strain of thought within our own American tradition. To this end we offer John Dewey's pragmatic vision of democracy as best suited to engage the realities of Chinese social practice and to support the realization of a "Confucian democracy" in China.

There is, of course, a significant irony occasioned by our selection of Dewey's thinking as the basis upon which to offer our proposals. Dewey's thought, which for a time was dramatically influential in determining the shape of Chinese educational institutions, was systematically uprooted after the Communist revolution. All of Dewey's books received line by line refutations, and millions of words were written in the effort to erase all traces of Dewey from the Chinese sensibility. We hope to demonstrate that placing Dewey under erasure in China was as serious a mistake as was the attempt to write Marx in bold letters across Chinese culture.

Finally, in part 4 we elaborate a model of "Confucian democracy." In these concluding chapters we offer an analysis of the senses of the individual, the role of ritual, and the issue of human rights entailed by Confucian thought. We do not ignore the serious defects of traditional Confucianism illustrated by the isolation of minorities, gender inequities, and an overall disinterest in the rule of law. In spite of these past failings, we argue that, on balance, there are resources within the Confucian tradition for constructing a coherent model of viable and humane democracy that remains true to the communitarian sensibilities of traditional China while avoiding many of the defects of rights-based liberalism.

One way of characterizing our work is simply to say that we are attempting to defend pragmatism against the "pragmatists." Pragmatic perspectives on the question of democracy in China may easily be misconceived as discussions motored exclusively by narrowly economic and/or political concerns. We would argue that this presumably "pragmatic" approach constricts the subject altogether too much, threatening to reduce our perspective upon the principal issues to that of the proverbial "frog in the well."

We hope to show in part that the most effective resort to pragmatism requires an understanding of the term in a distinctly philosophical sense. The pragmatic tradition in America is a philosophy of praxis which nonetheless requires that one take account of the complex set of values associated with peoples and institutions. This argues for an appeal to *culture*.

Discussions of Asian democracy from the economic or political perspective shy away from appealing to culture for a variety of reasons. First and foremost, such appeals seem to entail a kind of "culture is destiny" argument. The irony of this criticism is that deterministic arguments are far more likely to be found among political and economic theorists. Claims concerning the ubiquitous desire for power, or for profit, lie at the base of many such accounts of world events.

The pragmatic perspective that requires arguments be made on behalf of practical relevance rather than theoretical truth by no means enjoins an abandonment of cultural explanation. On the contrary, any attempt to ignore the broad range of cultural variables that might serve as guides or goads of action is distinctly *un*pragmatic.

Our interest in the pragmatic import of cultural factors will require occasional discussions of the conceptual background of elements relevant to a Confucian understanding of democracy. We must insist upon indulgence from the more practical-minded social and political theorists who can be indifferent to such discussions. While it may be possible to get along without much philosophical archaeology when dealing with the family of notions generally dominant within one's own cultural milieu, comparative Chinese/Western thought can benefit enormously from raising to the level of consciousness the rather dramatic differences between the conceptual clusters of the two cultures from out of which notions such as "individual," "society," "law," and "rights" emerged.

We agree with the more moderate political or economic theorists, that events are often shaped by specific decisions relevant to concrete circumstances that may or may not involve explicit appeal to so-called "cultural values." But we further hold that the influence of cultural values does not have to be explicit to be important.

In this work we shall be arguing, first, for the unsuitability of the central tradition of rights-based liberalism for the Chinese situation. Second, we shall suggest that traditional Confucianism contains elements that might well be translated into a communitarian form of democratic society. The combination of these two arguments may give our work the appearance of a rather idealistic apology for China against the Western world.

Our argument can be read in this fashion only if one forgets the difference between political and economic analyses on the one hand, and cultural analysis, on the other. Economic and political approaches are largely focused upon governmental institutions. Cultural analyses are concerned with a broad range of values embedded in social, ethical, aesthetic, and religious sensibilities. Our cultural approach permits us to recognize promising elements in Chinese society and culture that strictly political and economic analyses could easily overlook.

We are certainly aware of the egregious failings of the present Chinese government. With respect to the issue of human rights, for example, that government has compiled a sorry record. The widespread atrocities inflicted upon the Tibetan people over the last fifty years—"re-education," imprisonment, torture, execution—go beyond human rights violations. These abuses—government sanctioned criminality—are part of a general effort to eradicate Tibetan culture. In addition to the assault upon the Tibetan minority, Uighur Muslims in Xinjiang province are closely surveilled and tightly controlled. Moreover, there are countless instances of the PRC government's gross repression of the political actions of Han Chinese. The 1989 Tiananmen Square massacre has come to symbolize that repression to the world at large.

Neither are we innocent of the limitations of institutionalized Confucianism with respect to the possibilities of promoting a viable democracy in China. The rigid hierarchical structure of the family, the abuse of paternal authority, a depressed status for women, are clearly potential hazards of any society that attempts to implement Confucianism *tout court.* Even in its ideal form, certain elements of the Confucian sensibility must be adjusted in order to accommodate the most viable forms of democratic institutions.

Our reason for not including lengthy indictments of the failings of the Chinese government or of traditional institutional Confucianism while, nonetheless, criticizing Western attempts to export individualistic, rights-based democracy to China, is that our cultural perspective requires us to ask after the relative value to China of democratic institutions that may be read out of its own cultural base as opposed to those that have evolved from a contrasting cultural ground.

Our endorsement of Confucian values as the matrix out of which democracy might emerge is by no means an endorsement of either the Chinese government or of institutionalized Confucianism. The consideration is that we are not focused upon government or social institutions, but upon the broader cultural milieu. As the chief American spokesman for communitarian democracy, John Dewey, insisted: *Democracy is not about institutions and governments; it is about communities.* The principal obstacle to the realization of *effective* democracy in both Asia and the West lies in the failure to recognize this central fact.

In the following chapters we have attempted, doubtless with only limited success, to avoid three fallacies that inevitably threaten theoretical analysis of the sort we have undertaken. The first is *The Fallacy of the Single Perspective* which argues that, ultimately, there is really but one adequate manner of envisioning one's subject.

This fallacy is most often committed by individuals who reduce the consideration of a topic to a single disciplinary perspective. Such individuals claim that the responsible thinker must choose from among distinctive theoretical viewpoints—political, economic, sociological, philosophical—the one that permits one to "get it right." As pragmatists, we do not wish to exclude a priori any particular contribution to the ongoing discussion concerning the hope for democracy in China. We only wish to insist upon the value of our pragmatic perspective as one voice in that conversation.

There is a second, slightly more subtle manner that leads one to commit the Single Perspective fallacy. Theoretical discussions of the hope for democracy in China are conditioned far more by the political and cultural affiliations of the discussants than by any ideological conflicts that might be evident in their respective positions. For example, in a typical conference of the type often attended by the authors of this book, participants drawn from China (including Hong Kong), Taiwan, and Singapore meet together with Europeans and Americans. Two important polarities invariably emerge among such discussants.

Differences obviously exist between the Taiwan and Chinese representatives who, however politely, find themselves at odds over the Taiwan question. Taiwanese and Chinese scholars cannot but allow their distinct perspectives to shape their arguments and conclusions.

Europeans differ significantly from Americans in a variety of ways. America, envisioned as a liberal, rights-based, democracy conjoined with a highly developed corporate capitalist economy, is seen as the principal agent of the modernization and Westernization of China. This means that distinctly American dynamics constitute important elements of the "pragmatic present" from which to envision processes of modernization and Westernization. It is inevitable that American thinkers in particular should speculate on the future of China from this particular present. Europeans seem to feel at greater liberty to theorize about Chinese democracy without the same sense of complicity in Westernizing processes that many American scholars feel.

The arguments of this book are conditioned by the pragmatic present of contemporary American society. Our perspective is *American* in two quite specific senses. First, this work is written from a pragmatic present which acknowledges complicity in the events that willy-nilly are shaping China. Second, our book is American in the distinctly cultural sense that it relies heavily upon the thought of the principal American pragmatist—John Dewey.

In sum, our treatment of the hope for democracy in China is an instance of cross-cultural speculation and analysis that avoids any pretense to a dispassionate "God's-eye" view. Read in this manner, our work may find its appropriate place among others concerned with the future shape of democracy in China.

In addition to the Fallacy of the Single Perspective, we have sought to avoid *The Fallacy of Misguided Comparison*. This fallacy leads one to compare of the ideals of one society or culture with the practices of another. Asians often, with some justification, accuse Americans of judging their societies in this fashion. The constitutional guarantees of American society are contrasted with specific violations of the rights and freedoms in Asian countries. The "rule of law" is held high by Westerners who forget how often that rule is subverted by the fact that the law benefits the wealthy far more than the poor, and the Anglo-American far oftener than the Afro-American or the Hispanic.

Asians are hardly innocent with respect to this fallacy. The alienating effects of American individualism are often attacked in the name of a Confucian communitarianism that, decidedly humane in principle, *de facto* excludes and isolates minorities while placing undue burdens upon women.

A final fallacy, certainly implicit in all misguided comparisons, is *The Good Principles Fallacy*. This fallacy suggests that ethical and humane principles in the absence of relevant action are of greater value than concrete and specific actions unaccompanied by high-sounding principles. For example, in debates on human rights at both the national and international levels, there has been far more concern to articulate the specific status and content of rights, and the nature of the violations of rights, than to deal with the issue of how rights might be concretely implemented across societies. The mere rehearsal of a list of rights often seems sufficient to allay the crusading impulses of the all too many righteous among us.

Casual readers of our work may believe that we ourselves have run aground of the Good Principles Fallacy. For it is easy to presume that a theoretical work of the sort we are presenting is unconcerned with the questions of concrete implementation. Philosophers such as ourselves, concerned to note the contribution of culture to the shape of social and political circumstances, are more likely to offer models and principles, without an immediate appeal to concrete analyses. What is needed, so the more practical-minded claim, is specific analyses conjoined with equally specific prescriptions. For example, with respect to the issue of the hope for democracy in China, one needs to note the conditions with respect to human rights and to suggest ways of improving the situation through democratic processes leading to institutional reorganization, the restructuring of legal mechanisms, and so on.

Though we shall deal with our subject primarily at the speculative level, it will be no part of our purpose merely to advertise a set of ideas culled from the texts of two cultures, and to hold them high as occasions for inspiration and ennoblement. Exemplary principles, even when detached from particular circumstances, are truly abstract only if one treats them so.

The refusal to engage the practical world in order to maintain academic neutrality too often leads to the marginalization of the academic. The trick is to maintain something of a balance.[4] In this present work we are constructing distinctly philosophical arguments in relative detachment from the specifics of political and economic issues. We insist that general discussions of the sort this work represents may have real practical value if they are taken as productively vague conceptual models open to stipulation and application in a variety of theoretical and practical contexts. Seen in this fashion, our work becomes part of a collaborative effort involving all those who find the models and analyses we offer useful in their various endeavors.[5]

In the spirit of John Dewey, we intend to celebrate the ideas of democratic community expressed in Chinese and pragmatic understandings as a means of reminding ourselves that such ideas are deeply implicated in the most specific and local of the problems encountered by any engaged in the activities of living in and maintaining community life; that such ideas, in the form of relevant ideals, will always arise in the process of dealing with this problem and that, and that they then may serve as effective tools for intelligent action. Whether we actually employ these tools, or suppress their use by appeal to feigned necessities or covert interests will, of course, be largely a matter of choice.

The present circumstances clearly invite engagements at the cultural as well as the economic and political levels of discourse. However unimportant we in the West might initially assess appeals to the efficacy of cultural values, it is clearly the case that many Asian members of the conversation will be positively disposed to such appeals. To the degree to which we wish to accommodate this disposition, we will do well to recognize that the American pragmatic tradition offers resources for the construction of just such appeals.

The challenge to Western promoters of China's democratization is to articulate a model of communitarian democracy consistent with the profoundest values of traditional Chinese society. Such a model would promote a persistent concern for the protection of human rights that nonetheless avoids giving priority to the rhetoric of individual rights over the interest in implementing specific rights through communal effort. This model would likewise promote the rule of law without abstracting it from the moral suasion essential to the health of any community. A viable Confucian democracy must promote a conception of equality grounded in the communal sources of individuality rather than in the notion of atomistic individualism. We hold that American pragmatism in general and, in particular, John Dewey's vision of democracy as a "communicating community" provides the readiest assistance in the effort to develop such a model of democracy.

There is very good reason to believe that democracy in some form will inevitably come to China. Already, village elections are being instituted throughout the country, and the Chinese government has begun to show less reluctance to enter the human rights debates. We believe that distinctly philosophical assumptions associated with specific value commitments will help to shape the manner in which democratic institutions are implemented in China. Doubtless these commitments will be mixed together with political and economic factors devoid of explicit value concerns, as well as with the blind forces of brute circumstance. But to ignore cultural determinants expressed in terms of value commitments in favor of these allied factors is to refuse to provide the best hope for a humanized democracy in China.

# PART 1

# IDENTIFYING CHINA

# The 'Myth' of Han Identity

## 1. Myth and Cultural Narrative

The historical, geopolitical, and cultural differences that divide us from the Chinese make viewing China from the West a particularly challenging task. The most productive means of taking up that perspective seeks to identify China on its own terms before engaging its culture and its people. Our first step in attempting to do just this is to consider how China has presented itself both to the World and to itself as "the people of the Han." Subsequently, we shall characterize those factors and forces in contemporary China that are challenging the notion of Han identity.

One of the more important characteristics of Western culture is a concern for the origins of the world and its inhabitants. Behind the presumably scientific accounts of physical cosmology and evolutionary theory lies a rich tradition of mythical tales drawn from Greek and Semitic sources. These tales have shaped the psychological and cultural assumptions in accordance with which we envision our world.

Both Greek and Semitic versions of our founding myths share a common concern with the victory of the forces of *Order* over those of *Chaos*. Hesiod's *Theogony* tells how *Eros* overcomes the separation of Chaos and brings Heaven and Earth into harmony. The book of *Genesis* tells of Chaos as a dark, formless Void that God overcomes through a command—"Let it be." Plato's *Timaeus* suggests that at the beginning there was confusion and irrational disorder which the *Demiurgos* ordered through the agency of rational persuasion.

Whether construed as a yawning gap, an empty void, or a boundless confusion, Chaos is the enemy, and Love, Will, and Reason overcome Chaos and establish order. It would be difficult to overestimate the importance of our cosmogonic tradition and the primacy of agency it entails. These accounts have influenced our attitudes toward cosmological, psychological, and political interpretations of human experience.

Contemporary thinkers may underestimate the importance of cosmogonic myths since these seem to be merely crude attempts at saying what we have since learned to articulate in more scientific language. Such a view tacitly affirms the significance of our founding myths by taking for granted that accounts of the origins of things are obligatory means of making sense of the world. When, however, one encounters a highly sophisticated culture such as China, which is oddly uninfluenced by the Chaos/Cosmos dialectic upon which so much of our Western sense of rational order is grounded, one is faced with a real problem in attempting cogent cultural comparisons.

The agencies of thinking, acting, and feeling emergent from Western cosmogonic myths do not have easily identifiable correlates in the Chinese world, ancient or modern. This discovery suggests that mythological constructions may not have had the same culture-building force in China as was the case in the West.[1]

We are not concerned here to discuss in any detail the reasons for the relative unimportance of cosmogonic constructions in classical China. A much fuller treatment of this issue may be found in other of our works.[2] Briefly, the issues are these: Of the two indigenous patterns of thought forming the Chinese classical tradition—Daoism and Confucianism—the former does in fact contain a significant amount of mythical speculation. However, the terms most closely associated with the classical Western senses of "Chaos" and "Order" are not understood in pejorative and honorific senses, respectively. Therefore, the theme of bringing order out of chaos through harmonizing agencies such as Love, Will, or Reason does not shape the mythical materials. Moreover, the Confucian tradition has far less interest in myths of any kind, and seeks to explain the origins of the world in terms of the emergence of a human culture and a viable society constructed by individuals who are, at least putatively, historically identifiable.

In the absence of a highly visible cosmogonic construction, we are forced to look for alternative assumptions that ground and articulate the tradition. Performing this task allows us to recognize the principal features of a narrative which, though lacking in the imagistic and poetic features associated with Western mythologies, has functionally the same force in the foundation of Chinese culture as do our own Western cosmogonies. It will be difficult for one brought up on the cosmogonic tradition of the West to understand the importance of the principal narrative the Chinese employ to focus their identity. This is so because, unlike the Chinese, we construe the founding myths of a people as subsets of our more general cosmogonic tradition. For example, the founding narrative of the United States of America speaks of the special character of America as a "New Jerusalem," "a city set on a hill," and includes such metaphors as the "wilderness" and "manifest destiny." All of these mythical themes are specifications of the Greater Enlightenment narrative of the centrality of Reason and Freedom. This narrative in its turn may be seen to be a specification of the even more general cosmogonic tradition from our Graeco/ Hebraic past which celebrates the victory of Order over the forces of Chaos.

For the most part, the Confucian tradition has remained content with founding narratives that seem independent of any speculations about the origins of the world. This is to say that the Confucian tradition does not require an initial beginning from some transcendent source. The founding "myth" of Confucian China is a narrative that tells of the construction of the unifying culture of the Han dynasty (206 BCE–220 CE). As such it is no myth at all.

We shall continue to refer to the Myth of the Han, however, because in the following chapter we will argue that Han unity is a "myth" in the vulgar sense of the term—namely, it is a fiction, a half-truth. Having said this, the Myth of the Han must be taken with utmost seriousness as the principal means by which China presents itself to the world and to itself.

# 2. The People of the Han

The Chinese character for *han* is 漢. The character has a range of meanings, most of which derive from the river in central China that empties out at Hankou 漢口, literally, "the mouth of the Han." In classical texts such as the *Book of Songs* and the *Zuozhuan*, *han* refers to *tianhan* 天漢 and *yinhan* 銀漢: the accumulated brilliance of innumerable stars that stream across the night sky to form what we call the "Milky Way." *Han* is further an abbreviation for *hanzhong* 漢中, a territory in the pre-imperial state of Chu that takes its name from the Han river. In the late third century BCE, Liu Bang 劉邦 emerged from this area as *hanwang* 漢王, the king of Han. When he defeated Xiang Yu in 202 BCE to become the founding emperor of the Han, *hangaozu* 漢高祖, he lent the name of his local origins to a dynasty that would endure for some four hundred years. It was during the Han dynasty that a Chinese social, political, and cultural identity was consolidated. This cultural matrix served as the source to which Chinese people appeal when they call themselves *hanren* 漢人, "people of the Han." And just as America became "the land of the free and the home of the brave," *han* has taken on a qualitative significance, so that *hanqi* 漢氣, "the spirit of the Han," is courage, and a *nanzihan* 男子漢, "a man of the Han," is a brave fellow.

It was early in this Han period that the canonical texts were set, and Confucianism emerged as the imperial ideology reinforced by a civil service examination system that would continue to produce China's political and cultural elite until the end of empire in the early years of the twentieth century. While the Han dynasty has always been taken seriously when scholars have reflected on the political and social construction of China, the present generation of sinologists has shown an increased interest with the specifically cultural aspects of the Han. Examples of this increased attention are legion. What John Major in *Heaven and Earth in Early Han Thought*[3] says of the "relative obscurity" of the important Han text, the *Huainanzi*, applies equally to most of the textual materials from this syncretic period. Major's appreciation of the formative importance of Han cosmology in shaping the Chinese perception of its place in the world is part of an ongoing sea change in our perception of this era. Further, the contemporary Chinese thinker, Li Zehou, argues that the Han dynasty is far more important to the foundations of cultural and intellectual China than was previously acknowledged.[4]

*Hanxue* 漢學 or "Han learning" is the exegetical and evidential tradition that begins around the canonical texts during the Han dynasty, and with the post-hoc Qing dynasty exclusion of Song-Ming neo-Confucianism, continues down to this day. And the medium of *hanxue* is the *hanzi* 漢字: the Chinese character. The term *han* is used pervasively in the Chinese language to identify the distinctive cultural core of what is alternatively referred to in English as "Confucianism" or, by extension, "Chineseness." Importantly, however, it is not a static, essential core, but rather a dynamic cluster of significances, changing over time. Thus, to ask after the "myth of the Han" is to ask "What is the dynamic core of Confucianism?"

Over the past century and a half, "Confucianism" has experienced some rather wild swings in value on the stock market of world culture. At one end of this pendulum's arc, there is Hu Shi's early twentieth-century battle cry for the May Fourth reform: "Down with the House of Confucius!" At the other end of the pendulum's path is the banner of Tu Wei-ming's evangalizing promotion of "third wave Confucianism." Swinging back the other way, there is the *"pikong* 批孔 " anti-Confucius campaign during the Cultural Revolution when Confucius was thoroughly demonized. The most recent swing has led to the rhetorical rehabilitation of Confucianism in the later phases of Deng Xiaoping's reformist government, where it continues today to serve as the principal resource for "socialism with Chinese characteristics."

Confucianism has been reviled by many as yellow silt clotting the arteries of China, retarding the vital circulation of those new ideas necessary to enable it to emerge into the modern world. At the same time, it is celebrated by others as the indigenous dynamic making Asian economic development, in spite of periodic setbacks, the miracle that it continues to be.

Turning from the term *Confucianism* to that of *Confucianist*, Guy Alitto has called the twentieth-century scholar, Liang Shuming 梁漱溟, "the Last Confucian," thereby tolling the passing of this great tradition.[5] Today the Chinese academy is touting the same Liang Shuming as the first in the breed of "New Confucians" (*xinruxuejia* 新儒學家). For some, such as Joseph Levenson, Myron Cohen, and Marjory Wolf, Confucianism is an effete, patriarchal ideology whose welcome demise is making room for a long-needed cultural transformation.[6] For others, the same Confucianism is a *sine qua non* for "Chineseness," alive and well in the modern world if in no other form than that of a counter-discourse with which to challenge undesirable imports from the modernizing West.

Arif Dirlik rues what he takes to be an unholy alliance between Confucianism as an indictable "post-colonialist discourse," and the devil
himself—the *laissez faire* capitalist. For Dirlik, the revival of Confucianism in modern Asia is little more than Asian Orientalism. It is at best a
conspiracy between the State and freeloading intellectuals. In his own
words, Confucianism is "a foremost instance . . . of intellectual discourse creating its object."[7]

With the confusion that plagues the use of the term "Confucianism"
to express Han identity, it is important to determine, if possible, the
referent of all of these divided, conflicted, and mutually contradictory
judgments proffered by our best interpreters of Chinese culture. What
does it mean to be "the people of the Han?"

First, a methodological issue: We must avoid essentializing "Confucianism" or "Han" by treating them as technical terms. We cannot expect such precision when approaching an understanding of Han
identity. We need, rather, to begin from an awareness of the contingency and cultural specificity of those objectivist assumptions that have
driven the modern Western approach to self-understanding. Such assumptions underlie the belief that cultural understanding can be pur-
sued as an encounter between a self-contained subject and an independently given object. This belief stands in stark contrast to the
assumptions grounding the Confucian world view.

With the priority of situation over agency characteristic of the Chinese tradition, the agent is always embedded in a world and hence defined in terms of those constitutive relations that locate him. Such a
starting point defies familiar notions such as an essential identity. Analysis is thus not an appropriate approach for reading what is a fundamentally aesthetic tradition, taking as it does the uniqueness of the relational patterns of each and every situation as its basic premise.

Bracketing the "what" question, therefore, we need rather ask *how*
has "the myth of the Han" functioned to sustain the pattern of relations
it has constituted across time. Taking our cue from Chinese medicine,
we have to think physiologically rather than anatomically. That is to say,
in taking our reading and seeking to understand the world of the Han,
we might need to feel a pulse rather than locate an artery.

In contrast to the mainstream Western philosophical tradition, the
Chinese tradition is historicist and genealogical. As such, it is resistant

to articulation in theoretical and conceptual terms that presuppose unfamiliar notions such as objectivity and strict identity.[8] Conceptualization requires principles, univocal meanings, correspondence between propositions and states-of-affairs, and a sense of reference, all of which have had minimal relevance in the axiologically driven Chinese traditions of ethics, aesthetics, and religion. Approaching the story of the Han as a continuing cultural narrative rather than as isolatable doctrines and ideologies presents us with a rolling, continuous, and always contingent tradition with its own internal logic.

Perhaps an example taken from the dawning of Confucianism will help bring the difference between a *narrative* and an *analytical* understanding into sharper focus. How should we read the Confucian *Analects?* We could proceed with a conceptual reconstruction by isolating and attempting to stipulate the content of the key vocabularies *ren* 仁, *yi* 義, *li* 禮, and so on. Alternatively, we can construct our understanding in a much less formal way by proceeding analogically, associating one passage with another, and one historical exemplar with another. That is, we might do better to pursue a *narrative* understanding that highlights relevant correlations among specific historical figures and events.

Moreover, the *Analects* is a never-ending story. That is, in this reading strategy, the life experience of the reader and commentator is always brought to the interpretation, making each pass through it always specific and unique. The accumulation of commentaries around the *Analects* recalls those readers who were best able to make the text alive in their own historical moments. For example, *ren* 仁 is a central term in the *Analects*. It is often translated "human-heartedness" or "benevolence." Seeking a narrative, rather than an essentialist understanding of the term, would lead us to consider accounts of "authoritative persons." The presumption would be that the term "refers" to the ways of living and thinking of particular historical persons who have set an example for their own worlds, rather than an essence nameable by an abstract noun.[9]

We can further illustrate the notion of *narrative* understanding or reasoning by looking at the method of reasoning itself. If we reflect on the Chinese tradition broadly, we find that the terms most closely correlated with "reason" do not name abstract ideas or stipulate essential functions, but must be construed by reference to a shared reservoir of historical instances of reasonableness available for analogical comparison.

For the classical Chinese, knowledge is not as much representational as performative and participatory. That is, it involves, not closure, but disclosure; it is not discursive but is a kind of know-how which offers us an understanding of how to effect robust and productive relationships among things in the human and nonhuman realms. "Knowledge" is "know-how" evidenced in making *one's own* way smoothly and without obstruction in *this* particular locale. The knower is committed to *realizing* such relationships rather than envisioning the truth about the world.

Similarly, "culture" is *this* specific historical pattern of human flourishing as it is lived out in the lives of the people. "Logic" is the internal coherence of this particular community's narrative. "Truth" (or, better, its cognate, "trust") is a quality of relatedness demonstrated in *one's own* capacity to foster productive relationships that begin with the maintenance of one's integrity, and extend to the enhancement of one's natural, social, and cultural contexts.

The narrative character of Chinese culture arises because a cultural dominant in the tradition, now and then, has been the priority of process and change over form and stasis, which leads to a privileging of particular "thises" and "thats" over objective essences. Thus, it is the specific exemplars who provide the bearings for continuing community. In lieu of gods as a separate order of being, the Chinese tradition has seen fit to celebrate and elevate ancestral figures, cultural heroes, and supreme personalities over its long career. This need for models to emulate has required the philosopher to be a paradigmatic individual—an advance scout to reconnoiter and recommend a "way" for the generations to come.

As a narrative, then, "the myth of the Han" is constituted by the stories of formative models. In reflecting on the lives of these models, we become immediately aware that any account of the existential, practical, and historical nature of this tradition stretches it beyond the boundaries of what would normally be defined as intellectual culture. Both traditionally, and within contemporary China, philosophy is much more (and certainly in some ways, much less) than a professional discipline. Many Chinese philosophers of our generation continue the tradition of scholar-officials as institutionalized intellectuals who have the practical responsibility to forge a "way" for the daily workings of government and society.

Yü Ying-shih, a contemporary intellectual historian, makes this point when he draws a continuous line between the traditional literatus of imperial days and the contemporary intellectual:

> As much as I would like to distinguish the *shih* [*shi* 士] from the *chih-shih fen-tzu* [*zhishifenzi* 知識分子], I must point out that spiritually the latter has continued much of what had been cultivated by the former. For example, the idea that the intellectual must always be identified with public-mindedness is not a cultural borrowing from the modern West, but from Confucian heritage traceable ultimately to the sage himself.[10]

Intellectual endeavor in the contemporary Chinese context continues to range over the relationship between prevailing cultural values and the social and political lives of the people. Philosophers have been and still are the intellectual leaders of society. Hence, a reflection on Chinese philosophy from an internal Chinese perspective must be primarily practical. That is, it must involve a survey of the intellectual discourse as it has driven and shaped social, political, and cultural developments.[11]

However we might choose to characterize the "myth of the Han" or "Confucianism," we must distinguish it from any particular set of precepts or any potted ideology identified post hoc within different phases or epochs of China's cultural narrative. Confucianism is not an isolatable doctrine or the commitment to a certain belief structure, but is, in fact, the continuing narrative of a specific community of people, the center of an ongoing "way" or *dao* 道 of thinking and living.

Any particular doctrinal commitment or set of values that we might associate with Confucianism needs to be qualified by its porous nature, absorbing into itself, especially in periods of disunity, whatever it needs to thrive within its particular historical moment. This porous nature of Confucianism makes it a persistently *comparative* tradition. In fact, an argument can be made that China has been doing comparative philosophy since the introduction of Buddhism into China in the second century.

The resilience of the persisting values has often caused history to repeat itself. When Buddhism was introduced into China through a largely Daoist vocabulary, the foreign ideas were, in due course, overwhelmed by the vitality of the indigenous impulse, and Buddhism was effectively sinicized. In its Sanlun, Huayan, and Chan incarnations, Chinese Buddhism has a closer correlation to the early Daoist classics than it does to its South Asian origins.

Christianity in China was itself melded with popular religions to spawn one of the largest uprisings in human history—the Taiping rebellion (1851–1864). More recently, Yan Fu 嚴復 (1853–1921) stands out at the beginning of an ambitious project to translate recent Western philosophical classics into Chinese in the late Qing dynasty. And with Yan Fu's penchant for the arcane, evocative language of China's own philosophic tradition, the foreign ideas of modern Western thought were largely overwritten with more traditional Chinese values and sensibilities.

In this pattern of assimilation, China's Marxist experience is certainly no exception. Iconoclastic modernizers appropriated the Marxist heresy as a foundation for Chinese socialism. However, in its Maoist incarnation, Chinese Marxism has redefined a doctrine which, on most interpretations, owned universalistic aspirations into a kind of "neo" neo-Confucianism. On the other hand, any reference to Chinese "democratic" ideals introduces terrible equivocations: What is to be made of "individualistic values" in the absence of Western notions of the individual, autonomy, independence, human rights, and so on? As soon as we get beneath surface impressions, we realize that contemporary Chinese philosophical developments are deeply embedded within traditional Chinese methods of philosophizing. By and large, Chinese philosophers continue to be concerned with the creative appropriation of their own cultural tradition. Marxian rhetoric and liberal democratic values are largely heuristic structures through which more fundamental traditional Chinese values are revisited, reconfigured, and sometimes, revitalized.

In most traditions, patriotism is expressed as a kind of grudging conservatism, but in China, especially in this century, it has often driven radicalism, iconoclasm, and even revolution. "Nativism" in China has a similarly paradoxical shape. The best of our contemporary interpreters of recent Chinese history tell the story in terms of both change and persistence. In his research on the Chinese nativism in this century, Yü Ying-shih reports that "national essence (*guocui* 國粹)," a neologism coined in Japan, took on a rather curious profile when imported to China. In describing the 1920s scholars who identified themselves under this banner, Yü Ying-shih observes:

> It might at first sight seem strange that a group of scholars professedly devoted to the preservation of China's national essence should rely so heavily on Western conceptual schemes and methods for the study of their own history. . . . Criticizing the Japanese scholar Inoue Kaoru (1835–1915) who identified "national essence" as something entirely indigenous, Huang Chieh [Jie] remarked that "national essence" consists not only in what is indigenous and suitable, but also in what is borrowed and adaptable to the needs of our nation.[12]

Similarly, Chang Hao demonstrates rather persuasively that neither discontinuity (Levenson)[13] nor continuity (Metzger)[14] provides an adequate account of early twentieth-century China by telling the story of four of its most prominent reformist intellectuals—Kang Youwei 康有爲, Tan Sitong 譚嗣同, Zhang Binglin 張炳麟, and Liu Shipei 劉師培—in terms of change and persistence.[15]

"Confucianism" is *rujia* 儒家 in Chinese: the lineage or "family" of the Ru scholars. Perhaps, in our attempt to evaluate the role of "Confucianism" in recent Chinese history, we are paying too much attention to the "*ru*" and not enough to the "*jia*." That is, we might want to reflect on the singular importance of *jia*: "family" or "lineage."

The centrality of this idea of family as the grounding metaphor pervasive in Chinese culture arises from two Confucian insights. First, the family is that institution in which people give most wholly and unreservedly of themselves. Beginning with family, then, how do we extend this complex of roles and relationships to the community and the nation more broadly? How do we get the most out of our human resources? It is significant that speaking of "nation" in Chinese is to speak of "nation family" (*guojia* 國家); to speak of "everybody," the expression literally is "big family" (*dajia* 大家). Secondly, the continuity between humanity and the world—between culture and nature—leads to the singular importance of the family metaphor in the definition of relational order within Chinese cosmology.[16]

When we move from "family" to Confucianism as a cultural lineage, the question remains the same—namely, "How do we get the most out of the available cultural resources?" The production and appropriation of what is fitting (*yi* 義) that is characteristic of this Confucian tradition, late and soon, is justified as ingesting what can either be adapted to fortify a continuing past, or as reviving resources already present in China's ancient past. It is a syncretism that seeks to get the most out of its ingredients under always specific circumstances. The degree of appropriation is a function of opportunity. The irony is that "nativist" intellectuals, in turning their backs on the Confucian tradition as well as in borrowing whatever they need from non-Confucian sources to achieve "productive continuity" (in traditional language, *he* 和: "productive harmony"), instantiate what is most centrally the "how" of Confucianism.

This lineage called Confucianism can be imaged metaphorically in many different ways. It is this moving line—in calligraphy, the brush stroke (*yihua* 一畫), always moving, always centered: thick and ponderous, thin and darting, fast with a flourish, slow and deliberate. In philosophical literature, it is the "way" (*dao* 道), in ornamentation, the fabulous "dragon" (*long* 龍) and phoenix (*fenghuang* 鳳凰), that define the ever changing, ever provisional, cultural horizon. The most obvious image is the one, cumulative *dao,* the continuous moving line of culture that is under construction by the "road-builders" of each generation.

In the Chinese language, "the world" is *shijie* 世界, literally "the succeeding generational boundaries" which conjoin one's own generation to those who have come before, and to the generation that will follow this one; "cosmos" is *yuzhou* 宇宙, "the turning canopy of the heavens under which we live." That is, the Chinese world is expressed as an ever moving cultural lineage. The pursuit of wisdom is literally, "to know the way (*zhidao* 知道)." This pursuit has, from classical times, centered on finding a way to stabilize, discipline, and shape productively and elegantly the unstoppable stream of change in which the human experience is played out.

This way (*dao*) of the world for the Confucian tradition has been constituted by bringing a framework of formal roles, relationships, and institutions (*li* 禮) to regulate the process of communal living. *Li*, often translated as "rites" or "propriety," is an enduring yet always malleable syntax through which the human being can pursue refined and appropriate relationships. Absorbing the Daoist challenge early in its career, Han Confucianism cast the net of relevant circumstances beyond human community, sacrificing a degree of focused human intensity for an increase in width and diversity.

The regularities observable in nature such as the cycle of the seasons, the growth and decay of every life form, the turning of the heavens, the weathered striations on a piece of stone, are all synergistic models on which human beings can construct their path through life, walking in rhythm with the cadence of the cosmos.

Although this way of living, this *dao*, has historical antecedents, it is not simply to be discovered and walked. The *Zhuangzi* says, "A path is made by people walking." In the *Analects* we read, "It is human beings that can broaden the way (*dao*), not the way that broadens human beings."[17] The human being must be a roadbuilder because human culture is always under construction.

This passage should be read together with another passage in the *Analects:* "The people can be made to travel along the path, but they cannot be made to realize it."[18] That is, "making a roadway real" must be distinguished from simply walking along it. The role of the Chinese intellectuals is to be communal leaders. Some human beings build roads and others travel behind.

We have only suggested some of the many significations of the locution, "people of the Han." First, the locution refers to a historical period, not wrought from legend, but possessing identifiable cultural characteristics. Second, the term is symbolic of an ethnic and linguistic unity applicable to as many as 93 percent of the Chinese people. Third, in its most honorific sense, the Han tradition is an intellectual, sagely tradition that cannot help but give it a coloration of cultural elitism. This elitism is evident to both the 7 percent of the population constituting recognized minorities, and the majority of the 75 percent of the population living in rural areas, as well. Fourth, as a consequence of its intellectual character, Han identity is resourced in classical texts the mastery of which qualifies some to be transmitters of Han culture. Fifth, Han culture is porous, capable of responding with flexibility to internal and external influences that would reshape it. Finally, and most importantly, the people of the Han are *an exclusive family,* the members of which respond to outsiders with varying degrees of suspicion and anxiety.

Any responsible view of China must take into account the centrality of the myth of the Han in shaping the cultural self-consciousness of the Chinese. At the same time, it is important to note how that myth is being challenged in the contemporary period from both within and without Chinese borders. Indeed, the best way to understand contemporary China is to note how, politically and culturally, it is reshaping itself in response to these quite serious challenges.

# Challenges to the Myth of the Han

## 1. Waking Up to Diversity

Confucius observed that there was a single thread running throughout his teachings.[1] This thread is *shu* 恕, which may be translated as "deference"—literally, "putting oneself into another's place when determining how to act with respect to that person." *Shu* is captured in the famous negative golden rule: "Do not act toward others as you would not have them act toward you." As a strategy for constituting community through effecting patterns of deference, this "thread," *shu*, can be understood as yet another variation on the "continuity" effected by "the moving line."

In addition to the thread tying together Confucius's teachings, there is another thread, a silken one, that spans the breadth of China. Certainly one of the most romantic of all the ancient trade routes, the Old Silk Road stretched from Xi'an in China to the Mediterranean Sea, some 4,000 miles. Later in its history, legend has it that Marco Polo followed this route on his fabled journey to "Cathay." Retracing the Silk Route from Xi'an to Kashgar, skirting along the Taklamakan desert on the hottest of summer days, one is encouraged to ask whether Confucius's single thread will be strong enough to hold together the vast complexities that constitute the real China.

The Chinese continue to call themselves *hanren* 漢人: "the people of the Han," where the term "Han" today refers to membership in the principal ethnic group of China constituting over 92 percent of the population. Han Chinese are distinguished from the Tibetans, Manchus, Mongols, Huis, Uighurs, Miao, Zhuang, and the other fifty-odd officially designated "minority" ethnic groups. The two facets of the Han identity—ethnic and cultural—are the chief components of the unifying metaphor that Chinese employ to persuade the world and themselves that they are, in some sense of the word, *one*.

The casual tourist who restricts his travel to Beijing, Shanghai, and Guangzhou might be lulled into the sense that the characterization of an ethnic and linguistically unified China is on some level appropriate. But the trip along the Silk Road from Xi'an to Kashgar challenges our assumptions about unity with the most radical images of diversity. In the villages of Xinjiang, a province in Western China closed to foreign travel until 1990, it is possible to spend days without encountering Han Chinese. Indeed, it may be difficult to find anyone who speaks or admits to speaking Mandarin Chinese.

In its modern reconstituted form, the Silk Route may itself present a significant challenge to the myth of Han unity. China's new continental land bridge which will allow goods to move from Japan across China into Europe might well be as dramatic a contribution to historic change as was the Old Silk Road whose path the rail and truck routes will follow.

China's acknowledgment of and respect for the non-Han minorities is compromised by the enormous effort invested in a kind of "Oriental Orientalism," where the dominant Han group isolates and encapsulates its ethnic minorities as a way of reinforcing its own cultural identity.[2] The enormous diversity concealed by the myth of the Han makes such reinforcement essential. Any strong sense of "the people of the Han" is continually challenged by the mosaic of ways of living and thinking that is the real China.

So-called "Han" China is decidedly *local*. It is a continent constituted by a patchwork of ethnic, linguistic, and cultural localities. The very magnitude of its regional differences prompts the outsider to ask how this tenuous Han identity has ever managed to persist.

But ethnic pluralism is not the only challenge to the myth of the Han. Today, as never before, a number of factors and forces threaten the idea of Chinese unity. China's emerging relationship with the West has again forced it to open itself to the outside world, precipitating a conflict between tradition and modernity that China is ill-prepared to accommodate. In addition to its problematic relationship with the Western world, its relations with the world of neighboring states and "overseas" Chinese presents peculiar difficulties. Also, rapid changes in the socio-economic structures of China are producing serious strains on the sense of unity perpetuated by the myth of the Han.

# 2. China versus the World

The first threat to Han *Chineseness* is a result of the fact that China, never in any real sense a member of "the family of nations," is being forced, willy-nilly, to enter upon the world stage. While it is not altogether true that China has been isolationist throughout its history, it is a peculiar fact of Chinese history that the maintenance of stability within the Chinese empire has tended to preclude interest on the part of the government in exploration, conquest, and colonization.

Voyages of exploration took place in the Han dynasty and again, more extensively during the Tang period (618–906). The Han expedition took the Chinese all the way to the Indian Ocean, but did not lead to significant trade. The Silk Road was an important trade route, of course, but Parthia (roughly corresponding to modern northeast Iran) managed during most of the Han period to act as a buffer between China and the Roman Empire.

Explorations during the Tang dynasty led to active trade with the Middle East, but incursions of Muslim forces into Central Asia soon halted this experiment. In the fourteenth century there was a renewed interest in exploratory voyages. During this period, although India and Africa, among other sites, were contacted, these voyages were initiated as diplomatic ventures to appraise the foreigners of the existence of the Central Kingdom and its Emperor, and then only later as a strategy for developing international trade.

In the early fifteenth century, Zheng He 鄭和, the eunuch admiral, began a series of seven trading and diplomatic voyages that, over a period of some thirty years, took silks and Ming porcelains to trade for medicines, spices, and precious stones. Zheng He carried dignitaries and various sorts of exotica back to the Ming court, establishing a strong Chinese presence in a large part of the known world. He commanded a fleet of hundreds of treasure ships (*baochuan* 寶船), carrying tens of thousands of seamen and official personnel. Some of the ocean-faring junks measured four hundred feet in length—massive compared to the eighty-five-foot Santa Maria that, nearly a century later, would carry Columbus to the New World.

After trading throughout Southeast Asia and the Indian Ocean, Zheng He visited ports-of-call up the eastern coast of Africa. Himself a devout Muslim, Zheng He traded with the great Arab entrepreneurs, making a final excursion as far north as Mecca. Europe was not on the Chinese itinerary since Zheng He was persuaded by Arab travelers that the Europeans had only wool and wine to export—commodities of little interest to the Chinese traders.[3]

Given the size and compass of the voyages of Zheng He, it is remarkable that these expeditions are so little celebrated by Chinese historians. Indeed, if they are remembered at all, it is more often as an extravagance rather than as an achievement of any significance. Whatever the Chinese interpretation of these voyages, it is certainly true that the Chinese were, technologically speaking, better equipped than the Europeans to explore and settle the New World.

At its peak early in the fifteen hundreds, the Chinese navy boasted 3500 vessels. However, within a century of Zheng He's voyages, the entire fleet had been willfully and utterly abandoned. By 1551, with the Japanese *wako* piracy on the southeast China coast at its height, it had become a criminal offense to go to sea in a multi-masted ship. The Chinese concern about being known to others had overcome any curiosity they had about the existence and character of the world outside. The Ming court acted in a manner that has become characteristic of China into the modern period: It sought to rid China of unacceptable foreign influences by seriously limiting the construction of large seaworthy ships.

The nineteenth century spelled humiliation for China, from the Opium Wars to the ill-fated Boxer rebellion. Awakened from its isolationism by foreign incursions of every kind, China began to import Western technologies in a last ditch effort to defend its national integrity. The reforms leading to the May Fourth Movement offered yet one more window for China to enter the modern age on its own initiative. But Mao's eventual adoption of Marxism, and the subsequent victory of the Communist party, led once more to an anti-Western isolationism.

Again and again, China has proven itself immune to conversion by the West. Whether it be Christianity or capitalism, Western incursions have never finally taken hold. As recently as the turn of the last century, Yan Fu, one of the reformers trained in Europe, spent a lifetime translating Western philosophic, scientific, and economic classics, and took part in the unsuccessful "Bourgeoise Rebellion" of 1898. He died several years later in relative obscurity.

Yan Fu's career stands in rather stark contrast to his Japanese classmate at the British Navel Academy, Itô Hirobumi. One of the leaders of the powerful Meiji Restoration, Ito helped to bring Japan into the twentieth century as an influential member of the family of nations.[4]

The most recent example of China's ambivalence toward the outside world concerns the events surrounding the Beijing massacre, June 4th, 1989. In 1987 South Korea made its transition to democracy. Witnessing this development on its borders, Chinese reformers bent on democratization were emboldened to act. Today, Korean democracy is established and maturing. China, on the other hand, has not yet recovered from the student led protests that closed the eighties. June 4th, after all, was in part a consequence of the Korean development. Circumstances that have allowed neighboring cultures to embrace modernization never seem sufficient to allow similar developments within the Chinese subcontinent.

The liberalization that took place after the death of Mao Zedong was promising for a while. The resilient Deng Xiaoping seemed to possess the appropriate degree of pragmatism necessary to inoculate him and the country against ideological orthodoxy. But in the end, as June 4th so clearly demonstrates, the growing openness to Westernization was seriously challenged by the ever present fear of the disequilibrizing effects of foreign influence.

Two points need to be made at this juncture. The first is that, regardless of surface impressions, any expectation that China will easily accede to the *"Modernization = Westernization"* formula is, at least as seen through the lens of history, unwarranted.

But the second point is perhaps even more telling. The enduring xenophobia of China which has led it time and again throughout history to cleanse itself of the taints of foreign influence is as much a signal of the fragility of its national identity as it is of its potential for persistence. We in the West find it difficult to understand the cultural justification for such a convulsive response to foreignness. But that is because we forget that the comparable Western identity, associated as it is with "individualism," is forged from a different ore than that of the Chinese.

As we shall see in our discussions of the meanings of "modernity" in chapter 3, the dominant models of Western individualism are resourced in transcendent principles that do not directly depend upon any social or cultural institutions for their development. In China, individual as well as national identity, is realized through shared language, customs, and rituals.

Members of Western cultures can move beyond the borders of their homelands without the loss of their identity. Chinese individuals are more closely tied to the specifics of their culture. The rational identity of the Westerner, on the other hand, is deemed independent of any social grouping. Sustaining Han Chineseness, however, seems to require the perpetuation of an ethnically and linguistically closed community.

Han identity is parochial, dependent upon the integrity of the localized culture and community. To force this population into externally driven relations is threatening enough. But to insist upon its participation in modern political and economic structures grounded in assumptions about the universality of abstract individualism is disintegrative in the extreme. The first challenge to Han identity, then, is the mere presence of an outside world that demands modernization on its terms.

The sense of over-againstness that China has typically felt toward the rest of the world is only one of the ways in which China manifests the fear of compromising its Han identity. The threat of external influences is registered, as well, with respect to those ethnic Chinese who live beyond the borders of mainland China. Not only Taiwan and Hong Kong, upon which China has had legitimate political claims, but the Chinese of Singapore and the emigrant population of "overseas Chinese" are felt, if only in the vaguest of manners, to be within the sphere of Chinese cultural hegemony.

The notion of "Chineseness" is so powerful that for many overseas Chinese, the feeling of ethnic and cultural identity is maintained after many generations away from Mother China. This sense of connectedness is easy enough to understand once one recalls the Confucian stress upon family ties. Many Chinese émigrés have felt the obligation to maintain supportive connections to their families in China, and since the liberalizations of the post-Mao era, these connections are a significant factor in continuing the sense of Chinese identity. Indeed, the economic growth in parts of China, such as Guangdong province, currently China's richest, has been significantly impacted by the contributions of Chinese emigrants. It is no surprise that the major direct investors in Mainland China since the 1978 economic reforms are Hong Kong and Taiwan.

The reaccession of Hong Kong on July 1, 1997 was an event with various levels of significance for China. First and foremost, it was a step in China's reasserting its political control over the sphere of its cultural hegemony. In the minds of many Chinese leaders, the return of Taiwan is an essential next step in reasserting China's dignity and integrity. It is perhaps this sense of cultural integrity that will lead China, once reunited as a "Greater China," to increasingly exert influence upon those neighboring areas in which there is an important ethnic Chinese presence.

This vision of China's leaders is a consequence of the notion of Han identity. Chinese are first and foremost constituted by their linguistic and ethnic character. The "Chinatowns" of the world—from San Francisco and Vancouver to Paris and Sydney—have been relatively dormant enclaves in foreign lands that are becoming increasingly reanimated by China's growing international presence.

The modern Chinese diaspora has resolved itself in a manner not unlike that of the Jewish diaspora. Mother China is a homeland that serves as both reality and symbol of cultural identity. Anyone reflecting upon how the establishment of Israel has reinforced the economic and political influence of the Jews in Europe and America will have little difficulty recognizing the potential effects of the extension of Han identity at an international level.

This vision of Greater China is a troubled one. The Chinese of Hong Kong, Taiwan, Singapore, as well as émigrés in Europe and America, have been subject to those "foreign influences" China has so consistently deplored. Whatever happens in the future between China and the rest of the Chinese world, the Han identity will be significantly challenged by those Chinese who have, for some time now, existed in the "outside world."

# 3. Internal Tensions

There are a variety of centrifugal forces within China itself that exacerbate the difficulty it will have in sustaining a viable sense of Han identity. Principal among these are ethnic fault lines, the significance of growing regional disparities, the fragmenting effects associated with the creation of Special Economic Zones, and a growing class conflict occasioned by the recent emergence of the peasant class to a position of economic and political power. It is necessary to add to these factors an element that cuts across all of the others—namely, a climate of political opinion that will increasingly turn on the conflicting demands of tradition and modernity.

## *Ethnic Conflicts and Local Identities*

The most direct challenge to the Han identity within China itself is its ethnic pluralism and the reassertion of local identities, a familiar phenomenon across the centuries as the spire of dynastic unity becomes the gyre of interregnum. Although it is an oft-advertised fact of Chinese society that minorities constitute only 7 to 9 percent of the population, there are significant reasons why these ethnic groups, even in such modest numbers, can constitute a challenge to the Han identity.

First, there are the lessons of history. Border minorities have presented a threat to the integrity of the Chinese world reaching back to the conquest of the Shang dynasty by the Zhou peoples (1122–256 BCE), a federation of Wei River valley border tribes that invaded the fertile lands of the Yellow River valley.

The Yuan dynasty (1271–1368) established by the Mongol ruler Kublai Khan, and the Qing dynasty (1644–1911) in which the Manchurians ruled China, led to a significant influx of minority populations. Indeed, the modern-day provinces of Heilongjiang, Jilin, and Liaoning, comprising what was formerly Manchuria, have large percentages of minorities.

In contemporary China, the most visible of the minority populations—the Uighur Muslims and the Tibetans—are concentrated in specific areas of China. The Uighurs are largely in Xinjiang province, and the Tibetans in the Tibetan Autonomous Region. In the case of the Muslims, the province of Xinjiang borders with Kyrgyzstan and Kazakhstan, new nations born of the breakup of the Soviet Union which own significant Muslim populations. Though the Uighurs have no bordering "homeland" to which they might wish to return, this is not the case with the Kyrgyz and Kazakhs and Tajiks. Though a recent agreement between China and bordering Muslim states has resulted in these states agreeing not to support separatist activities within their own territories—which in turn would lessen the success of such movements from within the borders of China—the continuing instability of these same countries suggests that such agreements should not themselves be thought to be lasting or secure. Moreover, it is questionable whether Han China will benefit at all from its relationship with the new border nations. For either these nations will stabilize and grow into strong *Muslim* neighbors which cannot but be expected to support their fellow Muslims within China, or they will destabilize completely with this new source of instability serving to further weaken a tenuous peace within Muslim China.

Separatist activities in 1996 and 1997 were particularly strong among the Uighurs in Western Xinjiang. And the Chinese crackdown on those activities was most severe. Whatever form liberalization might take place in the future, the recently discovered oil reserves in Western Xinjiang and the consequent potential for increased economic connections with the Middle East precludes the possibility that Beijing will leave this area to its own devices. On the other hand, the entire Muslim Middle East has a vested interest in the welfare of the Chinese Muslims, and is not likely to be indifferent to perceived maltreatment of that population by the Chinese government.

The situation of Tibet is quite different, of course. Until recently, there were few areas as isolated, both geographically and culturally, as that country. The effect of the 1951 annexation of Tibet has been to raise the level of concern for the fate of the Tibetan people in the Anglo-European community. This growing awareness is largely a response to the worldwide Tibetan Movement led by the Dalai Lama. The pro-Tibetan forces have achieved a great deal of success in bringing to the fore the story of Tibetan suffering.

It is still too early to tell whether this growing public concern will translate into significant political support. It is rather clear that Tibet has few effective allies. Nonetheless, there will doubtless be increasing pressure on China from the Western world concerning the current "human rights debate." It is true that Europe and America did precious little to aid the Tibetans during and after the Chinese takeover. And, with the notable exception of India, China's neighbors tend to cooperate with the Chinese on the Tibetan issue. It is now thought to be to the advantage of Western powers to use the Tibetan issue as a token in the debates over human rights.

In addition to the officially designated ethnic minorities, there are an estimated 70 million Christians (50 million Protestants, 20 million Catholics) who constitute another line of division in China. The Western world cannot be expected to ignore their fate. The bottom line seems to be that, though the direct challenges to Han unity of the Chinese minorities are only marginally significant, the rhetoric of global community and the international considerations that attend it make the situation much more complex.

The minority populations of China are treated as exceptions in every sense to the Chinese Han mainstream. Though this treatment sometimes appears to offer advantages (for example, the "one-child" policy has not been applied to minority populations), the overall effect of the exceptional status of the minority populations is to increase resentment on the part of the Han Chinese, thus enforcing the isolation of the minorities and increasing the power of the Han majority.

In addition to the tensions created by ethnic pluralism, the phenomenon of local identities is another significant factor qualifying any presumption of Han unity. It is truistic that in China, *everything is local.* And it is not an exaggeration to say that there is a Shanghai culture, a Guangdong culture, a Shandong culture. The sum of these identities has no actual focus other than that celebrated by a mythic Han unity.

Guangdong (Cantonese) culture is in many ways the medium through which most of the Western world has experienced China. The majority of the Chinese restaurants opened in North America and Europe are "Cantonese" because most of the immigrants to these geographical sites have been from this region. Hong Kong, of course, was originally a part of Guangdong and the language of Hong Kong is Cantonese. In fact, the Cantonese language continues to be more identifiably "Chinese" outside of China than is Mandarin. Thus, the Cantonese influence upon China in recent history and in the future is incalculable—especially with Hong Kong added to the mix.

Characteristic of the Chinese individual is his or her identification with the place of origin. One might expect this characteristic to be submerged once one enters into public life, but it is clear from a consideration of Chinese politics how important identities are. Shanghai's newly acquired privileged economic impetus is in part a function of the fact that Jiang Zemin rose from his tenure as mayor of Shanghai, as did the current premier Zhu Rongji. And the fact that Jiang has promoted a number of Shanghainese into his government is significant for the shape of China's political future.

The net effect of both ethnic minorities and the presence in China of strong local loyalties is to increase the forces of regionalism and geographical disparity which in turn can lead to an increase in the counteractive centralizing tendencies. It is impossible to say where this continued raising of the ante will ultimately lead. It is fair to say, however, that whatever the ultimate effect, the tensions felt will be a continuing concern for the Han Chinese government.

Local identities in China are not simply cultural in the traditional sense of the word. Something very much akin to local identities have been created in an essentially ad hoc manner. Whole cities have been constructed almost overnight through migrations of hundreds of thousands of Chinese. For example, the city of Urumqi (Wulumuqi) in Xinjiang province is over 80 percent Han Chinese, most of whom were imported to insure Han dominance in the capital of this overwhelmingly Muslim province.

A far stranger example of the creation of local identities involves China's "floating population:" estimated to be between 10 and 20 percent of its population. In the city of Beijing, as well as other principal cities throughout China, millions of peasants have come looking for work. And characteristically, these populations live in provincially discrete districts throughout the city: "Zhejiang town" and "Xinjiang Road."

## Economic Competition

In addition to the regional tensions created by local identities, economic competition among various areas of China threatens the sense of Han unity. This competition has been further fueled through the creation of Special Economic Zones that resulted in islands of economic activity within China, each with its own operating rules. That is to say, there are a number of industrial and technological cities or regions whose laws, tax structures, and other institutional elements are tailored to the particular strengths of the entity.

For some years Guangdong province has received special economic advantages in the hope that it would become a "fifth Asian tiger." In 1984, in anticipation of the reaccession of Hong Kong (1997) and of Macau (in 1999), Deng Xiaoping issued an edict invoking the principle of locality in a sweeping manner. Rather than seeking a general rise in the economic level of economic productivity, each area of China was to develop in accordance with its own peculiar characteristics. What this meant, of course, was that those provinces poised for economic growth were to be given every opportunity to rise to the occasion. The subsequent development of regions such as the Pearl River Delta is most remarkable. The cities of Hong Kong, Guangzhou, and Shenzhen are the principal urban centers of this zone. A number of other cities and industrial areas have developed rapidly enough to create an urban-industrial complex that may soon rival any in the world. By 1992, when Deng Xiaoping made his second visit to the area, the Pearl River Delta had become the wealthiest region of China.

It is simply not in the interests of Beijing to seek too much control over this highly productive region. And though there have been any number of disputes with the region over issues of local autonomy, Beijing has not always won these power struggles. After Deng Xiaoping's death, the fortunes of Shanghai have improved vastly, in some ways to the detriment of the interests of the Pearl River Delta, but this is merely one more example of regionalism at work. As we have indicated, Jiang Zemin's relationship with that city is an important factor in its having been given its present privileged status. And, particularly in this post-Tiananmen period, Shanghai's politically conservative character makes it preferable to the much more democracy-oriented area of Southern Guangdong, which has had neighboring Hong Kong as a model for nearly a generation.

The creation of Special Economic Zones, the most recent being Hong Kong, leads to a situation which renders futile any attempts to develop a "rule of law" in China. Without the rule of law, tensions and conflicts will inevitably arise between a strong central government in Beijing and powerful local interests. And though, in the last analysis, autocratic, authoritarian governance has been the rule in China, the strength of the autonomous regions, provinces, and special economic zones often determines the outcome of conflict with Beijing.

It is difficult to see how the sense of continuity and commonality required by the myth of the Han can survive such intense internal competition. It is likely that this competition will increase in the coming years, a consequence of policies that attempt to bring China abreast of the Western world.

## Class Conflict in a "Classless Society"

Ethnic tensions, local identities, and Special Economic Zones all create strains on the presumed harmony of the Han Chinese. Ironically, especially for a nation that continues to claim that it has implemented a socialist society, class divisions, as well, threaten to become an increasingly strong factor in challenging the stability of Han culture.

Recent books by Kate Xiao Zhou and Elisabeth Croll tell the fascinating story of how the freeing of Chinese farmers from political and economic constraints transformed the face of China in a relatively short time.[5] These works are especially welcome since they provide dramatic evidence of the rather surprising fact that "peasant-power" was perhaps the principal force for China's recent economic surge.

The collectivization of farming in China under the communist regime created a very unusual circumstance. This was perhaps the first time in the long history of China that any such attempt at centralization had been attempted. The principle that "everything is local" cannot be so easily contravened, however. When the farmers no longer worked for themselves and their families, but for the State, there was little motivation to succeed. Freed from these constraints, however, there seemed no limits to their initiative.

The sensational success of the "town and village enterprises," officially begun in the seventies as joint ventures of rural communist leaders and farm entrepreneurs, was a surprise to everyone—except,
perhaps, the farmers themselves. As Willem Van Kamenade notes: "Already by 1981 collectively organized investments made by farmers ac-
counted for 37 percent of all state investments, and the number of em-
ployees in the TVEs had mounted to 30 million."[6]

An even greater surprise, perhaps, was the fact that the "democratic
experiment" begun at the village level has achieved such dramatic
results, both substantively and rhetorically.[7] Since the introduction of
"basic democracy" in 1988, elections have taken place in most of the
villages of China. Though there is indication that these elections have
yet to be fully regularized, there is one impressive statistic that should
be noted. In the last round of village elections, it is said that over 360
million Chinese voted. The turnout in the villages was usually about 80
percent, and even sometimes as high as 100 percent.

The urbanized Chinese intellectual (*zhishifenzi* 知識分子) is, in fact,
heir to the Confucian educated class (*shi* 士). These modern sages, like
their classical counterparts, are typically possessed of the fear of a peasant class that is the psychological manifestation of the insecure hold the
Chinese gentry traditionally has felt it had on any privilege it possessed.
Thus, even those urban intellectuals who verbally espouse the cause of
democracy constitute an effectively antidemocratic force by virtue of
their suspicions of the single group within which democracy is most effectively present. Fear of the peasantry—what Van Kamenade has
termed "peasant phobia"[8]—has any number of causes, but they all are
rooted in the reality that, unlike Japan and Korea, China is a rural country in which the political dominance of the peasant class is always a
possibility.

In a traditional Confucian society the great divider of classes was the
bureaucratic examination. This being the case, the relationship between the peasants and the urban intellectuals is historically problematic because rarely could rural folk succeed in a system that privileged
education above all. Hence, a class distinction between farmers and intellectuals is persistent in such a society.

But an always tense situation was made much worse with the Communist revolution. Mao instituted policies of collectivization that pur-

ported to follow the Leninist model in which individual farmers constituted the erstwhile grounds for a feudal system. Collectivization was to "free" the farmers to move beyond this feudal status. Ironically enough, this process actually reinforced feudalism.

A system of household registration was employed to prevent migration to the urban centers of China. The effect of the *hukou* 戶口 system was to tie the farmer to the land and their locale. Under this system all those registered as residents of a city could receive food and housing subsidies while farmers were expected to grow their own food and provide their own housing. Instituted by Mao in the fifties primarily as a means of controlling internal migration, the *hukou* system effectively bound the farmers to Communist cadres in a feudal relationship more strict and limiting than any heretofore extant in the history of China.

The *hukou* system made some sense as a short-term dodge to control the famine that constituted the most serious problem faced by the new Communist regime. However, it soon outlived its usefulness, and for some years functioned only to prevent the economic vitality of the peasant class from contributing to China's overall productivity. The peasants effectively owned the status of an underclass, set apart from city dwellers, who considered them to be basically undesirable.

The remarkable changes that led to the increased status of farmers in China began with reforms initiated less than two years after Mao's death. 1978 was effectively the year in which China moved self-consciously away from *revolution* and toward *reform*.

Mao Zedong had always seen his role, however cynically and stupidly he sometimes behaved, as a revolutionary whose aim was to dramatically transform China by uprooting it from its inertial past, thereby setting it on the road to a distinctive future. He was not interested in mimicking the development of the Western world. Rather, he thought he saw in the Marxian counterdiscourse to a capitalist West, a means of bringing China into its own. Long before the 1978 reforms were initiated, however, the realities of China's rural policies had begun to dawn upon many of its leaders. Even among the party ideologues there came the realization that the best hope for economic development lay in utilizing the energies and resources of the rural areas of China.

It would be easy to overestimate the extent to which changes in governmental policy were responsible for the transformation of the countryside. The most substantial changes likely came about through the initiative of the farmers themselves. Until the peasants were able to demonstrate the value of being provided new freedoms and incentives, there would have been little governmental cooperation. Farmers began to deal with their village cadres, obtaining permission to develop private enterprises from which both the farmers and the cadres benefited. As long as the farmers met their quotas, cadres were increasingly willing to allow peasants some freedom with respect to occupation and migration.

The greatest opportunities for the peasant class came from the factor of surprise. Neither the village cadres nor the government officials in Beijing had expected that these reforms gradually won by the farmers would eventuate in such a dramatic increase in productivity. Thus, the peasants had achieved a substantial amount of economic power before the bureaucrats had the opportunity to foul things up.

The change in the status of Chinese farmers has presented a significant challenge to the Confucian idea of the dominance of the urban intellectual in defining the Chinese identity. And to employ the idiom of our concerns in this book, the principal effect of these reforms was to enhance the dynamic of democratization. The villagers were perfectly aware that their economic interests, and their power vis-à-vis the central government, would be enhanced by village elections. And though the control of the villages by party officials is still guaranteed in principle, the effects of such elections has been to increase the wealth, power, and prestige of the peasants in China's overall economic and political spheres, and thereby to shift the balance of power within China.

## Ideological Tensions

A final dynamic that belies the myth of Han unity has to do with ideological disputes within China's governing elite. Of course, ideological tensions have existed within China from its very beginnings and are little more than those seen in any politicized society. Such debates in China are epitomized in the minds of most Westerners with the May Fourth Movement of 1919 and, later, with the democratization movement leading up the Beijing massacre of 1989.

It needs to be emphasized that, after the 1989 repression of the Democracy Movement, views most critical of the government and the

Party have been disseminated outside of China by Chinese exiles, Taiwanese intellectuals, and foreign China watchers. In other words, the diversity of opinion *on* China is to be distinguished from the relative lack of diversity *in* China proper. It should also be said that the discussion of these tensions is complicated by the fact that "revolutionary" rhetoric in China is the monopoly of the Communist Party.

As we have noted, the year 1978 was pivotal for the Chinese. It was then that Deng Xiaoping began his economic reforms in earnest. In fact, a major shift in the Chinese psyche dates from this period. The rhetoric of "reform" was to replace that of "revolution." The images employed were those of "Heaven (*tian* 天)" and "Earth (*di* 地)." In her work on rural reform in China, *From Heaven to Earth—Images and Experiences of Development in China*, Elisabeth Croll uses these images effectively to chart the transition from revolution to reform in the post-Mao period. Croll cites this line from a 1987 newspaper in China that summarizes developments after 1978: "We have finally come back from Heaven to Earth."[9]

The term "Heaven" (*tian* 天) has played an important role in China from the very beginnings of Confucian culture. It is *tianming* 天命, the "Mandate of Heaven," that guides the emperor in his actions and sustains his authority as *tianzi* 天子, "the son of Heaven." "Earth" (*di* 地) is associated with the people, particularly with the peasants who live next to the land and work the soil. To move from "Heaven" to "Earth" was, therefore, a shift in priorities away from increasingly distant revolutionary ideals toward the concrete and immediate problems of the people.

The movement from Heaven to Earth signaled by the introduction of rural reforms discussed earlier had the effect of decreasing the sense of *imperium* associated with Chinese leadership. Though by no means limiting the political power of the representative of central government, the actions of Deng Xiaoping and Jiang Zemin have promoted a return to the emphasis upon practical problems for which everyone is expected to shoulder their share of the responsibility.

As might be expected, this shift has not been complete. There are still those who hold on to the older revolutionary expectations associated with Maoist thinking. Party ideologues have time and again served as counteractive forces frustrating the aim of achieving more practical reforms. This is especially so when proponents of reform are seen as apologists for Western ideas related to economic and technical modernization. Thus, neither Deng Xiaoping nor Jiang Zemin could be associated in a one-sided fashion with the pragmatic aims of those championing "Earth" over "Heaven." Indeed, the effect of the democratization movements that led to Tiananmen is to push Beijing away from the language of modernization and back to the socialist rhetoric of past decades.

The rhetoric of reform has been complicated even more by the highly controversial 1988 television documentary, "River Elegy."[10] The ideological shift from Heaven to Earth was a theme instituted from within the government and the Party. "River Elegy," on the other hand, was a self-conscious return to the spirit of the May Fourth Movement on the part of essentially independent intellectuals. The documentary editorialized about the stagnation of Chinese culture as contrasted with the dynamism of the West. Here, in contrast to the Heaven/Earth comparison, the images of Yellow River and Azure Ocean are used. Specifically, the contrast is between the Western Ocean travelers and the Chinese river culture. And again, as was the case in the May Fourth Movement, the desire is to obtain from the West the gifts of science and democracy:

> The great yellow earth cannot teach us what a scientific spirit really is.
> The ruthless Yellow River cannot teach us a true awareness of democracy.[11]

By explicitly invoking the spirit of the May Fourth Movement, "River Elegy" was able to shift the focus of discussions of reform away from simply revising the Maoist form of socialism to the question of the use of Western norms, methods, and values as the means of reforming China. And the fact that Zhao Ziyang, the General Secretary of the Communist Party during the period of the broadcast of "River Elegy," supported the program insured that the lines were drawn more firmly between the conservatives and reformists within the Party.

"River Elegy" was aired about a year before the Tiananmen massacre. Already in 1986 and 1987 there had been widespread student protests. The text of the final part of the documentary expresses optimism with respect to the student movement:

The sudden eruption of the nationwide student demonstrations in late 1986 and early 1987 has for a while made everyone excited and tense. It might be too early to make an assessment of this student movement. Nonetheless, the form of the demonstration has been successful in attaining the objective of the overwhelming majority of the students who participated in the movement, namely the "transparency" of politics and policy making.[12]

The term "transparency" (*toumingdu* 透明度) is a reformist term indicating the imperative to open the political decision-making processes to public scrutiny. The tone of the entire documentary suggests how free the writers of the documentary felt themselves to be in expressing their concerns. On the other hand, the fact that most of the individuals associated with this program are now living in self-imposed exile suggests how much things have changed after Tiananmen.

Whatever else may be said of reformist sentiments in China, it is certainly true that one of the principal obstacles to reform lies in the fundamental importance tacitly accorded the myth of the Han. Reforms must in some sense leave the essentials of the culture intact—otherwise, how is China to remain China? "River Elegy" explicitly recognizes this barrier:

> The difficulty of reform lies perhaps in the fact that we are constantly worrying over "whether the Chinese will remain Chinese." We do not seem to have realized that in the last two or three centuries in the West having gone through the Renaissance, the Reformation, and the Enlightenment, the Western Europeans have not worried about whether after these reforms they would remain Italians, or Germans, or Frenchmen. It is only in China that this has always been the greatest concern.
>
> Perhaps this is precisely the deepest aspect of this yellow civilization, and also its shallowest aspect.[13]

Unfortunately, there is no advice given as to how the Chinese might overcome their constant worry as to whether they will remain Chinese. In order to follow the lead of the Europeans it would be necessary to be equipped with a sense of self and culture that is not so fragile that it would be threatened by venturing forth into new societies. It does appear, however, that the many challenges to the myth of the Han are strong enough to render moot any refusal on the part of the Chinese to compromise their "Chineseness." There may be little choice.

So far we have suggested two ideological conflicts based upon the reformist/conservative contrast. The first, essentially mainstream, is that of the movement away from the Mao inspired ideal of "permanent revolution" to that of economic and political reforms based upon practical and pragmatic needs rather than ideological principles. The second conflict is that which associates the notion of "reform" with a greater or lesser degree of modernization and Westernization.

Beijing, in the person of Jiang Zemin, will likely continue to promote economic reforms that allow China to move closer to a market economy. Since 1989, however, the cause of self-conscious Westernization has essentially been suspended, and little by way of explicit concessions to the Democracy Movement may be expected.

Having said this, forces associating Chinese economic enterprises with those of the West are leading to concessions with regard to human rights, contractual obligations, intellectual property, and so on. These forces can only move Chinese society from the rule of men in the direction of the rule of law. This movement urges an economically driven, legally sanctioned, rights-based democracy—the very sort that runs afoul of the communitarian traditions of Chinese society.

A third important ideological issue that further focuses the reformist/conservative debates is that of the "new authoritarianism." This issue became focused by debates between proponents of the Democracy Movement, and those supporting economic reform. It would be a mistake, however, to presume any simple contrast between these two camps.

Each of the two camps was represented by both authoritarian and nonauthoritarian positions. For example, many members of the Democratic Movement, now living in enforced exile, were proponents of the new authoritarianism, reasoning that the transition to democracy would require a strong guiding hand if success were to be assured. Likewise, economic reformers were divided into those who espoused the Asian model of economic development—identified most readily with Japan, Korea, Taiwan, and Singapore—in which a liberalized economy is conjoined with strong governmental authority and the "free enterprise" model that promotes (relatively) unfettered economic activity.

There is some sign that, at least at the economic level, the Chinese are moving away from government interference in business activity. Zhu Rongji, appointed in March of 1998 as successor to outgoing Premier Li Peng, has guided economic policy in China for the last five years. Zhu successfully proposed a one-third reduction in the central ministries and a dramatic 50 percent reduction of the 8 million government bureaucrats—thereby adding some credibility to Beijing's expressed desire to prevent government from meddling in business.

The conclusion one might draw from these considerations is that the current political authoritarianism may be practiced to a greater or lesser degree along side an increasingly liberalized economy. Reforms affecting the creation of Special Economic Zones and those associated with land reform and the village enterprise system may be allowed, even while the political freedoms of speech and media are severely curtailed.

The main issue, of course, is the debate between the democratic and antidemocratic forces in China. Presently, the antidemocratic forces are firmly in power. These forces, represented by the Beijing government, are ideologically committed to the rule of men over the rule of law, and to hard-line interpretations of "socialist dictatorship." There is no real question of nonauthoritarian interpretations of governance among these individuals.

The question for the future is whether the movement toward democracy, however faltering, will be enhanced or retarded by the authoritarian model. A complication exists in the fact that there is little by way of mass desire for democracy. The principal benefactors of democratic institutions have been the peasants of China. While they have been able to significantly shape their futures through the process of village elections, and have often achieved rather startling economic successes, they appear to have little motivation to see democracy generalized at the national level. "Heaven is high and the Emperor (and his urban intellectuals) are far away," and there is only a measured feeling of attachment beyond the level of one's village.

The intellectuals who favor democratization hardly constitute a mass movement and, moreover, are themselves quite suspicious of the emerging power of the farmers and village entrepreneurs. This suspicion and the attendant fear of the peasant class, as much as any other factor, is the reason many urban intellectuals see the necessity of an authoritarian transition to democracy.

A final ideological issue involves the question of Confucianism. Again, there is no easy way to sort out the pros and the cons. One can find both defenders and detractors of Confucian values among intellectuals, peasants, and Party officials. The motives for supporting Confucian values are quite diverse. Government officials and Party leaders employ Confucian slogans as anti-Western rhetoric. Some scholars recognize the need to advertise the sense in which Confucianism represents the true cultural self-consciousness of China. Economic reformers promote the virtues of order, discipline, frugality, and familial loyalty as basic to the success of an Asian capitalism with Chinese characteristics. And so it goes.

The use of Confucius as a foil with which to combat not only Western values, but also the entire process of Westernization, is not to be dismissed merely as an exercise in political bad faith. We must not discount the degree to which Chinese, both within and without the government, resent Western preachments directed against China. The very real dictatorial aspects of the Chinese government aside, much of the Western criticism of China is seriously misdirected because it presupposes that the Chinese people want what the Western people want.

The high degree of appreciation for individual autonomy found in Western societies is a puzzlement to many, if not most, Chinese. Whatever else Confucianism represents, it stands for the centrality of familial loyalties and obligations. The occasional celebration of "Western individuals" by Chinese intellectuals almost never carries with it the expectation of a lessened concern for familial loyalty and regard for one's community, natural tradeoffs of individualism. These "Confucian" commitments have functional equivalents in the communitarian traditions of the West, although they continue to wane in the Western world as individual autonomy becomes an increasingly uncritical value. In short, the Chinese might have a point were they to say, "We have values and qualities in our cultural resources which you in the West could do well to emulate."

The intellectuals' appeals to Confucianism are predicated upon the entirely reasonable recognition that a society or culture can not easily uproot itself from its own traditions. The naïveté of importing some alternative set of institutional imperatives is doubly naive for a culture in which "everything is local." The transformation and adaptation of Confucian values and institutions are far more preferable than the wholesale rejection of one's cultural heritage. In any case, as the unsuccessful Marxian experiment so well demonstrates, any such rejection is likely to fail.

Perhaps the most interesting endorsement of Confucianism comes from the economic reformers who argue that Confucianism is no barrier to the introduction of capitalism and a market economy, but a positive asset. In the minds of many, Confucian values make of Asian capitalism an even more viable economic model than Western-style capitalism. This argument is based upon a distinction between an earlier speculative, entrepreneurial stage of capitalism in which risk and individual initiative were prized, and the present state of a world capitalism that is labor intensive, mass-market driven, and depends for its success not so much upon competition, but upon the large-scale cooperation of its participants.

Arguments such as this from Asian economists dovetail nicely with the promotion of distinctly "Asian values" by politicians and intellectuals alike. Significant fluctuations in Asian economies notwithstanding, such arguments are not to be dismissed lightly. They require responsible Western economists and CEOs to take a serious look at Asian models of management and capitalist activity.

# 4. The Future of Han China

We have suggested that the myth of the Han is being severely tested both within and without China. The future of China will surely involve ethnic conflicts exacerbated by the attempts of other nations to influence official Chinese actions with respect to those non-Han minorities. There will be increased pressures upon the Chinese to modernize. And in the currently accepted idiom this can only mean to Westernize.

The special economic privileges allowed to local areas of China such as Guangdong, Shanghai, and so on, will continue to increase the power of these regions vis-à-vis the central Beijing government. Further, there may well be concessions demanded from other members of the Chinese world, principally Taiwan, for internal changes in China if there is to be economic and political cooperation among China and the outer Chinese world.

Farmers and village entrepreneurs are, as we have said, presently the most effective democratizing forces in China. They will continue to demand their slice of the political and economic pie. The rise of the peasant class may take place at the expense of the urban intellectual class. If this is so, the single most important model of the Han sensibility will be threatened.

Western nations will continue their rhetorical assault upon China, demanding greater attention to individual rights and freedoms. Insofar as it is consistent with the desire of Western-style businesses to exploit the mighty Chinese market, they will continue to press for the institution of dependable contracts within a system shaped by the rule of law. And consonant with the theme of the "River Elegy," China will have no choice but to open itself to the azure oceans through its recently constructed seaports, as well as to open itself to the "other" West in the form of its continental land bridge linking it to the outside world by rail and highway.

These are but a small number of the factors and forces that will conspire to shape the future of China. One can only imagine what must go through the minds of those who presently hold power when they rehearse, as daily they must, both the creative and destructive potential of these inexorable dynamisms.

The central question of this work is "What is the hope for democracy in China?" We have said something of what, in contrast to the received perception of China as "the people of the Han," we mean by "China." It is now essential to consider the meaning of "democracy." In the following discussions we shall argue that not only must we reject the myth of the Han, it is equally essential that the "myth of Liberal Democracy" be challenged. This will permit an understanding of the sense of democracy most relevant to the future of China.

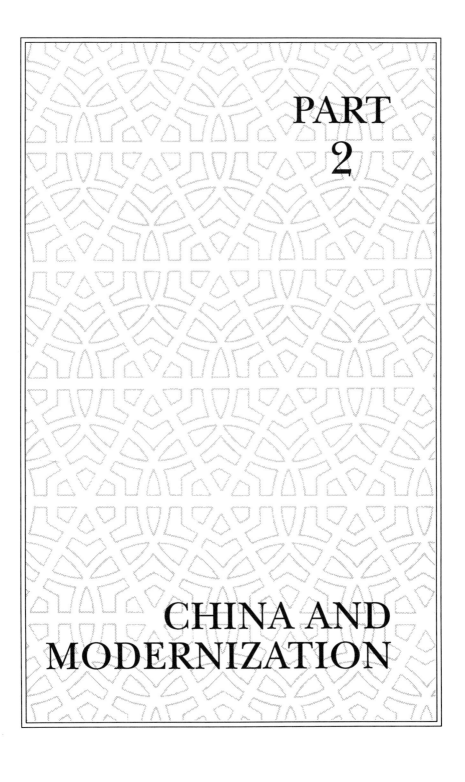

# PART 2

# CHINA AND MODERNIZATION

# 'Modernity' as a Western Invention

**3**

## 1. Politics, Economics, and Culture

The literature dealing with changes in Chinese and Western relationships is dominated by arguments which presume either an economic or a political determinism. Contrary to these approaches, we are discussing the present character and status of China from a distinctly *cultural* perspective. To prevent uneasiness on the part of readers who might be suspicious of such an approach, we should indicate why we believe arguments that attempt to assess a broad range of beliefs and value commitments are essential complements to those focused upon strictly economic or political activities. Indeed, as we shall demonstrate in this chapter, the presumption that political and economic explanations are not directly concerned with *values* and are not powerfully determined by broader cultural assumptions is dangerously naive. Language suggesting that economic and political arguments are to be distinguished from cultural explanations merely signals a contrast in *conscious intent* of the contrasted parties. Such language should not, however, obscure the fact that explanations drawn from the social and behavioral sciences are as much an expression of the culture from out of which they emerge as are theological, philosophical, and aesthetic arguments.

Theories of economic determinism, once expressed by proponents of both Marxism and capitalism, today tend to come in solely capitalist garb. Belief in the inevitable march of capitalism often presumed by Western economic interests precludes the necessity of considering the possible efficacy of any cultural *values* other than those associated with material needs and desires. Appeal to "market forces" is deemed an adequate explanation.

Individuals who accept political actions and decisions as the motors of social change are equally adverse to arguments that presume the importance of cultural values and institutions. As Edward Friedman notes, "political action can rapidly change the conditions that matter. . . . Politics changes faster than culture."[1] The presence of political pressure groups, or the unilateral decisions of a powerful leader, can effect changes in spite of any cultural conditioning features appearing to work against them.

There is certainly some truth in both economic and political arguments. One has but to look at China's recent past. Mao's often arbitrary decisions had long-lasting effects upon the face of China. His institutionalization of a brand of Marxism reconstituted the Chinese social landscape. Politics, indeed, makes a difference. The rapidity with which China appears to be making the transition to a capitalist economy clearly suggests the power of economic interests and motivations.

Proponents of cultural determinants are not altogether convinced of the efficacy of such dynamics, however. They are likely to respond to the arguments of both economic and political theorists by noting that, with respect to China, a substantial number of the political changes associated with Maoist rule lived only a few months longer than did he. And though it is too early to tell much about the fate of capitalism in China, there is evidence that the rebirth of Confucianism may in fact significantly influence the shape of Chinese economic institutions.

The point of the culturalist, particularly the historicist variety represented by the authors of this work, is that while politics is faster, culture runs deeper—and has far greater long-term efficacy. And while something like capitalist acquisitiveness may be generalized across cultures, such economic motives are to be inventoried differently in different cultural contexts.

Further, as historicists, we are as far as possible from arguing for the inevitable consequences of any set of cultural dynamics—including economic and political dynamics. Our argument is that both politics and economics are cultural expressions whose efficacy must be assessed alongside other cultural values. More particularly, we believe that liberal, individualistic, rights-based democracy and free enterprise capitalism, are specific products of the historical development of Western modernity. Any attempt, therefore, to generalize them across cultures is likely to be altogether too heavy handed an exercise.

Culturalist arguments have gained some increased recognition recently with the works of the political scientist, Samuel Huntington.[2] Huntington extends the argument of Daniel Bell's *End of Ideology* by proclaiming the dominance of cultural determinants over ideological factors in the form of international engagements. Such an argument is based upon the recognition that norms and values can remain implicit as long as we operate within a single cultural milieu. When the contrast between engaging countries is too great, however, as is certainly the case between Anglo-European and Chinese sensibilities, cultural norms and values are perforce raised to consciousness.

Our belief in the value of the distinctly cultural approach taken in this work depends in large measure upon the assumption that our approach is far more inclusive and less likely to lead to simplistic reductionism. In any case, the test is a pragmatic one. If what we have to offer provides suggestions leading to enriched and productive engagements between Chinese and Western interlocutors, we shall have done all that we could responsibly hope to do.

# 2. Meanings of "Modernity"

The most dramatic agencies associated with the notion of "modernity" are those of liberal democracy, capitalist economy, and rational technologies. In assaying the importance of modernization for China, we must not forget that these agencies are products of a long and complex history associated with the development of peculiarly Western institutions. They involve the contributions of Greek, Roman, and Hebraic sensibilities, further shaped by the dramatic migration to the American continent which allowed for several sets of new beginnings.

The three principal dynamics of modernity are directly traceable to themes allied with a variety of interpretations of modernity published over the past generation. These more philosophical interpretations presume conceptions of self and society that were allied with these dynamics and that, in time, were reshaped by them. The obvious implication is that the wholesale importation of such agencies into China would dramatically alter its character, actually transforming that society into the terminus of an alien historical narrative.

Few proponents of modernization, whether Chinese or Western, seem to have considered the implications of the rewriting of Chinese history that would be required were China to accept uncritically the agencies of modernization. The following pages are in part an attempt to advertise some of those implications.

The question as to how Asian cultures might balance the negative and positive impacts of modernization has only begun to be investigated in areas such as Hong Kong, Singapore, Taiwan, and Korea. Lately, this question is most dramatically and visibly addressed by the so-called "Asian Values" debates taking place in various venues around the world.

In considering a course for the future of a modernizing China, we must reflect upon at least the following three questions: First, "What does it mean to say that modernity is a peculiarly Western invention?" Second, "What would be the likely effects of China's acceptance of modernization and, therefore, Westernization?" And third, "What model of democratic development would allow the Chinese to set their own terms for entrance into the modern world?"

The first question may be more simply stated in this form: What, beyond the surface clichés familiar to us all, is meant by the equation, *Modernization = Westernization?* To answer this question we must clarify the connections between "modernization" and "modernity."

As a state or condition, modernity is a multivalent and richly vague complex that must not be too sharply defined lest, in the attempt to render the notion coherent, we omit some crucial elements. Thus modernity is not a concept but a conceptual cluster of overlapping and sometimes contradictory elements. That is to say, the notion of modernity is vague in the sense that it is open to a variety of distinctive associations. Modernization, as the shaping of institutions and societies along certain political, economic, and technological imperatives, carries a selection of these vague associations along with it, affecting values and attitudes in significant manners. Thus, in one sense, modernization is simply the process of institutionalizing certain aspects of the modern impulse.

Modernization has come to be characterized in terms of technology, rights-based democracy, and free enterprise capitalism. Conceptually, the connections between modernity and modernization are easy enough to establish. Modernizing processes receive much of their import from the matrix of ideas and attitudes constituting the phenomenon of modernity. Historically, the processes of modernization were furthered by those who purported to have little interest in or understanding of the broader intellectual and valuational components of modernity.

Often, as is particularly true of technological development, modernization seems to be an essentially mindless self-augmenting process that, while rational with respect to certain selected ends, is essentially uncontrollable, with largely indeterminate allied consequences. In the absence of conscious articulation, vaguer aspects of modernity are imported along with modernizing processes, and the long-term consequences of modernization for the members of the target culture are barely appreciated.

What aspects of modernity are carried in the modernizing process? Clearly, rights-based democracy stresses the autonomy of the individual at the level of both thought and action. Rights and freedoms are owned primarily by individuals and not by communities. Capitalism promotes the vision of *homo economicus* that defines society principally in terms of individuals with needs and desires. The value of individual autonomy is further celebrated by the element of economic competition. Such competition can seriously undermine the foundations of a communitarian social system.

Technologies are instruments of both production and of self-assertion, permitting increased control over human environs. The environment so controlled is increasingly that comprised by private satisfactions. One of the chief effects of technological development has been a shriveling of the public sphere and a bloating of the private. Private satisfactions increasingly take over from public duties as the defining character of the good life. The result, in principle, is a kind of default solipsism in which the Cartesian ego, free of physical and moral constraints, surfs virtual space and time.

Our concern throughout this work is to urge increased sensitivity to the consequences of suggesting to the Chinese that the political and socioeconomic institutions that lie at the end of their otherwise unique historical journey are essentially the same as those dominating contemporary North Atlantic democracies. To that end we now wish to unpack the various meanings associated with the rise of modernity in the West. We hope to show how naive is the presumption that the primary agencies of modernization are culture-neutral and, therefore, easily generalizable.

There are at least four fundamental strands associated with the principal interpretations of modernity.[3] As we shall see, the focus of all these interpretations is the notion of the self or individual. Thus, the cultural accounts that have produced the modern Western self involve, not one, but several tangled narratives. As a consequence of the coexistence of these strands of interpretation, the modern self is a richly vague pastiche of conflicting elements. Though the various strands contradict one another in important ways, modernizing impulses derived from Western cultural narratives tend, for the most part, to support the interpretation of the human being as a discrete individual. Thus, the most powerful consequence of modernization for China will be that the communitarian presuppositions upon which that society has been grounded since its very beginnings will be seriously threatened.

Contrasting understandings of the individual expressed in the various strands of modernity characterize the person in terms of either self-consciousness, or self-assertion, or the dynamics of production and acquisition, or creative expression.

The understanding of modernity in terms of the development of self-consciousness is perhaps the most familiar. René Descartes (1596–1650) provided the basic model of self-reflection in his famous *Cogito ergo sum*. The deepening of subjectivity in the articulation of the Cartesian "I think . . ." is balanced by the securing of the ego's existence through drawing the consequence, "I am." The consequence is that Descartes manages to objectify the subject, as well as subjective experience.

Descartes provided three other noteworthy contributions to the understanding of modernity. First, along with several of his contemporaries, he revived the Ancient Greek atomistic model as a means of construing the external world in material terms. Atomic theory, which characterizes the cosmos in materialist, mechanistic terms, is a principal motor of modernity, for it is the basis upon which the otherness of the world is both posited and overcome. Objectivity is grounded in the knowledge of objects. In each of the modern sciences—chemistry, physics, biology, psychology, and sociology—the knower becomes an object among other objects.

Second, the Cartesian discovery of analytic geometry provided a powerful tool demonstrating an isomorphic relationship between a mathematical mind and a mathematicized nature. This allowed for a sense of accommodation between the individual thinker and the natural world. One could now come to some understanding of the world by reflecting upon the structure of the mind and the nature of mental operations.

Finally, the incoherence of Descartes' treatment of mind and body allowed him to celebrate two primary sources of modern individualism—the self-conscious self and the physical body—each of which are to be understood as separate, distinct, autonomous units. As we shall see, contrasting visions of the "individual" of liberal democratic theory draw upon these two, mutually incoherent, definitions of individuality as "conscious mind" and as "material body."

Immanuel Kant (1724–1804) ramified the Cartesian element of personal subjectivity by developing a relationship between mind and its external ambiance which, instead of emphasizing merely the mathematical, stressed the importance of the cultural interests of science, morality, and art. Kant provided three highly influential analyses of these interests. *The Critique of Pure Reason* articulated the nature and limits of reason in terms of scientific judgments. The *Critique of Practical Reason* was concerned with moral experience and the distinctive character of ethical judgments. The *Critique of Judgment* discussed the notion of aesthetics and aesthetic judgments in terms that influenced the development of modern aesthetic theory. Kant's three critiques employed the cultural interests of science, morality, and art as media through which both self and external environs are to be understood.

Kant's refusal to accord religion an autonomous status on a par with the other three spheres was highly influential in determining the future role of the religious interest in intellectual culture. One of the consequences of Kant's treatment of religious interest was in providing autonomy for the moral interest, offering a means of setting it free from the hegemony of religion. Analogously, his third critique provided an autonomous sphere for the aesthetic imagination.

One reason for the importance of Kantian thought in contemporary intellectual culture lies in the fact that his promotion of autonomous value spheres was itself grounded in an interpretation of the individual as a moral agent owning freedom of will. Kant's positing of an "autonomous will" that exists prior to any particular desires or ends will later on provide some support for the interpretation of the human being as a self-assertive agent. In fact, the Kantian notion of the autonomous will is most prominent in rights-based liberal theory.

The distinctiveness of Kant's position, however, is that the autonomous will is subordinated to rational maxims or principles. That is to say, the Categorical Imperative enjoining that individuals be treated always as ends, and never merely as means, qualifies the exercise of the will in matters of choice. The individual remains a *rational* being.

G. W. F. Hegel (1770–1831) placed a capstone on the rationalist reading of modernity as the realization of self-consciousness. Like Kant, Hegel was essentially a philosopher of culture, and gave to the modern age an unexcelled example of the articulation of cultural self-consciousness. In this manner Hegel provided a *speculum mentis,* a veritable map of the mind—not of the Universal Mind he thought he had charted, but of the Graeco-Hebraic-Roman mind to which he was a most sensitive heir.

Already, with respect to this single strand of cultural development, one can begin to see how complex are the intellectual dynamics characteristic of Western modernity. Unless, contrary to all received interpretations of Chinese history, we can presume to discover equivalents of the Descartes-Kant-Hegel axis of interpretation in China, we must be cautious about entertaining the naive assumption that Western notions of rationality and self-consciousness are easily translatable into a Chinese idiom.

A second major interpretation of modernity is resourced in the construal of the self, not in terms of consciousness, but of volition. The modern individual is primarily self-assertive. Francis Bacon (1561–1626) is representative of this position. This model urges, not that "the rational is the real," but that "knowledge is power." Francis Bacon is the patron saint of that coterie of individuals who count self-assertive control of nature as the highest form of individual and social self-realization. Among Bacon's most influential writings are *The Advancement of Learning* (1605) and the *Novum Organum* (1620). Bacon's New Science, motored by an experimental method, was not to seek mere dispassionate knowledge. He wished science to serve the interest of human beings in attaining mastery of nature. Such mastery was, above all, to bring about improvements of human life on the surface of the planet. Bacon's self-assertive vision of science makes of him an early patron of the technological impulse.

Other representatives of the self-assertive interpretation of modernity include so-called "existentialists" such as Søren Kierkegaard (1813–1855), Friedrich Nietzsche (1844–1900), along with the sociologist Max Weber (1864–1920). The assessments of the self-assertive impulse by these thinkers ranges on both positive and negative ends of the scale.

The ambiguity of the notion of self-assertion can perhaps be seen most clearly in the work of Max Weber. Weber begins with the cultural problematic associated with Kant and Hegel. The autonomy and mutual articulation of the value spheres sets the problem for this interpreter of modernity. But Weber explains the dynamics of the problem in terms of the movement from traditional to rational societies, which he terms a secularizing movement. The secularization of society is a result of raising to consciousness the implicit character of the value dimensions associated with art, morality, science, and religion.

What traditional societies accommodate without deliberation, rational societies accommodate through conscious articulation. Thus the very project endorsed by Hegel—the attainment of a coherent cultural self-consciousness—becomes problematic in Weber's understanding of modernity. With cultural self-consciousness comes the "disenchantment" of the cultural domain. How are we to deal with this disenchantment?

When modern individuals become conscious of the character of the cultural interests that discipline their search for meaning, conflict inevitably ensues. This must be so since with this consciousness comes a recognition of contradiction. Implicit values are vague with respect to their meanings. Raised to consciousness they become concepts and theories that clash with rival notions. In place of subjective self-consciousness that recognizes a continuity between the mind and intellectual culture, there emerges the subjective as the agency of new cultural values. Cut off from the substantive, if often implicit, values of traditional culture, the decisions of the autonomous will tend to be empty and abstract— that is to say, *arbitrary*.

Weber holds that the true gift of modernity is freedom. This freedom is to be seen in the recognition of the autonomy of the will that lies at the basis of all decision-making. The few who manage to rise above the routines of an empty rationalized existence to exercise that freedom meaningfully are the creators of meaning and value for others.

In contemporary discussions, the interpretation of the individual as a self-assertive agent may be interwoven with the rational strand of modernity. Some readings of Kant have led to interpretations of individual autonomy that lean toward volitionalism. The economic interpretation of modernity that construes the self in terms of production and acquisition may also be allied with that of the self-assertive model. This alliance results when the economic and the political spheres are presumed radically distinct. This disjunction requires a separation of the concern for the mediation of individual wills motivated by diverse conceptions of the appropriate ends of the political life from the contentless economic realm motored simply by "desires" and "needs." The political realm becomes the arena of volitional activity; the economic sphere is construed in terms of material needs and desires.

The most influential understanding of the economic interpretation of modernity, however, is to be found in the legacy of John Locke (1632–1704), David Hume (1711–1776), Adam Smith (1723–1790), and Karl Marx (1818–1883). For in these thinkers the political sphere is seen to be derived from, and in the service of, the economic.

Locke's understanding of property as initially modeled upon ownership of one's self rehearses a new variation on the persistent theme of modernity—namely, *self-objectification*. This interpretation is further ramified by David Hume and Adam Smith. Hume begins with the essentially Lockeian presumption of a direct connection between individual psychology and personal property. The passions of pride and envy, and love and hate, are stimulated by the possession of lack of possession of property. Those who own or fail to own are the objects of the love or hate that are, ultimately, forms of pride and envy. Human passions, rather than serving to create a rich subjective experiencing, are both effects and agents of objectification.

Beyond the well-known difficulties associated with Hume's understanding of the self, personal identity is largely a social fiction deriving from the recognition of individuals as sources of pride and envy, and objects of love and hate. In addition, those legal and institutional structures that help to guarantee the stability of a system of property ownership further ramify the objectification of the self through the stipulations of persons as loci of economic and social responsibilities.

Adam Smith's familiar claim that "the patrimony of the poor lies in the strength and dexterity of their hands,"[4] and his arguments in favor of division of labor further ramify the objectification of the self in terms of specialized functions. The introduction of self-interest and competition into the economic analysis leads to a situation which both favors the owners of property and of the means of production and transforms the working class into functions to be coordinated through competition and the division of labor.

Karl Marx provides the final variation on the economic strand of modernity. He does this by attempting to provide an alternative to the Locke-Hume-Smith interpretation. Rarely in Western intellectual history has there been a better example of the function of theory as a *counterdiscourse*. The central agreement of Marx with Locke, Hume, and Smith lies in the importance each places upon the connections of property and selfhood. For Marx the objectification of the self through property is a process of alienation in which one makes of oneself a "strange and inhuman object." Nonetheless, the efficacy of property in the creation of the self is not denied.

A second agreement is the manner in which needs shape human motivations. Marx attempts to define *authentic* needs that would prevent the process, so familiar in advanced capitalist societies, of the multiplication of needs through the manipulation of a presumably indefinitely elastic set of desires. Marx finds artificially manipulated desires and the creation of needs to be primarily a process of increasing self-alienation.

The economic strand of modernity is not simply that of capitalism. The locution "free enterprise capitalism" includes within it, even in this presumably post-Marxist age, elements of the Marxian counterdiscourse. In his justly famous work on Marxism, Marshall Berman saw this clearly when he noted how capitalist society "inevitably produces radical ideas and movements that aim to destroy it." Its dynamism, however, allows it "to thrive on opposition" and "transform attackers into inadvertent allies."[5]

Thus far we have discussed "modernity" in terms of three rather distinct interpretations of the individual. Self-consciousness, self-assertion, self-gratification constitute alternative renderings of the self patterned upon three fundamental interests constituting modern culture. Reason, volition, and passion are fundamental modalities of the modern *psyche*. The incoherence of these interpretations reflects a basic incoherence in the modern Western individual who, in effect, possesses a soul at war with itself. Given all of the potential benefits of modernization Asian nations might receive, they have to reflect seriously upon the possibilities that modernity is a Trojan horse containing elements that may defeat the honest aspirations of the non-Western world seeking harmonious cultural development.

We have not quite finished our rehearsal of the principal strands of modernity. A final strand, the "aesthetic," is closely associated with the economic. This alliance of creativity and production is inevitable in a society whose Greek roots do not require a firm distinction between the making of shoes and the making of poetry. We see in both the economic and the aesthetic interpretations of modernity a concern for producing objects. The difference is primarily one associated with internal and external visions of the self. Economic individuals are created through objectification and the manipulation of desires by external objects. The aesthetic individual owns a self that serves as a mysterious source of creative expression.

The aesthetic interpretation of modernity requires that the distinction between the cultural interests of art and morality initially forwarded by Kant be fully realized. From Plato to the modern age, art served a fundamentally moral purpose. It comes into its own as a distinctive human interest only after a struggle on the part of Romantics and their epigoni to free the aesthetic from the moral impulse, and to celebrate the primacy of the former.

Charles Baudelaire (1821–1867) is the representative figure here. In his *The Painter of Modern Life*, Baudelaire provides the classic description of modernity as an essentially aesthetic event. Modernity is the experience of passing particularities *sub specie eternitatis*. It is "the ephemeral, the transitory, the contingent, the half of art the other half of which is the eternal and immutable."[6] The key to this understanding of modernity is the discovery of "the immediately actual existence of immediately actual time," and the recognition that "almost all our originality comes from the stamp that *time* imprints upon our feelings."[7]

This understanding of the ultimately temporal character of experience reinforced the internalization of human powers associated with the Romantic movement. The consequence was the increased separation of the aesthetic and the moral impulses. The concrete particularities of experience conceived as ends in themselves carry no moral message. The immediacy of aesthetic feeling permits no ethical mediation. The artist as amoral creator is a modern discovery.

The principal interpretations of modernity are resourced in and depend upon interpretations of the self. The self is primarily subjective awareness, or autonomous self-assertion, or as locus of needs and desires, or of aesthetic experience and expression. Given these four principal narrative strands which together tell the story of modernity, it would be impossible to understand the modern age in anything like a coherent manner. Attempts to do so merely select out one of the strands as dominant, thereby seriously under-gauging the complexity of the phenomenon. Self-reflection, self-assertion, self-gratification, and self-expression are the contrasting, and conflicting, means of fabricating the modern self. Responsible characterizations of modernity must surely be sensitive to the incoherence of this concept cluster.

If attempts are made to discuss the modern self in terms both of rational subjectivity and of self-assertiveness, what is the result? And what of the aesthetic impulse forcibly conjoined with rational and self-assertive elements? Subjective self-consciousness, political assertion, economic desire, aesthetic expression: Who is in the driver's seat of this modern chariot? In the attempt to avoid threatened contradictions, interpreters of modernity are tempted to select out a single strand of interpretation and argue for its adequacy. It is this that counts for the strong tendency toward reductionism on the part of so many modern intellectuals.

This brief allusion to themes of modernity indicates how difficult it would be to come to terms with the phenomenon in any theoretically adequate manner. But our purpose is not primarily to discuss the meanings of modernity; it is, rather, to demonstrate modernity's culturally contingent character. Our aim is to demonstrate the manner in which meanings of modernity are historically contextualized within Western intellectual culture.

We began this chapter with the claim that a broad analysis of the important beliefs and values characterizing a particular culture is more productive than an appeal solely to political or economic evidence. It is now possible to be somewhat clearer about our methodological concerns.

Economic and political interpretations of Chinese and Western engagement that rely on the efficacy of market forces or Western political institutions, or models of decision-making, to set the terms of the engagements seriously undervalue the richness of Western cultural resources. In addition, they seek to promote culturally specific values of questionable generality. Any attempt to argue that economic or political arguments are somehow less value-oriented and less culturally determined than are philosophic or aesthetic interpretations is both naive and counterproductive.

In subsequent discussions we shall demonstrate the connection of selected elements associated with the modernizing impulse with the interpretive strands of modernity. Our hope is to render more plausible the argument that exporting these elements to China will involve the exportation, as well, of a host of hidden assumptions that might have serious consequences with respect to Chinese individuals and their social organization.

One might search in vain for dominant strains of thought within the Chinese tradition that celebrate in the manner of Western intellectuals the central importance of the discrete and autonomous individual. More importantly, the values, behaviors, and institutions expressive of these strains of thought are equally absent. Later, when we have occasion to consider notions of social equality, human rights, the rule of law, and so forth, we shall see that it would be unreasonable to expect that these have received the same articulation in Chinese culture as in the modern West.

The tentative conclusion of our argument thus far, to be tested throughout the following discussions, is that a modernizing China will be asked to accept the presumed advantages of a capitalist economic system, a tradition of individual rights associated with liberal democracy, and the technological apparatus that will render more efficient the quest for increased material well-being. Of greater consequence, by effectively importing an alien history, a foreign tradition, China will also be asked to transmogrify the very conditions under which it has organized its way of life. It will be asked to accept culturally contingent, Western, presuppositions with regard to the issue of what it means to be human.

## 3. Modernity in Crisis

Ironically, China's avoidance of cultural disintegration through forced modernization may depend upon internal conflicts within Western culture. The "crisis of modernity" persistently proclaimed in the several movements huddled beneath the umbrella of "postmodernism" seems far more than a faddish *fin-de-siècle* malaise. The Western crisis is connected with the mutual incoherence of its cultural constructions. The complex of meanings associated with the concept of modernity is experienced as contradictory significances that tend to cancel one another out. Indeed, the internal contradictions advertised by the entangled strands of modernity have led to a significant cultural crisis.

The fading avatars of Enlightenment rationality—theoretical absolutes, universal values, scientism, metanarratives, logocentrism, and a host of totalizing discourses—have been broadly assailed by the new Romantic impulses of late modern society. These same impulses have led to a search for novel resources from which to construct counterdiscourses relevant to our altered circumstances. This search has been motored by two distinct dynamics: First, we have been urged to look within our own cultural stock for heretofore marginalized aspects of our tradition, hoping to discover fresh elements with which to construct alternatives to the outmoded aspects of our cultural milieu. The reevaluation of our cultural heritage has led to reinterpretations of classical sources at the very beginnings of our tradition, and to a shift of priorities with respect to contemporary philosophical movements. The former provides significant interpretations that challenge the standard rationalist *mythos* to *logos* interpretation of cultural development.[8] One consequence of the latter, most relevant to our present concerns, is a renewal of the tradition of American pragmatism, marginalized until recently within Anglo-European intellectual culture.

A second dynamic has thrust us outward, in the direction of alternative cultures, to discover whether marginalized elements of our culture are elsewhere present in a more developed form. This has brought about an increased interest in Asia, since Asian cultures, that of the Chinese in particular, have a sensibility shaped by distinctly *uncommon* assumptions—intuitions and beliefs little appreciated by the Enlightenment West. This sensibility is directly associated with the Confucian tradition.

Our argument is that interest in both the so-called New Pragmatism and the New Confucian sensibility of Asian cultures is the consequence of a search for counterdiscourses with which to critique the rationalist elements of modernity. This recognition itself is a result of the recent, rather surprising, discovery that the pragmatic sensibility has a long and distinguished history in Asia in the form of Confucian thought.

An important implication of our thesis is that the philosophical assumptions underlying the dominant modes of technical, economic, and political motivations for engagement with Asia, assumptions that comprise much of what we mean by modernity, are skewed in comparison with the most genuine elements of Asian cultural values.

This implication urges the likelihood that the counterdiscourse of the New Pragmatism may provide a more promising language with which to engage Asian, particularly Chinese, culture than that shaped by Enlightenment rationality. Indeed, for a variety of reasons soon to be rehearsed, the most significant East/West conversations may proceed between a Western New Pragmatism and an Asian New Confucianism.

Yet another implication of our argument is that the Chinese need not reject their classical past in order to enter the modern age since the West is itself looking toward novel sensibilities, some of which resonate rather well with classical Chinese perspectives. Therefore, instead of seeking modes of cultural accommodation in the institutions and rhetoric of the Modern West, China could with greater profit look to its own classical past and, ultimately, to intellectual movements such as pragmatism in the West to help resolve the very real tensions, conflicts, and contradictions attendant upon its entrance into the contemporary world.

# Accommodating Modernity

4

The deepening cultural crisis of "modernity" in the West suggests that the intellectual culture of the Modern West is in sufficient disarray as to be practically unusable as a resource for the development of coherent models of cultural accommodation. As a consequence, China need not necessarily be confronted by a monolithic set of demands motored by the processes of Western modernization. We suggest that a more appropriate resource for promoting the transmission of those elements of modernity China seeks to import might be found in the apparent compatibility of Confucian and Pragmatic sensibilities.

One way of arguing for the efficacy of an alliance of Confucianism and Pragmatism is to rehearse the history of attempts at Chinese and Western engagements. For this narrative clearly demonstrates the difficulties encountered by the Chinese in efforts to accommodate Western incursions into its politics and culture. The terms of accommodation which have guided Chinese/Western contacts to date have essentially been set by the West. There are, however, reasons to hope that contemporary engagements might take place on more equal terms.

In this chapter we wish to consider the character of Chinese and Western engagements since the sixteenth century and then to note the current models of engagement with the Modern Western World being forwarded by the Chinese. After that discussion, we will indicate that what appears to be novel in the contemporary situation is that cultural influence is a two-way street. That is to say: In addition to processes of Westernization affecting China, the consequences of Easternization are increasingly felt in the Western world.

# 1. Modes of Accommodation

The belief that China has a serious long-term commitment to the project of entering the Modern Age is comforting to many, challenging to some, and a source of anxious bemusement for others. The majority of these opinions seem to have been formed by individuals who have casually and unreflectively identified "modernity" with the institutions of liberal democracy, capitalist free enterprise, and the spread of rational technologies.

Doubtless these are aspects of modernity which form the heart of contemporary Chinese interests (and anxieties) with respect to the West. The deepening cultural crisis of "modernity" in the West, however, bespeaks a far richer, more complex, and more consequential "modern condition." It would be foolish, therefore, for any modernizing nation, the Chinese included, to ignore the broader cultural accouterments associated with and embedded in the more practical elements of the modern impulse. For some of these allied aspects carry with them such disruptive potential as to suggest that the Western cure may be more deleterious than the Chinese ailment.

In the past China has, periodically, made precisely this assessment in its rather half-hearted attempts at modernization and has sought on these occasions to reject all forms of Western influence. But for a variety of reasons associated with our present global situation, it does appear that China now has little choice but to modernize, no matter what the risks might be. The success of this modernizing enterprise, however, will depend upon the recognition on the part of both the Chinese and the Anglo-Europeans that the very notion of "modernity" has been called into question. Under the banner of "postmodernism," cultural critics have raised questions about the viability of the present forms of those very institutions of capitalism, democracy, and technology which seem to promise to the Chinese the opportunity to again become one of the great nations of the world.

Past encounters with the Western world were forced upon the Chinese through the agencies of religion and commerce. These were accommodated for a time, often until the threat to the Chinese way of life was so serious as to require concerted action, and then the West was forced to retire, usually at some tremendous cost to the Chinese. At the present juncture, the economic and political power of an awakened China is better matched to the agencies of Westernization. It is less likely, therefore, that the West can repeat the past; China is not simply to be proselytized, and then overrun. There must be mutual accommodation.

China is a land of many walls which together have preserved itself as "Chinatown-of-the-world." When the Church first engaged the Chinese in the late sixteenth and seventeenth centuries, the Jesuit Fathers had to traverse a natural wall of mountains, deserts, and oceans, only to be blocked in their mission by a far more formidable wall of alternative cultural presuppositions and values which they and the Western culture they represented were never able to breach. The more familiar artificial wall of mud and stone which snakes across China both geographically and chronologically has become an enduring symbol of China's physical and cultural isolation, and of its persisting goal of self-sufficiency. In spite of the best efforts of Western internationalism, both charitable and otherwise, China today remains very much a world unto itself.

Following Rome's establishment of the China Mission in the seventeenth and early eighteenth century, a protracted debate ensued in which Rome seriously reflected on whether it could allow the Chinese to remain culturally Chinese and still embrace Christianity. More than a century of heated deliberation was brought to closure with the Papal Bulls *Ex illa die* (1715) and finally *Ex quo singulari* (1742), both of which formally and specifically rejected any accommodation of Chinese cultural practices.

In the nineteenth century, Western commercial interests asserted themselves with a magnitude of force that the Qing dynasty was in no position to challenge. The Opium War (1839–1842) was a humiliating defeat for the Chinese at the hands of the British, with the annexation of Victoria Island and the extorted opium market setting the pattern of China's foreign relations for the next three-quarters of a century. Britain had begun to assemble Hong Kong.

Foreign incursions continued throughout the nineteenth century, putting China's territorial integrity increasingly in doubt. The protracted Taiping challenge to the impotent Qing court in the middle of the century exposed the nation's underbelly to the forces of imperialism, and before the "Christian" Hong Xiuquan was finally crushed by local militia in the mid-sixties, Britain had acquired a second piece of Hong Kong, the city of Kowloon. With the Sino-Japanese War (1894–1895) ending in the scuttling of the Chinese navy, the Japanese victors annexed Taiwan, and Britain, always ready to take advantage of China's weakness, extorted the New Territories from the Manchu court to make Hong Kong complete.

The Boxer Rebellion (1900) was the next in the seemingly endless chain of humiliations suffered by the Chinese when a famine-stalked population turned its enmity on the Western intruders. And in 1904 to 1905, even without Chinese participation, the Japanese and Russians fought their war almost entirely on Chinese soil. These and other such events continually demonstrated the impotence of China in any of its attempts to resist the aggressions of the international powers.

Largely motivated by the need to survive, China was forced to seek a new level of integration. The nationalistic impulses of foreign powers led the Chinese, contrary to their tradition, to develop their own form of nationalism. Nationalism, of course, required the Chinese to promote Westernization, since the West was the source of those economic, technological, and sociopolitical forces which, it was hoped, might make China a power among powers. The momentum of a series of events of the early twentieth century at times energized and at other times enervated the Chinese: the abolition of civil service examinations in 1905; the Chinese protests against the American Exclusion Act of that same year; the 1911 revolution which ended the Qing dynasty and introduced the Republican era in China; the intellectual movements associated with 1915 to 1919, collectively designated by the event which brought them to fruition, "the May Fourth Movement." Ironically, these events heated the blood of a growing Chinese patriotism at the same time that they threatened to undermine national integrity at a concrete social, political, and especially cultural level.

For twelve years (1916–1928), warlords dominated Chinese political life. This political free fall was accompanied by a social disintegration consequent upon the dissolution of the civil examination system before any adequate substitute could be put into place. The May Fourth Movement led to an increasing influence of Western ideas, but in no coherent form. There was a proliferation of competing agendas, with so little hope of consensus that the ideas tended to cancel one another out before receiving anything like practical implementation. This was the period of John Dewey's influence upon China, a result of his twenty-five month lecture tour. Dewey's influence led to many initial reforms, particularly in education. But with the rise to power of the Communist party, Dewey's influence rapidly faded.

After the defeat of the warlords in 1928, two influential political parties vied for the role of the agent of unification and reintegration: the Guomindang or Nationalist party and the Communist Party. The former was a revitalized party tracing its roots to the rebels of 1911 who had successfully extinguished Manchu rule; the latter had been formed in 1921 with only fifty-seven members and had grown rapidly in influence during the brief intervening period.

What we ought to learn from this brief rehearsal of historical events associated with the "Westernization" of China in the nineteenth and early twentieth centuries is that the desire for national survival was the defining motive in accepting Western influences. China, after all, coming quite late to the conversation, and then only under duress, had not been part of those post-Enlightenment developments which have defined "modernity." Nonetheless, many Chinese intellectuals by the time of the May Fourth movement had begun to recognize that seeking the power of the West would inevitably commit China to a *form* of democracy, a *kind* of capitalism, a *sort* of technological development, qualified by some appreciation of human beings as rights-bearing individuals possessed of individual autonomy and a legitimate appetite for private property.

From a Chinese perspective, of course, this recognition was a cause of real concern. As a developing nation, the Chinese were increasingly troubled by the corrosive effects upon their culture and social fabric associated with and embedded in the modernizing impulse. It is not an exaggeration to say that modernization of the sort assumed by the heirs of the Western Enlightenment carries with it such disruptive potential as to be broadly unacceptable to the Chinese.

This recognition, more than anything else, led Mao Zedong to insist upon adopting Marxism: "a Western heresy with which to combat the West." The reason for Mao's selection of Marxism as the putative basis of his revolutionary program should not be overlooked. He hoped to avoid the worst of the corrosive effects of Westernization by adapting an ideology which functioned as a counterdiscourse within the context of Western Modernity. Parenthetically, we must say that our selection of Deweyan pragmatism is based upon essentially the same insight—namely, that we must find a marginalized counterdiscourse in the West with which to confront the worst dynamics of Westernization. We are, of course, promoting a program of evolutionary reform rather than revolutionary transformation.

In the past, China has successfully avoided the worst consequences of the Westernization process by periodically ejecting from its lands those agents who have successfully breached "the Wall." But no more. For a variety of reasons associated with the globalizing effects of present-day economics and its attendant industrial, transportation, and communication technologies, China will have little choice but to accommodate modernity in some sense, whatever the risks. For the inertia of public events is such as to suggest that only by accommodating the institutions of capitalism, democracy, and technology, may China assume a role commensurate with her size and growing global importance.

How does China look at this crisis? This is not an altogether new situation. On a smaller scale the issues of accommodation were raised when the Jesuits entered China beginning in the sixteenth century. Discussions were enlarged with the Western incursions of the nineteenth and twentieth centuries. And today, as one might well imagine, one of the principal issues among Chinese intellectuals is the development of an adequate plan for accommodating what now appears to be the inevitable modernization of China. Recalling the discussions of the last chapter, however, it is doubtful that the Chinese understand the complexity of the modernizing dynamics they must confront.

A new intellectual discourse has emerged in contemporary China since 1978 that has attended the rebirth of China's spiritual identity. This conversation has moved from the discussions on the criteria for "truth" (where, in Marxian terms, "practice is the sole criterion of truth") in the late seventies, to the great debate on China's cultural construction ("whence and whither Chinese culture?") which began in the early eighties and has continued with varying degrees of intensity down to the present historical moment.[1] In the gradual awakening of a humanistic self-consciousness and the cultural consciousness which has attended it, several sometimes overlapping yet clearly discernible modes of accommodation may be mapped.

The 1980s in China were, until late in the decade, defined philosophically by a healthy climate of debate unprecedented since the founding of the Peoples' Republic in 1949. Far ranging cultural discussions, often appealing to Western vocabularies, methodologies, and philosophies as their frame of reference, revealed many differences of opinion on the spirit and values of traditional culture. In retrospect, there have been several discernable postures.

First, one extreme position was occupied by those aging political leaders who, in spite of the proliferation of faxes and satellite dishes throughout the country that breached the wall in an entirely novel way, still believed that China was self-sufficient, and could remain isolated and insulated from Western culture. The Great Wall can preserve China as the Chinatown of the world.

A second way, with a future for China only slightly less naïve and unlikely than the first, is represented by the radical iconoclasts whose concerns culminated in Tiananmen. These impassioned intellectuals expressed profound reservations about the viability of the Chinese cultural legacy, and in many ways have reiterated the critical posture of antitraditionalism in which the irony of "patriotic iconoclasm" prevails. They have rejected established values as being unsuited to the realities of modern Chinese society, and have advocated "countering tradition" as a means of advancing the tradition. Like the conservative guardians of the Great Wall, these usually young scholars have asserted that traditional Chinese culture is self-sufficient, but have drawn the unexpected conclusion: so much the worse for traditional Chinese culture. China cannot achieve renewal through self-criticism, and must abandon the attempt. This radical "antitraditionalism" led to the "River Elegy" television series and its bitter attack on the perceived negativity and inertia of the tradition. The most extreme statement of this position, often posited by idealists who have a jaundiced appreciation of the Chinese tradition and a romantic perspective on Western society and institutions, rejects "Chineseness" utterly, and recommends the wholesale importation of another culture's future.

Among these critics of China's cultural legacy, there is a cohort who, although less strident, have also seen the tradition as largely unadaptable, describing Confucian culture in terms of "structural stagnation" and "conservatism strangling individuality."

Advocates of a third way called "creative synthesis and synthetic creation," have promoted a "creative transformation of Chinese culture" through a full and thoroughgoing convergence of Chinese and Western cultures. Rejecting the assumed antagonism between Chinese and Western thinking, they have encouraged a scientific analysis of theory and practice to identify and assimilate all advanced and outstanding cultural achievements into a new tradition.

A fourth identifiable way has been "selective inheritance," a less radical, more academic trend that affirms the spiritual values of traditional culture. This group has opposed the more popular "introspective criticism" and "thoroughgoing reconstruction" and has sought to make a positive appraisal of the tradition so as to identify, select from, and carry over the cultural wealth of the past. These scholars are committed to a tradition-based scenario for China's cultural reconstruction. A leading and early voice in this movement, defining itself as a "revival of Confucianism (*xinruxue* 新儒學)," was the late Liang Shuming. As this impulse took hold, it was joined by many representatives of the Western-based diaspora on China's periphery who had themselves been trained by a generation of often self-exiled intellectuals: Tang Junyi, Mou Zongsan, Xu Fuguan, Fang Dongmei, Qian Mu. It is this way, with its strong ties to Western society, that has in some degree rekindled the long-stalled process of trying to reconcile the Chinese tradition with global culture.

Tu Wei-ming of Harvard University is one of the more prominent interpreters of the Confucian sensibility to the Western world. Tu presents his "New Confucianism" as a world philosophy, capable of engaging Western intellectual voices on equal terms. But maintaining such a balanced perspective is difficult at best.

Other scholars associated with this group such as Tang Yijie and Mou Zhongjian have championed a syncretic "selective inheritance" which goes beyond simply Confucianism, looking for a broader and deeper philosophical base for cultural renewal. This group has advocated traditional values which extend well beyond the confines of Confucianism per se, invoking an eclectic "Chineseness" rather than just "Confucianism" and forwarding notions such as "cultural China" (as opposed to geographical China) with its "Chinese" citizenry determined by cultural sensibilities rather than political allegiance.

A fifth way is really the more radical extreme of the fourth in that, while being sharply critical of the voluntarism that culminated in the insanity of the Cultural Revolution, it is still tradition-affirming. It is represented by Li Zehou's exploration of China's rediscovered humanity—"the subjectivity trend." What distinguishes this track most clearly from the fourth is the radical degree of transformation not only anticipated but readily embraced in the convergence of Chinese and Western culture. Li Zehou's quasi-Marxist revision of the familiar "Chinese body and Western function" to advocate "Western body (read 'modern industrialized materialism') and "Chinese function" as the model of China's cultural future, acknowledges (perhaps naively) the overwhelmingly positive value of Western-born ideological drives such as practical rationality, personal autonomy, and modern science, and the social, economic, and administrative institutions which issue from them.

In response to the obvious question: "Beyond the institutions of Western liberalism, what else is there?" Li Zehou might well reply that while the contribution of Western cultures tends to be formal in structure, and hence is articulated and more readily discernible, the contribution on the Chinese side is more fluid, more particularistic, and more easily undervalued. At the same time, it is of enormous importance. For example, one might celebrate the centrality of rights in pursuing the goals of human dignity and personal realization. But rights-talk without appeal to "rites" *li* 禮—the concrete and specific roles and relationships which constitute the fabric of community and which generate the sense of shame *chi* 恥 necessary for social living—is hollow and meaningless. Laws are not more real than ritual practices, and both are necessary for effectively realizing a healthy society. It is the tension and the achieved balance between formal and informal procedures which is difficult to sustain.

We must presume that it is some combination of the fourth and fifth ways which not only the majority of Chinese intellectuals prefer, but which will provide the best hope for persuading Western nations of the value of mutual accommodation. This is but to say that these two mod-

els of accommodation provide the basis for offering Chinese resources
for engagement with the two prominent Western dynamics—namely,
the modernizing impulse associated with Anglo-European economic
and political individualism and the communitarian counterdiscourse of
American pragmatism. Our arguments in this present work are most
closely allied with these two modes of accommodation.

Below we shall articulate the communitarian pragmatism that resonates with the Confucianism which we, along with Tu Wei-ming and
others, conceive to be the gift of China to global culture. In the discussion immediately to follow we will provide some realistic basis for believing that the Chinese/Western engagements which will help shape the
political and cultural events of the next century will involve not only
Westernization but *Easternization*, as well. Further, we hope to offer
some support for the view that the Westernizing impulses to which
China will be exposed may include important elements of the heretofore marginalized pragmatic sensibility.

## 2. Westernization and Easternization

Our discussion of the manner in which China and its champions in the
West are attempting to meet the challenges of Westernization has led to
the recognition that, particularly with regard to the New Confucianism
in China and the United States, Chinese culture has significant
communitarian resources with which to meet the individualistic influences of Westernization. This fact makes it important to recognize that
along with the processes of Westernization that currently dominate Chi-
nese/Western engagements, we might expect to see the increased significance of the countertrend of Easternization. Presently, that trend is
modest in comparison with its opposite. But if conversations between
Confucianism and pragmatism become as important as we believe they
might, we should expect that the trends of Easternization and Westernization will reach a position of greater parity.

To speak of Easternization, or more particularly of the Asian presence in America, presupposes the more general topic of globalization.
Globalization is generally characterized as a process by which geographical constraints are increasingly mitigated and, as a consequence,

social institutions and cultural values are no longer limited to a particular political locus.

Until recently, *Westernization* was thought to be the only significant trend in our globalizing world. For example, the last generation of American historians, led by scholars such as John Fairbank, read the modern Western and Asian encounter in the manner of Toynbee as first-world "impact" and third-world "response," couching their discussions in terms which assume that all cultures follow a necessary, univocal process of development at the end of which stands a Western-styled modernity.

In the nineteenth and twentieth centuries, religious, political, economic, and cultural institutions were exported broadly across the world by a colonizing West, secure in the belief that civilization was largely an Anglo-European monopoly. Free-market capitalism, autonomous individuality, rational technologies, along with putatively democratic systems of government, were imposed with varying degrees of violence upon Asian nations.

It was less than two decades ago that Paul Cohen in his *Discovering History in China*[2] took exception to this institutionally entrenched orientalism, insisting that Western scholars must pursue an "internal" perspective on Asian history that gives appropriate notice to the indigenous dynamics shaping Asia's cultures.

Perhaps the principal barrier that has impeded a Western understanding of Asia on Asia's own terms is the persistence in Western cultures of a "transcendental pretense,"[3] an assumption of rational objectivity, culturally sanitized science, or most recently, the universality of human rights, that empowers the contemporary heirs of the Enlightenment to evangelize other cultures.

In a post-colonial world, these dynamics have weakened enormously, and Westernization continues now mainly at the level of commerce and popular culture. Culture and economics have in fact forged a strange alliance in which Western culture, reduced to a complex set of images, is marketed to the world with the assistance of the media of advertising, movies, satellite television, and the Internet. The West does not merely, or mainly, export commodities; it exports *images*. Western shoe companies are not so much in the business of selling running shoes as they are of selling the prowess of Michael Jordan or a trip to "Planet Reebok." Along with the trivialization of Western influences upon Asia, and partly as a consequence of the void created by the present American cultural malaise, the debate concerning Asian values has suddenly taken the world's center stage.

In its neutral sense, globalization means that the world's cultures are becoming, in increasing degree, symbiotic. In principle, cultural narratives may overlap. They can shape and be shaped by one another. No one doubts this fact when it comes to the issue of Westernization, but the possibility that the West might be fundamentally shaped through its Asian encounter has yet to be entertained by most Westerners.

In the past, Asian influences have been little more than the result of simple curiosity or superficial indulgences on the part of a very few: Leibniz's interest in the *Yijing*, Voltaire's celebration of the virtues of Confucius, or the early twentieth-century fascination with Ming vases.

Of slightly greater significance is the little-known influences of Asian culture upon the arts. European impression was significantly shaped by Ukiyoe wood-block prints. In literature, members of the Bloomsbury circle were fascinated by Asian poetic forms and Noh drama influenced Yeats and Brecht.

More recently, resonance between philosophical Daoism and the philosophies of Alfred North Whitehead and Martin Heidegger has been noted. Military strategists have paid increasing attention to the sources of the Asian arts of war such as the *Sunzi*, and the newly recovered *Sun Bin*. In American business culture, Asian management practices have become increasingly of interest. The fascination with contemporary Asian literature and the avant-garde films born of it, at both artistic and popular levels, signals an increased influence that reaches beyond mere popular culture. And the interest in Asian foods, once directed principally toward Chinese "take-out," has grown into a far more sophisticated awareness of the complexities of those styles of cuisine.

In America today, with Europe receding as the cultural horizon, "sophistication" is slowly, almost indiscernibly, being redefined as the ability to deal with Asian cultures and languages, and is geographically moving the American center from New England to the Western states. And this Asian influence will become increasingly pronounced as the importance of Asia continues its dramatic rise, perhaps nowhere in greater evidence than in the demographically fluid new world as the face of America becomes increasingly Asian in its features.

What it means to be an American is being redefined. For example, university student bodies have altered profoundly. Asian and Asian-American students are, on the whole, consistently among the best students in American universities, and are a presence to be reckoned with. Moreover, Asian students who once came to America in order to seek residence and a job here are increasingly choosing to return to their homes. In fact, there is the beginning of a reverse "brain drain" in which American students are studying at Asian universities and then choosing to live and work in Asia.

Easternization is not simply a change in the physical and cultural presence of Asia in America. The most profound change involves an anxious recognition of the psychological presence of Asia. The popular media often plays to this anxiety with its waves of Japan bashing and the unrelenting demonizing of China. And the dissolution of this anxiety is no longer made possible by a belief in the invincible superiority of Western values.

This acknowledgment of an Asian presence is thus complicated by the fact that most Americans really do not understand Asian culture nearly as well as they must. This ignorance is the direct consequence of having the luxury heretofore of being able to ignore this part of the world, and it exists at the highest and lowest levels of American society.

A surprising number of Americans have only the vaguest understanding of Korea, Japan, and China—usually only enough to be made uncomfortable by the growing Asian influence. Among politicians, the situation is not much better. These individuals too often look at Asia through lenses darkened by old prejudices and outworn ideologies.

With regard to China, there is the belief on the part of the average American citizen that it is a communist, totalitarian dictatorship in which a long suffering people are denied all freedoms and are completely without rights. China is Tiananmen. This caricature of the Chinese world has most recently been in evidence in the way in which China's resumption of sovereignty over Hong Kong was reported as a "take-over" by the popular media.

Americans by and large know Japan through its automobiles and electronics, and have a grudging respect for their quality, but have little interest in understanding the culture of Japan. The prevailing image of Japan hardly goes beyond the assumption that it constitutes an economic threat. And recent economic woes in Japan have occasioned an undisguised glee on the part of many American businessmen and politicians.

The American understanding of Korea is vaguer still. There is the connection through the Korean War which leads most Americans to see Korea as an ally whom we assisted after World War II and to whom we brought the gift of democracy. Very little is known of Korea's dynamic economy, of its multinational corporations, or of its joint economic ventures, and virtually nothing of its complex culture and values.

The general ignorance of Asia on the part of most Americans has not been much of a barrier to processes of Easternization. Indeed, it is more likely than not that this process has been accelerated by it. Uninformed actions on the part of businessmen and politicians have allowed the more canny Asians, who understand the importance of gaining an accurate understanding of the strengths and weaknesses of their competitors, to increase both economic and political capital in their regions and beyond.

Another reason why the process of Easternization promises to become increasingly important is related to the malaise currently pervading American life. This lassitude, which is inhibiting effective social progress and seriously threatening the survival of civil society, has created a spiritual vacuum into which dynamic aspects of Asian cultures are being drawn. It is with respect to the revitalization of community that processes of Easternization can have their most lasting value in America.

Before discussing further how Asian values might manifest themselves in American society and, more importantly, how they might be used to revitalize the sense of community in America, something needs to be said about the general dynamic of cross-cultural encounters.

A productive engagement of two or more cultures proceeds through two principal stages. There is, first, a vague sense of "otherness" when encountering a novel set of cultural expressions. The comparativist initially tries to overcome this otherness by resorting to familiar interpretive concepts and categories. For example, in Asian/ Western encounters, Western philosophers and theologians have employed the general notions of "God," "Rationality," "Individuality," "Freedom," "Natural Law," and so forth, to interpret Confucian, Daoist, and Buddhist sensibilities. The second stage begins with the recognition that these notions somehow do not work. You cannot simply translate "*dao* 道 " as "God" or some functional equivalent without doing serious damage to both Daoist and Confucian thought. This leads to a search for alternative notions which better serve the ends of translation in the only resource available—namely, one's own cultural experience. This stage leads one to seek out elements in one's own cultural past that have been largely deemphasized or ignored. It is these unsowed seeds and discarded scraps that enable us to anchor and articulate the otherness of an alien culture. The happy consequence of moving through these stages of cultural comparison is that not only is one better able to understand the alternative culture, there is an increased understanding of the richness of one's own culture, as well.

Comparative Asian/Western philosophy is just entering the second phase of intercultural comparison. We are at last beginning to see the novelty of the Confucian sensibility and are at the same time being forced to learn new things about ourselves. The consequence is that many scholars are at least beginning to see that Asian understandings of democracy not only make sense, but some even believe that these alternative understandings may serve as models for a renewal of our own commitments to democracy. And, in accordance with the "seeds and scraps" method, Americans are being directed to elements in our own culture that resonate with the Confucian understandings of society and community.

We can illustrate this important by-product of comparative philosophy specifically with regard to our own collaboration, which began with a book published under the title *Thinking Through Confucius*. At the beginning of this project, like most Western philosophers, Hall had little appreciation of Confucius and, furthermore, would not have thought him an interesting subject of study. While Ames knew something of Confucius, he had no idea of the relevance of Confucianism to the Western cultural narrative, and no tools with which to pursue cultural comparison. In the course of our investigation of Confucius, however, we became fascinated by what is, at least from the perspective of Western philosophy, a truly *strange* manner of thinking. In our attempts to translate this thinking into a language that would facilitate a conversation with our Western audience, we have been led away from both the speculative and analytic vocabularies of traditional philosophy to the more concrete and practical modes of American pragmatism. Thus, in our own cultural repository we have discovered a vocabulary that seems best to resonate with the Confucian sensibility. It was specifically in the communitarian thinking of John Dewey that we found what was needed. Until that time, again not unlike other American philosophers, we had neglected American pragmatism in favor of British and Continental philosophies.

To summarize this personal illustration: We do not exaggerate in the least when we say that it was Confucius who introduced us to John Dewey. Nor do we exaggerate when we say that the recent cultural encounters with Asia might well contribute to the rehabilitation of pragmatism in America. And it is definitely no exaggeration to say that our personal illustration could be supplemented by any number of other Western scholars who in the last generation have begun to discover Asian thought and, as a consequence, have learned new things about their own culture.

We need to stress once again that our interest in Asian culture is not a mere intellectual exercise. There are very real problems in America for which solutions stimulated by an understanding of the Asian experience can be sought. One of the most direct ways of focusing the problems in American society and culture which may be profitably addressed by Asian cultural values is by referring to Daniel Bell's classic work, *The Cultural Contradictions of Capitalism.*[4]

According to Bell, capitalism has from its beginnings contained three significant contradictions which have shaped its development. The first concerns *the conflict of asceticism and acquisitiveness.*

This conflict involves the tension between the self-disciplined work ethic that capitalism enjoins, and the need to acquire, own, and consume upon which continued economic growth is predicated. The work ethic conjoined with acquisitive desire well expresses the spirit of capitalism.

The second contradiction is that between the *bourgeois tradition and modernism*. The tension between tradition and modernity is expressed as a conflict between the need to ground one's intellectual and social life in the conservative elements of the past, and the need to experience the novel, ever-changing, ever more progressive characteristics expressed in elite culture, from art to technology.

The third contradiction is to be found *in the separation of morality and law*. The need to ground individual actions and social relations in the informal mechanisms of a community ethos is, in late capitalist societies, superseded by the need to codify a set of rules and procedures as legal mechanisms which formalize social relations as basically contractual in nature.

Bell's claim—repeated in the Afterword to the twentieth anniversary edition of his work—is that acquisitiveness, modernization, and the recourse to legal mechanisms have come to dominate Western capitalist societies at the expense of self-discipline, tradition, and informal ethical relationships.

Now, in each of these instances, Confucianism, with its stress upon self-discipline, tradition, and the priority of morality over positive law, might offer the needed corrective measures. Increasingly this recognition must dawn upon American intellectual, political, and economic communities. It is anticipated with the introduction of Asian management practices in business, the rapidly increasing presence of Asian cultural and political studies in American universities, and the dramatic rise in the number of scholarly publications on Asian topics by American presses.

The result of this influx of Asian values into American society is that no longer can it be fashionable to scoff at the notion of a distinctly *Asian* democracy. Asian models of democracy, on the contrary, must continue to seep into the consciousness of American philosophers and political scientists to challenge entrenched assumptions about the equation of modernization and Westernization. This recognition of the potential value of Asian resources has, in turn, challenged Asian scholars to dig more deeply into Confucian sources to discover indigenous roots of truly democratic experiences.

Subsequently, we shall discuss the notion of "Confucian Democracy" in some detail. We shall prepare for that discussion by considering, in the next two chapters, the contrast between Liberal and Communitarian versions of democratic theory. Confucian democracy will be seen to have many similarities with the Deweyan form of communitarian thought that, we believe, offers the most productive understanding of democracy for America.

# PART
# 3

# THE CULTURES
# OF DEMOCRACY

# The Irrelevance of Rights-Based Liberalism

In this chapter we wish to lay the foundations of our argument that the general assumptions underlying the model of rights-based liberalism currently dominating contemporary understandings of democracy, particularly in America, are broadly irrelevant to processes of democratization most beneficial to the Chinese. In the contemporary debates between proponents of rights-based liberals and their communitarian critics, the majority of Chinese stand with the latter.

Those familiar with contemporary social and political theory might be initially confused by our method of characterizing rights-based liberalism. Our primary concern is to consider the character of rights-based perspectives on democracy within the context of theoretical interpretations of modernity. This will permit us to argue that rights-based understandings of democracy are as culturally specific as the peculiar understanding of modernity from which they are derived.

Some may initially wish to cry "Foul!" when they see how starkly we have characterized liberal, rights-based theory. Over the past few years, in response to their critics, liberal theorists have attempted to modify their positions in the direction of an increased appreciation of communitarian concerns: association, interdependence, social welfare, the contribution of tradition, custom, and morality in setting limits on recourse to legal mechanisms, and so forth. Were we concerned to engage the liberal/communitarian debate strictly as a theoretical exercise, it would, of course, be necessary to deal with such qualifications. Our pupose, however, is to demonstrate the unsuitability of certain principles generally associated with rights-based theory for the development of viable democratic institutions in contemporary

Chinese society. Our arguments are not directed against this or that particular theory, but against any position in which the most recognizable principles of rights-based liberalism remain intact. Thus, as long as one hews to the belief that the individual is somehow prior to the society to which he or she belongs, that individual rights must take precedence over common goods or interests, and the rule of law must be allowed to trump nonlegal mechanisms presupposing the existence of social empathy, it matters little how far one goes in the attempt to accommodate communitarian concerns. It is these fundamentals, however well masked by concessions to communitarian critics, that we find irrelevant to the most productive processes of democratization in China.

Our efforts in this chapter must be promissory, since we will only be able to anticipate some of the defects communitarians, Chinese and Western, would find in rights-based liberalism. Specific discussions of the Confucian and pragmatic critiques will begin in the following chapter. There we will consider John Dewey's communitarian theory of democracy. Subsequently, we shall attempt to demonstrate that Dewey's pragmatism comports well with the New Confucianism (*xinruxue* 新儒學) recently emerging in China and other Asian nations.

# 1. Rights-Based Liberalism

The cultural sensibility of modern Anglo-Europeans is expressed through a set of overlapping articulations of the self or individual. Such articulations are distinctive termini of separate strands of historical development, and the unsorted complex they comprise places a stamp of incoherence upon the social, economic, and technological elements of modernity. Focusing upon the political and social elements of modernity directs us toward the institution of rights-based liberalism, and the understanding of democracy it entails. Like the other significant elements of modernity, the dominant sense of democracy associated with the narrative strands of modernity is dependent upon historically contingent constructions of the self or individual. Specifically, with respect to the development of liberal democracy, the various senses of the self rehearsed in chapter 3 are divergent and mutually reinforcing sources of Western individualism.

One source of notions of the discrete individual presumed by liberalism is found in material atomism. This interpretation is rooted in classical Greek and Roman philosophy, and was expressed in the modern world by thinkers such as Thomas Hobbes, David Hume, and Adam Smith. A second principal strand is represented by classical thinkers, from Plato to Kant and Hegel, who were concerned with the nature of rational mind as the medium of philosophical reflection. The former mode of individualism gives rise to the modern *homo economicus* motivated by pleasure and profit. The latter, particularly in its Christianized form, argues for the integrity and privacy of minds as "souls" or "rational selves."

Liberal democracy reveals a strange alliance of these two contrasting understandings. The rational vision provides a formal basis for the claim that the individual is a "rights bearing creature," and the materialist ideology urges that the content of those rights be spelled out in terms of the good life of pleasure and profit. These two models are reinforce the close association of liberal democracy and capitalist economics. While it is true that theories of rights-based liberalism are often constructed in abstraction from explicit economic assumptions, in practice something like *laissez-faire* capitalism appears to be the economic model most congruent with such speculations.

Of the other models allied with the development of modernity, that of the self-assertive individual also resonates well with the dominant strands of individuality associated with liberal democracy and entrepreneurial capitalism. Again, notions of autonomy central to liberal political theory are usually grounded in the Kantian model of the autonomous will guided by rational maxims. But appeals to the strictly self-assertive models are often unconsciously imported into constructions of the liberal individual.

Rights-based liberals are least likely to invoke interpretations of the human being deriving from the organic model of the self. This model is ignored because its characterization of the individual in terms of organic interdependence conflicts with interpretations of the individual grounded in the central liberal value of *autonomy*.

Definitions of the self in terms of creative self-expression have also been marginalized in rights-based, liberal theory. The aesthetic model of the self is a variant of the economic model wherein "productivity" is replaced by "creative expression." And since the model of economic productivity dominates in capitalist societies, which, *de facto,* frame the institutions of liberal democracy, there is little emphasis upon theories that promote creative expression.

This situation renders the work of John Dewey immediately pertinent since these marginalized elements are central to his form of pragmatism. As we shall see, Dewey stresses the organic model of self and society, as well as the aesthetic character of social interaction and communication.

The principal strands of modernity entail individualistic, rights-based, interpretations of democracy. This is so much the case that the term "liberalism," which has carried a number of diverse meanings since the nineteenth century, has finally, for all practical purposes taken on the coloration of rights-based theories.

Liberalism emerged in the nineteenth century as a doctrine focused upon the notion of "liberty" and has since suffered the same transmogrifications as have the principal understandings of liberty, or freedom. If liberty is associated with the Kantian "autonomous will" which exists prior to any desires or ends that might otherwise shape the individual, then liberalism assumes highly individualistic associations. This is, in part, the ground of what has become rights-based liberalism.

The dominance of this understanding of liberalism is relatively recent. In fact, at the height of his influence, the communitarian John Dewey was the very epitome of the "liberal." Liberalism was then dominated by an essentially left of center politics and a community-oriented sense of obligations. The individual celebrated by such liberalism is someone who

> is thoroughly engaged with his or her work, family, local community and its politics, who has not been coerced, bullied, or dragged into these interests but sees them as fields for a self-expression quite consistent with losing himself or herself in the task at hand.[1]

Though this essentially communitarian understanding of the "liberal" is still a part of our informal vocabulary, as a term of art in political

theory, "liberalism" refers to individualistic, rights-based, understandings.

But even if we highlight rights-based meanings of liberalism, we can
find a significant differences among its principal forms. The liberal/
conservative contrast that is usually reflected in comparisons of "leftwing democrats" and "right-wing republicans" is focused upon debates
concerning the extent to which the state must remain neutral with respect to guaranteeing economic rights. For example, ideologues of the
left assume that some redistribution of wealth, usually through
taxation, is essential to guarantee the right to a dignified life for all.
This is by no means a communitarian view; it is simply a claim that individual rights presume minimal material benefits if they are to be successfully exercised. Conservatives, on the other hand, count on the
overall beneficial effects of the market to raise general standards of
living, claiming that redistribution always involves a violation of individual rights.

When we discuss the irrelevance to the Chinese of the specifically
rights-based form of liberalism, we intend to include those who stand
on either side of the liberal/conservative debates. Other senses of the
term "liberal" which still might legitimately apply to individuals such as
John Dewey envisioned shall be bracketed.

# 2. The Rights-Bearing Individual

Rights-based liberalism assumes that the individual is the fundamental
social unit out of which societies and states are formed. This individual
is, prior to her entrance into society, the bearer of fundamental rights. *Hs self*
Such an understanding of the primordial self entails the necessity of an
appeal to a "social contract" as a heuristic device accounting for the
founding of the state. Separate individuals, existing in a "state of
nature," or an "original position," possess sufficient rational self-interest
to discern the advantage of yielding some of their otherwise unfettered
freedom for the sake of security and mutual benefit.

Something like a social contract makes sense only if one begins with
the notion of separate, reasonably self-sufficient, individuals as the basis
from which to build a society. To anyone who finds such a sense of the

individual difficult to comprehend, the idea of a social contract seems unnecessary, even as a useful fiction.

Interpretations of the discrete individual underlying liberal democratic theory can certainly be overdrawn, and this is often the case in communitarian critiques. The best way of thinking of the individual in liberal, rights-based, terms is as one defined essentially by his or her individual autonomy, but conditionally by his or her relationships. This means that the liberal individual, like the communitarian, will be conditioned by social relationships. The difference is that the relationship is voluntary for the liberal in a manner distinct from that of the communitarian.

Another way of saying this is that, in a rights-based society, the right of free association is a right of *disassociation*. The freedom of the individual to choose the character of his or her relationships must include the option to cancel any of those relationships. Michael Walzer makes this point as follows:

> The central issue for political theory is not the constitution of the self, but the connection of constituted selves, the pattern of social relations. Liberalism is best understood as a theory of relationships which has voluntary association at its center and which understands voluntariness as the right of rupture or withdrawal. What makes a marriage voluntary is the permanent possibility of divorce.[2]

While it is true that political theory is more concerned with the "connections of constituted selves" than with the "constitution of selves," it is certainly the case that the conception of the possibility, if only in principle, of a self as conceivable apart from its relationships goes a long way toward permitting the breakdown of social unions. Since the solitary individual, sustained by no significant social bonds, is a fiction, it cannot be presumed that the right of rupture is total. It is not clear in principle the extent to which one might exercise that right before losing any viability as a putative member of a society.

The specific character of the society or the nature of the state will be different depending upon which of the various families of views of the individual one stresses. The understanding of the self as a solitary desiring machine motivated by the need to maximize pleasure and minimize pain is the vision underlying both the materialist view of the state, and of *laissez-faire* capitalism.

It is also quite reasonable to hold the Kantian view that individual autonomy is a function of will guided by rational maxims consciously entertained. A rational view of the individual will often lead to the assumption that there is an analogy between some transcendental source of meaning and value and the individual mind such that self-evident truths, natural laws, human rights, and so on, are discoverable or certifiable by the reasoning individual.

It is from such an understanding that the belief in absolute and inalienable human rights is most often explicitly derived. Quite often, however, materialistic assumptions influence those liberal societies framed by the model of free-enterprise capitalism. Inalienable rights of individuals are not granted by the state, but the state is charged with the responsibility of guaranteeing and defending those rights.

One of the chief features of the contemporary democratic theory that derives from rights-based liberalism is that of the priority of "right" over "good." The argument of John Rawls supporting this position is best known.[3] In opposition to utilitarian theories promoting "the greatest good for the greatest number," Rawls proposes an essentially deontological theory that makes the search for the principles of justice an investigation into how individuals would conceive the rules of social and economic fairness under conditions that precluded the exercise of self-interest. Here, in a hypothetical "original position," and under a "veil of ignorance," the fairest rules could be conceived.

This approach to justice must abstract from notions of goodness since there are an indefinite number of viable conceptions of what constitutes a good life while this can hardly be true with respect to "right." Conceptions of rightness and justice must be common to all members of a society, or there can be no real justice for all. Thus, basic political and economic arrangements that guarantee the protections of rights for all individuals are essential. For justice to prevail, these arrangements must be neutral with respect to notions of the good life.

This view of the autonomous individual as the basic unit prior to social union, contrasts readily with any understanding that would find the individual to be born out of, and continually dependent upon, its relations with others. This leads communitarian critics to charge the rights-based liberal with the illegitimate promotion of notions of the good life, which tacitly exclude the creation of viable communities. For in the liberal understanding, rational self-interest is presumed to dominate over sympathy or fellow-feeling. Given the economic arrangements of most liberal societies, decisions made by appeal to rational self-interest often involve material desires and interests. A serious defect of rights-based liberalism is that the notion of the autonomous individual it presumes comes to look like the political equivalent of the *homo economicus* of eighteenth- and nineteenth-century economics.

The priority of right over good insures the predominance of individual autonomy over community-based values since the individual is the only bearer of rights. Rights are accorded to individuals; goods tend to be goods-in-common. A fundamental problem with rights-based understandings of democracy is that they have few mechanisms preventing individuals from becoming alienated from communities since the rights serving as the fundamental signs and rewards of a just society are so often enjoyed in private. Such rights do not prevent individuals from joining together in communities or social unions, but neither do they enjoin or stimulate community building. Community building is normally a consequence of a need to promote goods-in-common.

Though the possession of rights does not per se militate against the formation of meaningful associations, there is no *obligation* to promote community-building. In a rights-based society, obligations must perforce be quite minimal. Otherwise, the right of choice with respect to goods may easily be mitigated.

For John Rawls, there are natural duties to promote justice, avoid cruelty, and assist one another. Obligations in a liberal society exist only when they are voluntarily accepted. According to Rawls, "there is . . . no political obligation, strictly speaking, for citizens generally."[4]

In liberal democratic theory rights are borne by individuals, not communities. The construction of the good life is primarily the responsibility of the individual who, possessing an autonomous will, is at liberty to choose his or her ends. Moreover, the individual is under no strict obligations to others save to act justly, avoid cruelty, and recognize the need, *in extremis*, for mutual aid. Any other obligations must be voluntarily accepted. Arguably, the absence of any notion of obligations grounded in the recognition that the promotion of viable communities is essential for individual growth and development is a serious defect of rights-based liberalism.[5]

# 3. The Status and Content of Rights

The assumption that the issue of rights is solely a political concern effectively indifferent to cultural influences is altogether too naive to permit responsible reflection. Not only do politics and culture always interact, politics must itself often take a back seat to culture. Politics is seldom successful in subsuming cultural issues. It is as likely that culture may be treated as the generic category in terms of which politics is shaped.

The understanding and articulation of the rights owned by the individual may be undertaken only when a governing institution takes seriously its responsibility to defend the rights of citizens. To this extent, politics is almost always the more immediate consideration. But the reasons for political decisions often are deeply embedded in cultural determinants.

With respect to the question of abortion, for example, one might argue that the Roman Catholic position of opposing abortion is a political position, which in turn leads the majority of Catholics to act in accordance with the Church. And to the extent that Catholics oppose abortion simply because it is the position of the Church, one could argue that the action is primarily political. The fact that the theological values of the Church are rooted in the Thomistic synthesis (itself based upon Aristotle's organic vision) argues that cultural determinants are responsible for the teachings concerning abortion.

Cultural determinants are most important with regard to the question of human rights, especially issues surrounding their *status* and *content.* The status of rights is addressed in the debates between liberal and more historicist types of communitarian theorists of democracy. The question is whether rights are objectively grounded. That is, are there *natural* rights, or are rights merely the contingent products of a particular form of community?

As we shall see in our discussion of John Dewey's understanding of democracy, the pragmatist would deny the strictly essentialist interpretations of rights. For the pragmatist and historicist, human rights are historically derived concerns resourced in the community that accords and protects them. Essentialist views of rights find them resourced in the very nature of what it means to be human. Historicist understandings see no possibility of, nor any need for, theological or metaphysical guarantees. Presently, the issue of the status of rights, rather than the more immediately significant understanding of the actual content of rights, occasions the greatest amount of debate.

Liberal democratic theorists have traditionally argued for the necessity of grounding political understandings in essential characteristics about nature and human beings. Visions of the world and the self drawn from Cartesian or Lockeian or Kantian or Hegelian principles inform claims to the universality of reason and of human rights. This is true, of course, whether or not proponents of human rights recognize this fact.

The great anxiety of the architects of the Enlightenment was expressed first and best by Descartes in his search for certainty amidst merely contingent and relative truths. The logico-mathematical method of Enlightenment thinkers was intended to insure the objectivity and universality of beliefs in the face of culturally relative, all too corrigible, beliefs based upon political or ecclesiastical authority.

In the Enlightenment narrative, there is clearly a content/status problem of the sort we have been discussing. If the proposition "All men are created equal" entails a claim concerning status, then one cannot feel easy about admitting the claim to be contingent and historically grounded.

The question of the ontological status of human rights is important only to the essentialist. For the pragmatist, there is less concern to ground any particular list of rights than there is to demonstrate their value in practice. Thus, the pragmatist places community ahead of the individual, at least in this regard: The principal issue is not the specific belief in an antecedently existing individual as a bearer of this or that set of rights. It is, rather, the actual practices of a society or community that validate or fail to validate the value of any set of beliefs.

Of course the pragmatist might conceivably find some value in the Enlightenment narrative of absolute rights. Granted that the defense of rights in practice, not their grounding in theory, is most important, a narrative of essential rights based upon a belief in a universal human nature might energize some in the defense of relevant rights. But this will not do. The pragmatist who accepts the *content* of the rights espoused by the liberal democracy on purely historicist grounds, is committed to a kind of openness of inquiry that precludes dissimulation and promotes sincerity of belief. This sincerity is grounded in a concern of the pragmatist for transparent communication, a concern we shall find central to the Deweyan vision of democracy. In fact, Dewey defines democracy first and foremost as "a communicating community."

John Rawls, formerly considered to be a traditional liberal, has clarified the position taken in his highly influential *Theory of Justice*, which appeared logically dependent upon Kant's metaphysical speculations about nature of the self.[6] Explicitly eschewing Kant's metaphysics, Rawls now claims that his understanding of justice as fairness, and of the need to promote the "right" over the "good," is based upon the contingent fact that individuals in a democratic society disagree about the good life. A neutral state is, therefore, required to protect plurality and diversity. This view recognizes a strong distinction between the private self possessing moral obligations and the public self who must remain neutral with respect to any conceptions of goods or the good life.

Rawls's nod in the direction of a more pragmatic interpretation of liberal theory is most welcome. On Rawls's clarified formulation, it is an empirical question as to whether a distinctly communitarian society ought to be reformed along the lines of rights-based liberalism. For if the concept of justice is indeed political and not metaphysical, then it is a contingent, culturally specific question whether a conflict with respect to goods requiring a rights-based public domain of the sort Rawls recommends actually obtains. The presumption of significant pluralism with respect to the notion of goods precludes the communitarian vision that goods are primarily goods-in-common. On Rawls's present account, that presumption is no longer necessary.

No one would argue with the fact that American society, for example, is patterned by the sort of pluralism attendant upon significant disagreements about the good life. The hope that American society can be transformed along ideal communitarian lines is altogether utopian. But if we do not envision the pluralism of American society as the only desirable norm, then we are free to match the form of social organization with the empirical conditions of the society under consideration. What this means with respect to China, of course, is that we are likely to find some form of the communitarian vision, not rights-based liberalism, more congruent with the actual conditions of Chinese society.

When we move from the question of the status of human rights to that of their *content* we are led to ask whether everyone having the opportunity to think about the issue of rights would agree as to the kind of rights that are desirable. The majority of rights-based liberals would answer this question in the affirmative. But this conclusion is certainly controversial and is continually challenged by those who fall nearer the communitarian end of the spectrum.

We can easily see this with regard to the distinction between "first-" and "second-generation" rights, a topic currently of some importance in liberal/communitarian debates. First-generation rights—civil and political liberties such as life or liberty—are the bedrock of most rights theory. Such first-generation rights are often challenged in the name of second-generation rights associated with economic welfare and cultural development, especially in the emerging Asian democracies. Communitarian societies such as China claim great success in generalizing second-generation rights, often at the expense of the freedoms of some segments of its people.

Second-generation rights of economic welfare and cultural development are difficult to maintain in a rights-based society. The underlying assumption of such a society is that individuals are not naturally associated, and that primary obligations to others are minimal, at best. On liberal grounds it is difficult to conceive of a manner that the state could promote cultural self-development without canceling its neutrality and espousing some form of the good life.

Whether liberty is more fundamental a right than economic welfare or cultural self-development is not a simple matter of taste. The overlapping of the right to liberty and the right to cultural self-development is evident when one asks the question whether the former includes the right to be vacuous and uninformed. It would appear that just such a right is assumed by rights-based liberalism. For example, when university professors suggest that, in the classroom one has the right only to an informed opinion, this invariably leads to the question of who gets to decide what an informed opinion is. And though, in the classroom context, the professor has that limited "right," it is presumed that students have voluntarily accorded her that right by virtue of their membership in the class. There is something unsatisfying to the communitarian in having to receive permission before ideas or behaviors may be effectively challenged. Many opportunities for mutual education are lost under such conditions.

The communitarian is likely to claim that so-called second-generation rights of economic welfare and cultural development are likely prerequisites of the appropriate exercise of first-generation rights. Such an argument may definitely be made with regard to economic welfare. Freedom from material want is directly related to a number of positive factors, such as level of education, and inversely related to criminal activity.

Even though there may be broad agreement in Western societies about the content of rights that ought to be accorded members of a society, one cannot be too specific about detailing such rights. Theoretical differences determine strong semantic divergences in the understanding of specific rights. Moreover, with respect to the issue of an alternative culture such as China, differences of cultural context and historical narrative preclude the presumption of commonality. Thus, the preference for first- or second-generation rights, as well as the specific contents of either class of rights, is a culture-specific issue.

Having said that, the preference for first- or second-generation rights is largely dependent upon one's liberal or communitarian commitments. In communitarian theory, welfare interests may often be given at least short-term priority over *individual* free speech. Liberals would never allow goods or interests to trump individual rights.

We have argued that modernity is a Western invention, and that liberal democracy, as one of the principal products of modernity, is itself a historically contingent factor. Our consideration of the anatomy of liberal democracy has attempted to show how the various elements associated with that theory are connected with the understanding of the self as individual—one of the defining characteristics of modernity. By further defining what is meant by liberal democracy, we hope to call into question any attempt to forward cultural values specific to Western culture as universals presumed necessary to any reasonable intercultural conversation regarding democracy. Our point will be that topics such as "liberty," "autonomy," and "equality," are historically determined notions and are, therefore, culturally negotiable.

By "culturally negotiable" we mean that interactions among different societies or cultures based upon the sincere desire to communicate openly and transparently may achieve results based upon the pragmatic value of the issues under consideration and not upon an appeal to absolute principles. With respect to the question of human rights, this is true both with regard to their status as well as their specific content.

## 4. Liberty, Autonomy, Equality

Is "liberty" or "freedom" a right essential to a democratic society? The issue is complicated by the fact that there are so many important meanings associated with these terms. Like all philosophically important terms, "freedom" is *semantically vague*. It is defined as "power," "knowledge," "conformity with natural law," or "the determinations of material nature."

A volitional understanding of the self entails a different kind of understanding of the content of the right of freedom than would one grounded in natural law. In fact, the abortion question is often focused here. Whether a woman has the right to dispose of her body in the manner she sees fit is more easily answered in the affirmative if the person is conceived as first and foremost a volitional agent. Rights then become questions of legitimate self-assertion and the decision to abort is more easily seen as a personal decision.

Conceiving the primordial, rights-bearing individual as a biological entity raises a different set of expectations. The person, as a natural being, is fulfilled by conforming to the biological laws that define health and optimal organic development. Abortion now can be seen, not as a natural right, but as the contravention of a natural law.

If one conjoins the notion of freedom with that of "autonomy," a term rights-based liberals closely ally with liberty or freedom, the gap between the liberal form of democracy and more communitarian varieties is widened. Whereas there are understandings of freedom that do not necessarily assume an atomistic individual, dominant understandings of the term "autonomy" suggest a mode of personal independence that the community-minded theorist might eschew.

The notion of autonomy is dependent upon a conception of rationality and/or reasonableness which suggests that the individual is capable of making decisions with respect to those issues most crucial to his or her welfare. The motive behind the promotion of the value of autonomy is the insurance of the inalienability of one's fundamental rights. The autonomous person is not dependent upon any other source to authorize his or her decisions and actions. Seen in this light, the notion of autonomy as attached to the conception of freedom asserts the responsibility of individuals for the decisions that affect themselves or others. Thus, freedom and autonomy are characterized not only in terms of action, but in terms of that sort of action based upon rational choices among presented alternatives.

Given the centrality of the notion of the self or individual, one might expect that choices are to be aimed at the fulfillment of the individual. Such fulfillment will, of course, depend upon the specific manner in which one conceives the person. If an individual is construed primarily in materialistic, economic terms, the proposed alternatives among which one is to decide are likely to be those which fulfill the sorts of desires the *homo economicus* is thought to possess. A more idealist vision of the self would likely lead to the promotion of broader educational and cultural opportunities.

In liberal democratic societies choices are construed more in terms of the quantitative rather than the qualitative model. This is largely the result of the alliance of liberal democratic societies with capitalistic economic systems, which disposes toward quantitative rather than qualitative considerations. The quantitative character of capitalism promotes choices relative to material goods serving to realize a chosen good.

Free enterprise capitalism is more compatible with liberal democracy than most other economic systems because both are nourished by conceptions of the discrete individual. Socialist economic theory, the chief rival of capitalism, presumes a fundamental interdependence of the members of a society. Such a conception, as we have repeatedly seen, is without merit to proponents of liberal democracy.

There is little concern in rights-based liberalism to render freedom of choice qualitatively efficacious by insuring the presence of a variety of putatively "meaningful" and "fulfilling" alternatives. The liberal argument for not constructing a society in which specific notions of the good are promoted is that this contravenes the very notions of freedom and autonomy upon which a society is based. In the mind of the liberal, such an effort smacks of a condescending and paternalistic state that quite conceivably could move toward totalitarian excess. Insofar as goods come into play, it is up to the individuals in a society to decide, through majority decisions, which values are to be represented. Such decisions, of course, may never set aside those rights held to be fundamental.

"Equality" is another culturally negotiable characteristic of democratic theory. The rights-based liberal understanding of "equality" derives from the basic notion of the individual. There is nothing on liberal democratic principles to distinguish one individual from another. This is true whether the individual is construed either in materialistic terms as a *homo economicus* defined primarily by the motivation to maximize pleasure and minimize pain, or as an individual mind or soul whose essence reflects the essential features of Universal Reason or the Mind of God, or as a self-assertive agent defined by the exercise of will.

The sorts of things that count as differences within society itself—greater effort, higher degrees of intelligence—are not considered essential defining features of the individual. As a consequence, the notion of equality is understood quantitatively. Qualitative distinctions are considered accidental.

It is certainly possible to sympathize with the first theorists of rights-based, liberal democracy. Historically, their strategy was to defend the members of society against the invidious distinctions perpetuated by monarchical traditions. Seen in this light, liberal understandings of "autonomy" and "equality" make a great deal of pragmatic sense. However, the historical conditions occasioning these interpretations have altered so significantly as to lead one to question their contemporary relevance. Certainly, their application in a Chinese context would, as we shall see, be an exercise in old-fashioned colonialism.

We can summarize our discussion of rights-based liberalism by indicating how the presupposition of discrete individuality serves to ground each of its allied conceptions. The liberal understanding of the "state of nature" is an implication of the belief that individuals exist independently of, and prior to, any social groupings. The necessary resort to the notion of "social contract" is obviously entailed by the priority of individuals to society. Rational choice is presumed by the positing of social contract, since the notion makes no sense were individuals not, already in the state of nature, capable of forming contracts. Liberty itself is presumed by the notion of contractual relations into which one freely enters. Autonomy is entailed both by the positing of individuals existing in a state of nature and the need to account for the individual locus of the "responsibilities," "duties," and "obligations" associated with the exercise of freedom within a social context.

A final element of rights-based liberalism shaped by the presumption of discrete individuality is a commitment to the "rule of law." Individuals dissociated in principle are best ordered by appeal to norms that abstract from any differences. Commitment to the rule of law might appear a necessity for any democratic society. On communitarian principles, this commitment would be qualified by a belief in the importance of the community in defining the character of the individual. A too ready resort to the rule of law could be thought a symptom of the failure of custom, tradition, and habitual patterns of deference to educate and shape behavior prior to any need for recourse to legal sanctions.

Due to the overriding importance of individuals as autonomous agents, it is to be expected that the interdependency and mutuality of communal associations would be mitigated in a liberal democratic society. Quite apart from the ethnic and cultural differences that actually obtain in modern liberal democracies, there is an inherent disposition toward *dis*-association in the very fact that the individual, not the community, serves as the fundamental social unit.

The foregoing consideration of rights-based liberalism is intended as a prelude to the discussion of John Dewey's theory of democracy that immediately follows. Our ultimate purpose is less to critique liberal democratic theory per se and more to suggest that it is largely irrelevant to Chinese society as traditionally constituted. Deweyan social theory, on the other hand, resonates in a striking manner with much classical and contemporary understanding of Chinese society insofar as Confucianism informs it. Our concern with the hope for democracy in China leads us to promote resort to the Deweyan version of democratic theory in future conversations with the Chinese.

# John Dewey's Democracy

One of the remarkable features of recent philosophical activity in America is the reemergence of John Dewey, whose thought appeared to have been well nigh eclipsed in America after World War II.[1] A principal reason for Dewey's resurrection is the renewed interest in communitarian discourse in the face of a growing dissatisfaction with the limitations of rights-based liberalism. We have urged that an added benefit of the communitarian turn is that it will provide an effective discourse with which to engage an awakening China.

Having outlined crucial elements of liberal democratic theory, we turn now to a dramatically different conception of democracy. We have selected Dewey's "communitarian" vision, rather than attempt to contrast the liberal and the communitarian positions per se, for three important reasons: In the first place, there are, in our estimation, no contemporary communitarians whose insights are nearly as profound as those of John Dewey. Second, recent communitarian discourse tends to be less constructive and more a series of critical assaults upon the excesses of liberal, rights-based democracy. Dewey's thought, never dialectical in the manner of many philosophical theorists, provides novel and constructive proposals accompanied by a minimum of harsh rhetoric.

Finally, there is a distinctly historical reason for selecting Dewey's thinking as a means of developing comparisons between Chinese and Western democracies. Dewey was one of the first modern Western intellectuals to visit and lecture in China. His rather dramatic, if short-lived, influence on China's social and educational institutions argues for the relevance of his thought to the Chinese context.

# 1. The Contingency of Democracy

The first thing to say about Dewey's understanding of democracy is that it is decidedly historicist. Though the ideal of democracy is as old as civilized discourse, modern experiments with the implementation of democratic ideals were made possible by the confluence of a series of historical circumstances. Among these were the spread of Enlightenment ideas and the widespread effects of the French Revolution. In addition, the potentialities of democratic development were greatly enhanced by the translation of dissenting sects to a distant geographical site in which unwanted constraints could be effectively abandoned. To these factors one may add the ascent of industry, which helped to undermine the institution of slavery, as well as to promote a shift from a mentality shaped by the threat of scarcity to one stimulated by the possibility of abundance. These and other forces attending the rise of democratic institutions are contingent elements of an historical narrative that easily might have been altogether different.

Popular understandings of democracy are decidedly nonhistoricist. Roberto Unger has outlined three central elements presupposed by an essentialist understanding of democracy:

> The idea of a science of human nature or of morals that would lay bare the basic laws of mind or of behavior . . . , the idea of a set of constraints rooted in practical social needs to produce, organize, and to exchange, . . . [and] the idea that these transformative constraints had a certain cumulative direction of their own.[2]

Classical political economy resulted from the combination of the first two of these elements; the belief in a manifest destiny for ideological movements such as Marxism and capitalism resulted from a combination of the second and third. These three assumptions have often operated in tight conjunction with the ideal of democracy.

Dewey clearly held that democracy is not tied to any essentialist view of human nature, certainly not one that construes the human being as an acquisitive atom or a desiring machine. Whatever one may say about the biological nature of human beings, it is the *cultural* elements of a given society—expressed through it's science and technology, industry and commerce, law and politics, arts of expression and communication, its most prized values, and its general modes of individual and corporate self-understanding—that shape the meaning of the human being. At the level at which it truly counts, the differences among cultures are of much greater importance than are the similarities.

Dewey strongly affirmed that no particular set of constraints could define an economic order peculiar to normative socialization. There are simply too many ways of organizing for the same practical ends. Thus, there can be no intrinsic connection between capitalism and democracy. From Dewey's communitarian perspective, capitalism generally impedes and undermines the formation of democratic communities since the assumptions of the former include notions of independent and autonomous individuals and those of the latter (at least in its communitarian forms) the *interdependence* of individuals.

The idea that the advance of democracy, capitalism, or Marxism, will be inexorable is fundamentally at odds with pragmatism's historicist conception of the development of attitudes and institutions. Recognition of the sort of historical contingencies that allowed for the implementation of democratic institutions argues against wholesale attempts to export democracy. Indeed the victories of democracy in the nineteenth century that were won in an accidental manner can now only be maintained through "deliberate and intelligent endeavor" which meets the various problems that arise in a given society one at a time.[3]

As Dewey well recognized, the assumption that democracy is intrinsically tied to the capitalist economic system is historically connected with the confluence of the industrial revolution and the articulation of modern democratic institutions. Specifically, this assumption derives from confusing the active force of industrial and technological development with the adjunctive or parasitical activity born from an economic system that combines a certain set of property rights with the motivation to acquire individual profit.

Scientific and technological advances that promise freedom from scarcity are only loosely connected with a capitalist system motivated by the need to concentrate the benefits of such advances in the hands of a few. The dynamic of science and technology is cooperative effort leading to the most efficient and effective instrumentation of a set of ideas. The dynamic of capitalism, still motivated by the eighteenth- and nineteenth-century notions of individualism, is that of pecuniary profit. Technology, unsullied by entrepreneurial demands, is shaped by the aim of efficiency in the longest term permitted by the volatility of its augmentation. Capitalism is grounded upon desire for short-term profit, measured by brief segments of the productive life of individual entrepreneurs. It is only by tacitly including science and technology within one's definition of capitalism that one can argue for an intrinsic connection between it and democracy.

Dewey's point is that technological sophistication has led to a society that could potentially ground its aims and values in a sense of abundance rather than scarcity. Technology can free individuals from attitudes long shaped by the need to wring from nature sufficient sustenance for the moment and to renew the struggle daily.

This is an important point if one is to understand the difference between Dewey's vision of a democratic community and that of liberal democracy. Liberal democratic theory is much more likely to celebrate the value of capitalism since capitalist activity is consistent with the understanding of the self as discrete and autonomous. Beginning from the assumption of the discrete individual as the fundamental social unit, the liberal theorist finds competition well-nigh inevitable. Further, freeing the individual to articulate his or her needs and desires, and providing a field within which actions aimed at satisfying those needs and desires may be undertaken, appears to the liberal theorist to be a reasonable exercise in guaranteeing fundamental rights of the members of a society.

For Dewey, the difficulty with this manner of thinking lies in the fact that alterations in the relations between economic institutions and scientific and technological instrumentalities have rendered the notion of the discrete individual even less viable than before. In its early phases, the industrial revolution benefited from the imagination and courage of individual entrepreneurs and the industry of individual workers. Rewards were distributed for individual effort.

Two factors have rendered the notion of the discrete individual obsolete: First, capitalist activities and enterprises outgrew the capacity of any individual entrepreneur to determine the shape of the enterprises, and the complexity of the interactions required among workers in industry led to a lessening of the sense of other than monetary reward for individual effort. Second, and directly related to the first, scientific and technological sophistication allied with economic activity set up a tension between the individualistic and communal aspects of social actions.

Dewey considers this second factor most essential. Succinctly put, science and technology conduce to cooperative behavior while capitalism still follows the myth of the discrete individual. The guiding principles of capitalism and technology—profit for the former, efficient and effective realization of ends for the latter—are at odds with one another. The sort of individual required by the capitalist enterprise is radically distinct from that found desirable in scientific and technological activities.

We alluded to this point in chapter 4 in the discussion of the Asianization of capitalism vis-à-vis Daniel Bell's arguments in his *Contradictions of Capitalism*, but the point bears further elaboration. According to Dewey:

> The chief obstacle to the development of a type of individual whose pattern of thought and desire is enduringly marked by consensus with others, and in whom sociability is one with cooperation in all regular human associations, is the persistence of that feature of the earlier individualism which defines industry and commerce by ideas of private pecuniary profit.[4]

This is one of the fundamental distinctions between Dewey's vision of democracy and that of most liberal theorists. Not only do scientific and technological activities of the sort that legitimate the ends of democratic community swing free of capitalist motivations, capitalism is actually counterproductive in creating such a community.

> The tragedy of the "lost individual" is due to the fact that while individuals are now caught up into a vast complex of associations, there is no harmonious and coherent reflection of the import of these connections into the imaginative and emotional outlook on life.[5]

Dewey's understanding of democracy requires that we conceive it in terms of a reversal of the dynamics that allow economic motivations to shape democratic institutions, with the consequent dissolution of community. Democracy is to be understood in terms of the development of a community in which the economic and technological elements are disciplined by the goal of individual access to the ideals and goods of the community. Until this is the dominant motive, to say that one lives in a democracy is to play with words in the most cynical way.

Dewey believed that strictly technological developments could promote freedom of access to the products of a community for all individuals. The final end of this process would be that, one day, when shuttles weave without economic incentives determining what they weave and how much and to whom their products are affordable, then democracy in some finer form would be possible.

It should be clear how Dewey would respond to the celebrated thesis of Francis Fukuyama in his *The End of History and the Last Man*.[6] Dewey would find Fukuyama's argument that liberal democracy is the inexorable goal of human history defective on two grounds: First, the historicist tendencies in Dewey's thinking would undermine the claim that *any* form of social organization is inevitable. Second, and more importantly for our purposes here, Dewey believed that the press of modern circumstances had led to a situation in which the corporateness of social life had rendered largely irrelevant the individualistic assumptions underlying rights-based democracy.

Thus far we have argued that Dewey's characterization of democracy must be understood as a historicist one. In summary form:

> *There is nothing inevitable about either the existence, the form, or the fate of democratic societies. Specifically, Deweyan democracy presumes that, not only democratic community, but the scientific and technological activities supporting that community, have conditioning features that preclude the dominance of capitalist motivations.*

## 2. A Communicating Community

In the rhetoric of Western democracy, democratic institutions have been considered among the highest attainments of *reason*. This is so in part because of the rather unrealistic understanding of the rationality of classical Greek society, as well as the association of democratic institutions with the Enlightenment sensibility.

If we conceive reason in objectivist and essentialist terms, Dewey's democratic ideal is precisely *not* a rational one. For Dewey, "emotion and imagination are more important in shaping public sentiment and opinion than information and reason."[7]

"Democracy" names a context in which human beings function principally in the support of things-in-common. It is these things that motivate the creation of groups such as families, governments, churches, scientific associations. The process infusing all these forms of association is that of communication, what Dewey calls "the miracle of shared life and shared experience."[8]

For Dewey, democracy, regarded as an idea, "is not an alternative to other principles of associated life. It is the idea of community life it-self."[9] Further, the realization of democracy as the expression of communal association is the precondition for the development of true communication. Such communication, expressed in the form of free and open inquiry, grounds the employment of that intelligence which alone can promote the achievement of the ends of associated living. This insight is captured in Dewey's understanding of experience as "the result, the sign and the reward of that interaction between organism and environment which, when it is carried to the full, is a transformation of interaction into participation and communication."[10]

Dewey's characterization of experience in terms of "participation and communication" indicates that *language* is the central determinant of experience. But language as productive of community is not to be conceived as rational discourse, but is fundamentally aesthetic in character. In Dewey's words: "The expressions that constitute art are communication in its pure and undefiled form."[11] This is so because aesthetic language appeals to the imagination and the emotions in ways that most directly promote shared experience.

> The language of art is not affected by the accidents of history that mark off different modes of human speech. . . . The difference between English, French, and German speech create barriers that are submerged when art speaks.[12]

It is equally true that the separating effects of class and occupational differences and differences in political ideologies or religious beliefs can be mitigated by shared aesthetic experience. For example, this is shown to be true to the extent that the music, iconography, and architecture of a given society assist in the expression of both national and local identities. Thus, in addition to the U.S. Flag and the National Anthem, various sections of our nation are identified by more specialized cultural associations—for example, New England-style architecture, Country and Western music, and so forth.

Given Dewey's understanding of democracy in terms of aesthetic communication, it is not surprising that democratic modes of association and the organizations that sustain them have as their implicit aim the protection and refinement of artistic pursuits.

Aesthetic pursuits preclude any appeal to a distinction between "fine" and "applied" arts. The *production* of art involves "any activity that is productive of objects whose perception is an immediate good, and whose operation is a continual source of enjoyment of other events."[13] The *enjoyment* of art involves the perception of immediate good of objects. Such enjoyment is fundamental to the most ordinary events in human experience. To be effective in the enrichment of human experience, aesthetic activity requires both production *and* enjoyment.

Thus, for Dewey, art is not divided within itself, nor is the artist separated from participants in other occupations. The occupation of the artist is intended for everyone, and every occupation potentially has aesthetic character.

Aesthetic activity as both production and enjoyment promotes the development of a democratic community by providing occasions for shared experience. Emotional sharing is both more profound and more productive than the sharing of common principles entertained in separation of any common feeling. Thus, contrary to those who would relegate Dewey's concern for art to some higher cultural realm, art and aesthetic activity in their most fundamental forms are essential to a functioning democracy.

Experience in its highest form is expressed in *language* in the broadest sense. Such experience constitutes communication, which presumes a communal context. The healthiest individual is one who lives in the healthiest society, which is, in the words of Dewey, a "communicating community."[14]

The pragmatist wishes to promote those forms of social engagement and interaction that optimize communication. This effort requires a general interest in the character of communication, from its fundamentally evocative and aesthetic modes of expression to the institutional forms and technologies that promote or retard creative interactions.

Dewey's idea of democracy is not constructed in terms of strictly rational modes of association and communication. Nor is it primarily a *political* idea, if we associate the term "political" too directly with governmental institutions. Government is only one of the groupings, and generally not the most efficacious one, promoting the aims of association and communication.

✳  *For Dewey, the sine qua non of a democratic community is the presence of widespread and effective communication. Such communication can only exist within a community pervasively informed by aesthetic activity.*

## 3. The Democratic Individual

Pragmatism is a philosophy of social engagement best expressed in its distinctive understanding of "individualism." In contrast to the liberal democratic individualism that dominates modern Western thought, American pragmatists such as George Herbert Mead and John Dewey provide a distinctly *social* characterization of experience which determines that the fullest form of human life is *life together.* Dewey claims that "assured and integrated individuality is . . . the product of definite social relationships and publicly acknowledged functions."[15]

The loss of a sense of identity associated with such relationships and functions leads to a confusion of roles and their attendant motivations. Dewey felt the loss of a sense of duty to be one of the consequences of a capitalist economic system: "The business mind . . . is divided within itself . . . [since] the results of industry as the determining force in life are corporate and collective while its animating motives and compensations are so unmitigatingly private."[16]

If such divisions are to be healed, it can only be through a recognition of the corporateness of social life. In Dewey's democracy, the integrity of the individual would be a function of the coherence of a community of shared experiences. The fullness of the individual's experience can only be guaranteed by that community. A consequence of this recognition would be that the achievement of an individual's principal rewards would be realized through her roles and the functions she performs rather than through private pecuniary gain.

The centrality of the notion of communication in normative social relationships assists in the identification of those occupations which best enrich individual existence and which are more likely to be undertaken because of the intrinsic satisfactions they offer. The academic life, for example, is very satisfying for the vast majority of individuals who choose it, even though it offers rather modest material rewards. The life of the teacher and scholar offers the opportunity to participate in a communicating community of students and other academics, and often of the public at large, in ways that express the more enriching aspects of social life.

Again we encounter the essentially *aesthetic* character of Dewey's vision. The individual is *particular*, but not *discrete*. Individuals are unique elements in a community where members serve in mutually satisfying ways to enrich the experiencing of one another. Interactive, participatory behavior is the mark of a viable democratic community, and this provides the context within which an individual is constituted.

Notions of freedom and autonomy take on radically different meanings for Dewey than for proponents of liberal democracy. Freedom is freedom-in-context in which actions and decisions are rendered effective by drawing upon experiential resources derived from shared existence. Dewey is concerned that freedom be efficacious, not abstract.

In the abstract sense we are free when there are minimal constraints precluding any particular action. In the *effective* sense of freedom, an individual is free only when conditions promoting a given action are present. Members of communities are responsible for maximizing their fellows' opportunities to make decisions and perform actions that, in turn, enrich the community. Further, in a democratic society, government officials are enjoined to promote these same ends.

The enrichment of the community is not an end in itself. The individual, as a participant in the community, benefits from the enriching context. That benefit is shared with the community to the extent that resources for further enrichment of other individuals are augmented. The end of communal interaction is the enrichment of the individual.

Dewey's understanding of *autonomy* contrasts readily with the rights-based liberal vision. By analogy with economic assumptions of *laissez-faire* capitalism, rights-based liberalism asserts a "trickle down" theory of social enrichment. The efforts of the individual in accordance with his or her conscience and capacities will lead to a situation in which some will be the producers and others the consumers of meaning and value. Autonomous actions of individuals are purported to contribute to the overall health of both individuals and society as a whole.

Proponents of such an understanding are usually as sanguine about their faith in cultural "trickle-down" as they are about the economic form. However, there is no real evidence that either form is anything more than a convenient fiction. By failing to recognize the means whereby the enrichment of individual experience actually takes place, the proponent of autonomous individuality contributes to the increasing impoverishment of individual experience.

For Dewey, autonomy would have to be construed from within the context of a communal understanding of experience. This would require that the moral obligations of individuals are not primarily to their individual consciences but to the communal context to which they belong. It is, after all, the individuals, quick and dead, forming that community, who have authored both the content of that conscience and the means of maintaining one's integrity with regard to its claims. Being true to one's self is being true to the resources, capacities, and propensities that constitute the self-in-communal-context. *Being true* means nurturing the *terminus a quo* of the self (the community as experiential resource) as well as the *terminus ad quem* (the particular focus of the community. In effect, it means to understand the self as by no means separate from the communal context within which persons emerge as foci of experiencing.

We must ask how individual actions may be coordinated so as to contribute to the overall harmony of the community. The answer, from Dewey's perspective, lies in two principal factors: First, in *culture*, as a complex of a variety of potentially harmonious interests and aims, and, second, in the *aesthetic interpretation* of culture.

Substituting the notion of "culture" for that of "experience" renders Dewey's fundamentally teleological perspective a bit more coherent. The fulfillment of experience is found in the activities of participation and communication that comprise complex social experiences. The *telos* of rudimentary experience is *culture*. Given this sense of culture, Dewey would not appreciate standard understandings of the concept that distinguish culture from politics or economics or technology. Culture is the manner in which varieties of complex interactive experiencing are brought together with respect to a particular social context. Politics, economics, scientific and technological activities, aesthetic, moral, and religious sensibilities are all elements of culture.

If democracy is primarily to be understood as a communicating community, then the health of a democratic society is a function of both the pervasiveness of communication and the character of the communicated content. There are two important issues to be addressed in this context. Culture is to be construed primarily in terms of aesthetic activity. Effective culture is always "local" and "focal." We shall find that these two propositions, in fact, amount to the same thing.

In his *Freedom and Culture*, Dewey discusses issues of individualism and freedom as distinctly cultural problems, as opposed to issues of human nature. His concern is that atomistic interpretations of human nature have pervaded those societies which aspire to be democratic. These interpretations construe the human being as *essentially* an independent, prospectively autonomous, agent. The freedom of the individual is then wrapped up in the notion of *absence of constraint*. The abstractness and simplicity of such an understanding foils any attempt to see the individual as a product of the complex communicative interactions that characterize culture.

If cultural context is taken into account, the story is strikingly different. If the individual emerges from out of an interactive context, the self is always contextualized. In such a situation notions of freedom and autonomy are no longer defined in terms of independent agency, but of *interdependent activity*.

Reductionistic explanations of human nature arose *pari passu* with the development of modern democracy. These explanations we associate with Hobbes's understanding of the state of nature as "a war of each against all," and with the constructions of Hume and classical economic theory that subject the rational to the passional aspect of human beings. The influence of this reductionist model broadened with the application of Darwinian notions of "survival of the fittest" to social and political contexts. A further ramification was provided by the Freudian understanding of civilized society as the sublimated products of libidinal impulses. This understanding added support to the activities leading to the stimulation of desires by the production of objects satisfying those desires. Consider, for example, techniques of advertising and media stimulation that are capable of creating desires previously unmanifest.

Rather than promote a disjunctive nature/culture dichotomy, Dewey would likely claim that so-called "naturalistic" understandings are in fact defective modes of cultural understanding. The cultural interests of economics and the sciences, naively construed from a mechanistic perspective, have combined to provide an understanding of human nature which is hardly naturalistic, merely culturally reductionistic.

The cure for this truncated vision of the human being is to appeal to cultural interests distinguished by a direct and explicit concern for *values*. In place of a predominant interest in the economic and political aspects of culture, we ought turn to the aesthetic, moral, and religious impulses to supplement our understanding of the human being. This move would be consistent with a *teleological* as opposed to a *reductive* understanding of culture.

The most important contribution of such a move would be a shift away from understandings of the individual grounded in notions of *pleasure* and *power*. The narrower forms of both the political and economic interpretations of the independent individual are drawn from the age in which *scarcity* rather than *abundance* was the presupposition of social existence. In principle, this presumption is no longer relevant to contemporary technological societies. Its continued employment stands in the way of developing truly democratic societies.

Appeals to the value interests of a culture as a means of characterizing the individual are essential if we are to make those changes necessary to build a viable democracy. The most significant changes are the shifts from the presumption of scarcity to that of abundance, and from the presumption of the individualistic, as opposed to the corporate, character of social life. The second presumption depends in large measure upon the first. In times of scarcity it is more difficult to moderate the competitiveness for survival characteristic of societies in which "every man for himself" promises life for at least some. A society grounded in the notion of abundance, however, is better suited to cooperative endeavors.

Art, morality, and religion depend upon an understanding of life-in-common. Emotions beyond those of the rawest forms of pleasure and pain depend upon the commonality of shared experience. The conditioning features of a satisfying life-in-common necessarily include sensitivity to the aesthetic, moral, and religious sensibilities. In a society which realizes its aim as a communicating *community*, it is these value interests that are most abetted.

For Dewey, art acts to kindle emotions. But art in itself is insufficient. The aesthetic elements of experience are directed first and foremost to one's immediate situation. Only in this manner can art sustain the growth of effective individuality. Effective individuality is achieved when one has knowledge of, and some control over, his specific circumstances. Communicative activity that substitutes the "sensational" for the effectively emotional parodies and undermines democratic association.

In this context, Dewey's analysis of the communications media seems eerily prophetic in character:

> The press, the telegraph, the telephone, and radio have broadened indefinitely the range of information at the disposal of the average person. It would be foolish to deny that a certain quickening of sluggish minds has resulted. . . . [But] before we indulge in too much pity for the inhabitants of our rural regions before the days of invention of modern devices for circulation of information, we should recall that they knew far more about the things that affected their own lives than the city dweller is likely to know about the causes of his own affairs.[17]

Without the presence of effective emotions, associated with a belief that we can control to some degree the causes and consequences of our own affairs, it would be unlikely that we could ever extrapolate outward to events dominating larger contexts. Dewey's point is that the sensationalism of "news" is often the direct result of stimulation by the presentation of images and ideas that characterize events over which we have no control. Our lack of control is a consequence of the inability to see the connections with our own immediate circumstances.

Dewey's comment that "democracy begins at home, and home is a neighborly community"[18] has lost all but it's nostalgic force. In the absence of neighborly communities that serve as the touchstone of democratic action, the best we are able to do is shift back and forth between the abstract and impotent extremes of individual absoluteness and individual relativity. Witness the liberal/conservative seesaw of the last several elections in the United States, which threatens to turn Washington D. C. into the Jurassic Park of democratic nations.

If there is no local or focal identity born of face-to-face encounter then the extrapolation of experience from the local to the national or international levels cannot take place. If our primary interest is in world events, the absence of a sense of connectedness can only lead to a feeling of impotence. We should begin at the local level and extend our sense of control over our local contexts to ever-broader contexts. Art and aesthetic experience schools us in the immediacies of experience, and as such allows us to ground our sense of self first locally, and then to see that local identity as *focal* with respect to ever larger contexts.

To summarize:

> *A democratic community is a communicating community. Such a community is both "local" and "focal." Effective individuals in this community are constituted by distinctive social relationships and publicly recognized roles. These individuals realize their greatest satisfactions through these roles and relationships. A democratic community is characterized by modes of communication which promote an understanding among individuals of the causes and conditions that most affect their lives.*

## 4. Tradition, Intelligence, and Education

Our depiction of Dewey's understanding of democracy will proceed with some comments on the relation between democracy, tradition, and "intelligence"—this latter term representing Dewey's understanding of the principal dynamic of productive social change.

As radical as were Dewey's reformist ideas, he well recognized the determinative power of customs and habits, particularly when they function in support of circumstances that allow for the most relevant employment of intelligent action in the furtherance of community.

Dewey quotes admiringly the oft-celebrated words of William James:

Habit is the enormous fly-wheel of society, its most precious conservative influence. It alone is what keeps us within the bounds of ordinance,
and saves the children of fortune from the uprisings of the poor. It
alone prevents the hardest and most repugnant walks of life from being
deserted by those brought up to tread therein. It keeps the fisherman
and the deck-hand at sea during the winter; it holds the miner in his
darkness, and nails the country-man to his log cabin and his lonely
farm through all the months of snow. It protects us from invasion by
the natives of the desert and the frozen zone. It dooms us all to fight
out the battle of life upon the lines of our nurture or our early choice,
and to make the best of a pursuit that disagrees, because there is no
other for which we are fitted, and it is too late to begin again.[19]

Ultimately, in fact, Dewey claimed that there is no moving beyond
tradition:

The essential continuity of history is doubly guaranteed. Not only are
personal desire and belief functions of habit and custom, but the objective conditions which provide the sources and tools of action . . . are
precipitates of the past, perpetuating, willy-nilly, its hold and power.[20]

If we are free ourselves from the inertia of old habits and institutions,
much effort must be expended in developing those attitudes conducive
to communitarian democracy.

"Habits, customs, and systems can remain viable only when they are
the objects of intelligent thinking."[21] There must be strong traditions
which serve as the objects of intelligence, or thought will be insub-
stantial. Paradoxically, intelligence must employ the very traditions it
seeks to overcome as a means to their overcoming.

Here, the role of education in democracy is to be acknowledged.
Dewey understands education to be truly conservative. Its function is
"to conserve and transmit the best of our traditional cultural heritage
[and, at the same time,] cultivate individuals who can cope with their
environment."[22]

Dewey discusses the principal means of coping in terms of a theory
of intelligence. Democracy is the chief end for which intelligence serves
as the means. As "the perception of relationships between what is done,

and what is undergone,"[23] intelligence is brought to maturation, not at the beginning but at the end of the process of social development.

Intelligent action is a presupposition of democratic development. As such it possesses a number of conditioning features: Intelligence requires social engagement. It involves the pursuit of ends-in-common. This feature is a function of the experiential context that provides the richest of resources for individual development that can only be created through the mutual recognition of needs.

Intelligent action requires a problematic and experimental perspective. *Problematic thinking* begins with a particular problem to be addressed and seeks methods of resolution suited to the specifics of that problem. Such thinking is never aprioristic. The best one can have is rules of thumb that have suited similar situations in the past and may be relevant to the present situation. The experimental attitude is necessary since the optimal means of resolution may only be discovered by recourse to continued social experiment.

Finally, it is likely that attitudes shaped by traditional habits and customs may no longer be relevant to changed social conditions. According to Dewey, "the underlying persistent attitudes of human beings were formed by traditions, customs, institutions, which existed when there was no democracy."[24]

All of the conditioning features of intelligent action are focused here. Specific problems associated with a democracy-in-the-making are often occasioned by the inertia of attitudes and dispositions. Intelligent action seeks to alter interpretations of a social environment in order to insure a more harmonious engagement of practice and interpretation.

The problem of the "lost individual" discussed earlier well illustrates the disengagement of practice and interpretation. Changes occasioned by the growth of industry and technology have led to an environment most conducive to corporate and cooperative behavior. The attitudes associated with free enterprise capitalism remain based upon a belief in the value of competition among independent and autonomous individuals. Intelligent action would lead to experiments demonstrating the manner in which the conscious promotion of corporate activity would maximize the ideals of a democratic way of life. Adjustment in traditional economic arrangements would follow.

There is, of course, an apparent circularity involved in such an argument. This understanding of intelligence depends on the assumption of communitarian engagement. Concepts of liberal, rights-based democracy, and of free enterprise capitalism, are already dismissed as legitimate goals of intelligent action. So, what is Dewey's point here?

When Dewey claims that attitudes are outmoded, he means that objective conditions have truly changed. With regard to the notion of the creation of an optimal member of democratic community, he means, for example, that the recognition of the shift from conditions of *scarcity* to those of *abundance* is not significantly qualifying the attitudes of individuals. His point is that a general recognition of such a shift would lead to forms of social existence more satisfying to all. Further, the failure to recognize that shift promotes social interactions that cause disharmony and frustration.

The disjunction between objective social conditions and attitudes permitting one to cope with those conditions presents one of the central challenges to the implementation of democratic ideals. Ingrained traditions, which perpetuate attitudes, habits, and institutions incongruent with democratic ideals, are the primary obstacles to social reform. And since "great change in events and practical affairs is attended with marked cultural lags in verbal formulations,"[25] we may lack a proper language to characterize the ideals freed by the social changes that make democratic developments possible.

Here we come face to face with a most important consequence of the pragmatic interpretation of ideas and ideals. Unlike his contemporary, A. N. Whitehead, who accepts the efficacy, if not the primacy, of ideas and ideals in the "slow drift of mankind toward civilization,"[26] Dewey believes that this drift is itself the context from which the articulated ideal (clothed now in appropriate beliefs, habits, and institutions) emerges. Whitehead's accession to the positive influence of irrational forces illustrated by such factors as "steam and the barbarians" is met by Dewey's belief that it is "steam"—that is to say, technology—which is the primary causal agent in the development of mankind's potential. And it is the potentially barbarous employment of technology, a consequence of habits and institutions we should long ago have outgrown, that presents the fundamental obstacle.

Changes in social circumstances may be more rapid at some times than at others. Circumstances attending the founding of America produced a situation that, though by all means cumulative and evolutionary, gave the appearance of sudden and rapid transformation. This process had led to the disintegration, among some, of old beliefs and the perpetuation, among others, of beliefs broadly irrelevant to the changes taking place.

The West's situation remains one significantly shaped by free enterprise capitalism, individual autonomy, and rational technologies. Dewey finds in rational technologies the element that has contributed most to the altered circumstances associated with the possibility of a shift from the presupposition of scarcity to that of abundance and from that of individuality to corporateness. A combination of capitalism and individual autonomy has, however, served to perpetuate old habits.

An allied consequence of the latter is a disturbance of the balance between morality and law. This imbalance is, as Daniel Bell has claimed, largely a consequence of the development of capitalism. Increased dependence upon legal mechanisms has replaced reliance upon moral bonds as the basis of social interactions. This movement is a function of the desire to maintain a rationalized economic system. The alliance of capitalism and the liberal concept of democracy insured the transition from a custom-based morality to the artifice of a legal system ordered along contractual lines.

"The rule of law," a catch phrase of liberal democracy, is hardly the aim of a communitarian democracy. The greater the number of laws on the books, the more we recognize a decline in our internal sense of things-in-common. This is accompanied by a decline in endeavors aimed at realizing shared goals. According to Dewey, "all laws except those which regulate technical procedures are registrations of existing social customs and their attendant moral habits and purposes."[27] As the recent history of our nation sadly proclaims, attempts to legislate morality are doomed to fail since, at best, they involve efforts to force the standards of one moral grouping upon the society as a whole. A far better method of attaining social harmony is to sensitize individuals to the needs of their fellows.

Recourse to legal surrogates for customary and traditional social interactions is detrimental to the aims of a democratic society. Not only does it perpetuate the dominance of economic interests over communitarian concerns by essentially codifying the interests of the wealthy, it transforms social relations regulated by law into abstract modes of interaction in which the feelings of shared commitment to common goals is effectively lost.

Dewey often claimed that his work, *Democracy and Education,* contained the best summary of his broad-ranging philosophy. This is not surprising since Dewey characterized his thinking as reflections upon the democratic experience and understood the meaning of democracy wholly within the context of the community life in which education served as the central means for promoting the optimal form of social existence. "Democracy" is the name of that optimal form of communal existence, and "education" names the process that sustains such a community.

Dewey's educational theory is based upon two significant assumptions: The first entails a denial of any disconnect between mind and body. Education involves the entire person. The second characterizes the individual as embodied in a transactional community.

In a Deweyan democracy, the individual emerges from, and acts to promote, social transactions. Education goes on within those associations that focus the normative activities of the larger community. Basic modes of association such as the family and voluntary groupings all have an educative function.

Deweyan education is not premised upon the notion of *preparation,* but is conceived to be both an ongoing process and an end in itself. Education serves the aim of growth, which has no proper culmination. Growth is a function of the ability to extract significant meanings from experience allowing it to be reconfigured so as to promote habits and character that serve one's self and the larger community.

All education is *moral* in the sense that it seeks to realize common goods. Moreover, morality is social since moral actions are always tacitly or explicitly predicated upon responses to the anticipated or perceived intentions and behaviors of others. Education always seeks to sensitize individuals to goods-in-common.

The moral goods of a democratic society are straightforward: Education for democracy promotes habits of sympathetic identification, cooperation, and deference to realized excellence, rather than those of autonomy and competition. Such education promotes the development of a critical attitude toward enterprises such as *laissez-faire* capitalism.

Education for democracy teaches individuals to look to the benefit of their fellows. Such a concern is not motivated by self-sacrifice, but self-interest. The richest possible resources for individual experiencing create the best context for a satisfying life for all. Since the creation of such community interest requires the promotion of aesthetic modes of communication, education for democracy will have a strong aesthetic component.

Education for democracy aims at sharpening the tools of intelligent action discussed above. Intelligence is grounded in the present, but requires an appropriate recognition of the value of the inventory of habits and traditions characterizing a given social context. Further, as there are no essential truths whose content is to be transferred to the minds of students, intelligence is grounded in historicist understandings which require the highest degree of flexibility in shaping the means/ends relationship.

Sound education is measured in part by the manner in which individuals in a democratic society are able to discern the relevance of present attitudes to present modes of social organization. The growth of society requires the adaptation of attitudes and beliefs to altered social circumstances. Further, there is a concern in embodied education of the sort Dewey espouses always to be aware of the connection of idea and affect, of thought and its guiding emotion.

Education is aimed at maintaining the sense of the *local* and *focal* character of experience. We begin always with the immediacies of experience and only after reckoning with the first-handedness of things do we extrapolate outward to large fields of experience beyond our face-to-face encounters. Such education militates against the sense of disconnectedness that is endemic in a society whose sources of information are predominantly patterned by a sensationalizing news media. Education for democracy must prepare individuals to forge connections between apparently isolated events and their own fields of experience. This, in turn, permits a recognition of the causal forces that impinge upon them, and offers some possibilities for gaining effective control over those causal elements.

Finally, education for democracy helps to maintain a balance between the harmonizing effects of morality and the regularizing effects of law. Legal mechanisms are signs that harmony has broken down and that some quick fix is necessary. The creation of effective modes of civility that will allow for the workings of habit, character, and moral suasion in the maintenance of a viable community is a high priority of educating for democracy.

Our final summary characterization of John Dewey's democracy is this:

> In a democratic community, habits, customs, and traditions are essential grounds for the use of intelligence. Intelligent action requires a concern for the relevance of beliefs and attitudes to the social conditions they interpret. Intelligent changes in tradition are evolutionary rather than revolutionary. Maintaining a productive balance of the disciplining impetus of law and the sensitizing influences of morality is crucial to such development.
>
> Education for democracy is practical, aesthetic, growth-oriented, historicist, and communitarian. If we recall that, for Dewey, the self is irreducibly social, then we may say that the central aim of education is self-cultivation. Self-cultivation captures the life-long nature of the educational process, as well as its essentially moral character. Self-cultivation is the cultivation of democratic community.

## 5. Dewey and Rights-Based Liberalism

Finally, it will be helpful to connect our discussion of John Dewey's democracy with the consideration of rights-based liberalism in the last chapter. The principal distinctions between Dewey's vision of democracy and that of rights-based liberal theorists are as follows:

First: Dewey's thought eschews any notion of the discrete individual underlying liberal democracy.

Second: For the notion of human rights as essential possessions of individuals prior to entering society, Dewey substitutes the notion of rights as accorded by the society of which an individual is a part.

Third: Rights-based liberalism seems to accede to the employment of the capitalistic economic model as a primary determinant of the modes of social and political association. Dewey finds such an economic system detrimental to his communitarian form of democracy.

Fourth: Rights-based liberalism depends upon government as a regulatory agency that, effectively, is morally neutral. Dewey claims no mode of association or regulation can or should maintain moral neutrality, since the aim of a democratic society is to promote and sustains goods held in common.

Finally: Given its concerns for moral neutrality at the level of regulation, rights-based liberalism promotes the mechanism of legal sanctions over those of moral suasion as a means of maintaining social harmony. Dewey's democratic theory reverses this emphasis.

# Confucianism and Pragmatism

## 1. Dewey in China

Pragmatism officially came to China on May 1, 1919, the date John Dewey arrived for his twenty-six-month visit. Since his was a decidedly peaceful entry, unaccompanied by warships, and not the consequence of coerced treaties, there was reason to believe that he might meet with some success. Only three days later, however, the May Fourth uprising occurred in Beijing.

The New Culture Movement associated with the May Fourth reforms was initially quite open to new ideas, particularly Western ideas, and most particularly those concerning social reform. Since Dewey had announced that the central subject of his lectures was to be that of "democracy," interest was initially quite high. Soon after his arrival, efforts were begun to transform the Chinese educational system along pragmatic lines.[1]

Within a very short time, however, Dewey's influence came into question. The New Culture Movement was initially anti-Confucian, and Dewey's thought was seen to be in radical opposition to traditional Confucian ideas. Ironically, this was true in spite of the fact that in 1920 Dewey was awarded an honorary degree from a Chinese University accompanied by a citation which named him "Second Confucius." When Sun Yat-sen and the Guomindang—the Nationalist party—promoted a return to many of the traditional Chinese values and institutions, Dewey's thought was deemed unacceptable due to its foreign origin.

When the communists came to power, Dewey's thought was roundly condemned as an expression of Western imperialism. After the establishment of the People's Republic, a purge of Deweyan pragmatism was begun. Literally millions of words were written refuting Dewey's works.

The effort to erase Dewey's presence from the face of China was finally completed only in the mid-fifties.

After the episode of "Dewey in China," pragmatism was studied only here and there throughout Asia. Continental philosophy represented by Kant and twentieth-century figures such as Sartre, Heidegger, and Wittgenstein, were much more attractive to Asians interested in learning about the Western world.

There is a real irony here, of course. For, as we shall see, American pragmatism and Asian Confucianism are more dramatically similar than one might reasonably expect intellectual movements born from such disparate historical experiences to be. Lately, scholars in both Asia and America have begun to recognize this and a most interesting intercultural conversation is gradually beginning.

The reasons for Dewey's failure finally to influence China were largely associated with his refusal to take a wholesale approach to social problems. Always warning the Chinese against the uncritical importation of Western ideas (including, of course, his own), as well as the uncritical rejection of traditional Chinese values, Dewey, in spite of his radical reconstruction of the popular democratic ideal, was simply too moderate for a China in search of revolution. It was practically inevitable, therefore, that Marxism's wholesale ideology would replace Dewey's decidedly retail philosophy.

While his ideas are neither pro-capitalist nor anti-Confucian, the popular idea of democracy with which Dewey was wrongly identified entails both of these characteristics. Moreover, as Dewey and his ilk were hardly successful in reshaping the actual understanding of democracy and democratic institutions in the North Atlantic countries, it is not surprising that it is the popular, rather simple-minded, idea of democracy that many are currently urging upon China.

Given Dewey's insistence that democracy is expressed in attitudes rather than institutions, and that the sort of democratic attitudes entailed by his vision of democracy are both gradually formed by, and reinforced through education, it would appear foolish to suggest that present-day hawkers of so-called democratic ideals will have any real influence in these decidedly less auspicious circumstances. Potential exporters of Western democracy to China seem satisfied that internal changes among the peasants, the entrepreneurs, and some intellectuals, or the pressure of other so-called democratic nations, or the demands of the world market, will work in a manner that Dewey's intelligent, patient, and altogether sensitive efforts did not.

Dewey's ideas have been effectively purged in America as well. Shifts in philosophic interest within the American academy, abetted by the importation of emigré European philosophers prior to World War II, altered the intellectual landscape of America in the direction of exoteric modes of thought. Dewey's thought, and pragmatism in general, were effectively erased from the intellectual scene.

Dewey's educational reforms, badly misunderstood and only partially applied from the beginning, have long since been effectively abandoned. His understanding of democracy was never altogether in the mainstream. In many ways, the opportunity to introduce a reconstructed idea of democracy seems to have been lost as surely in America as it was in China.

Recently, however, there has been a rather dramatic renewal of interest in pragmatism. In America, this is most obvious in the work of the New Pragmatist, Richard Rorty. But, perhaps of greater long-term significance is the amount of energy expended upon the resurrection of Dewey himself along with other classical American pragmatists. These efforts are part of a general shift away from European and toward American intellectual culture. The result thus far has been the renewal of philosophical self-understanding on the part of American intellectuals.

The renewal of interest in American thought is fortunate with respect to our present international situation for John Dewey's vision of a democratic society demonstrates surprising affinities with the traditional Chinese understanding of social organization.[2] Moreover, judged in terms of its resonance with many of the most pervasive Chinese beliefs and values, the Deweyan vision of democracy should be such as to engage the interest of a modernizing China.

We certainly realize that, even if dialogue between communitarian pragmatism and some form of leftwing Confucianism were to come about, it would likely be drowned out by the voices of those engaged in other sorts of conversation. At the relatively innocent level of intellectual culture, self-proclaimed "postmodernists" from the West, celebrating Zhuangzi as the first true deconstructionist, are engaged by Chinese thinkers who argue for the relevance of Kant and Western modernism to the reconstruction of China. In this conversation, a modernizing China engages a postmodernizing West—and nobody wins.

Of course, the main conversation may proceed at the far darker level of practical politics and economics—where deals are made. In this dark place, where "democracy" is synonymous with a jerry-rigged form of market capitalism and nineteenth-century party politics, a seedy capitalism faces an effete Marxism—and everybody loses.

In spite of the apparent practical futility of the exercise, we shall proceed with the effort to demonstrate the similarities between elements of Dewey's conception of democracy and Chinese understandings of community. Such a comparison may at the very least succeed in provoking some, on both the Chinese and Western sides, to introduce Dewey's ideas into future conversations concerning China and Democracy.

There is, in fact, some hope to be found in the increased interest in "Asian Values" on the part of both Asians and non-Asians alike. Academic institutions and organizations in Europe, the United States, China, and Korea have committed a great deal of energy to a variety of discussions, which include detailed consideration of models of "Confucian Democracy." Those who are enamored of the quick-fix will always place their faith in political and economic factors and forces. But, the efficacy of cultural dynamics manifested in the consequences of ideas and values should not be ignored.

In this present chapter, we intend to initiate a demonstration of the manner in which a Deweyan vision of democracy may contribute to an assessment of the hope of democracy in China, thereby justifying once more Dewey's right to the title, "Second Confucius."

## 2. Shared Marginality

The separate emergence in America of the "New Pragmatism," associated with the celebration of central elements of the thought of John Dewey and other classical pragmatic thinkers, and of the New Confucianism (*xinruxue* 新儒學), championed by a number of scholars throughout Asia and America,[3] are phenomena of signal importance for both America and Asia. This is so for two basic reasons: First, each of these ideological expressions is perhaps the most authentic interpretation of the sensibility of its home culture. Secondly, and somewhat surprising, is the fact that Confucianism and pragmatism share a number of important philosophical assumptions, and may thus serve as resources for intercultural conversation.

By saying that pragmatism and Confucianism are authentic cultural expressions of their respective cultures, we do not mean to claim that the presence of these sensibilities in America, on the one hand, or in China, Korea, Japan, and Vietnam, on the other, is unproblematic. We only intend to suggest that Confucianism and American pragmatism uniquely speak the cultural languages of their home environs. It is certainly true that, until recently, Enlightenment modernity, associated with rights-based liberalism, free enterprise capitalism, and the unchecked spread of material technologies, has threatened to efface not only Confucianism in the developing countries of Asia, but the philosophical pragmatism of American society, as well.

The claim that a modernizing Asia has threatened Confucianism is hardly controversial. But to assert that American pragmatism has itself suffered from the strictures of modernization may seem more unusual. After all, the grotesque parodies of American pragmatism at the hands of some European and Asian thinkers have influenced many to view it as an instrumental "any-means-to-an-end" kind of thinking, distinctly nonintellectual and altogether unrefined. Pragmatism is wrongly considered by the philosophically uninformed to be a simple offshoot of a kind of capitalist and technological frenzy masked by the overworked phrase of President Calvin Coolidge: "The business of America is business." In fact, it is the social, economic, and technological expressions of the modernist impulse in international economics and politics that has marginalized both Confucianism and American pragmatism. In the senses of the words "Western" and "Modern" normally used in contemporary cross-cultural comparisons, American pragmatism is as distinct from modern, Western society as is Confucianism itself.[4]

As we have insisted, modern forms of liberal, rights-based democracy carry with them either an understanding of atomistic individualism consistent with the economic views of Locke, Hume, and Adam Smith, or a Kantian stress upon categorical principles. Each of these perspectives is significantly at odds with classical American pragmatism.

John Dewey was a consistent critic of the autonomous individualism entailed by classical views of liberal democracy, and he was quite explicit that there are no such things as categorical principles defining human beings as rights-bearing creatures. Individual rights are resourced in the community that assigns them. Further, the alliance of democracy with capitalism and technology is a European, essentially a British, phenomenon associated with a misconceived alignment of the activities of the industrial revolution with the articulation of modern democratic institutions.

Contrary to the interpretations of democratic development that see it as an assured consequence of economic progress, philosophical pragmatists such as John Dewey argue that the growth of democracy must be realized independently of any economic system that combines a concern for property rights with the motivation to acquire individual profit.[5] Likewise, pragmatism sees science and technology as potentially cooperative activities, leading to the most efficient and effective realization of selected ends. Too close an alliance between technological development and the motives of classical capitalism militates against the value of technology in promoting community.

Our point is simply that American pragmatism is in serious conflict with the motivations of modern Western societies insofar as they are dominated by the elements of rights-based democracy, free enterprise capitalism, and material technologies. In fact, American pragmatism is a counterdiscourse to the mainstream ideology that defines modern Anglo-European social, political, and economic sensibilities.

The situation is far more complex in Asia since Confucianism has had a longer history and, traditionally, a stronger hold on the principal Asian countries. Nevertheless, in the twentieth century, Confucianism has been significantly marginalized in many Asian nations. In a more important sense, Confucianism, like pragmatism, has had only peripheral status on the broader world scene.

Marginalization has been the consequence of a number of challenges to Asian autonomy and identity: most dramatically expressed in the late nineteenth century by Western and Japanese expansionist and colonial policies; by World War I, culminating in the infamous Treaty of Versailles; by the Chinese civil war, followed by the institution of Marxist policies in Maoist China; by the American support of the nationalist

Chinese in Taiwan; and by the Japanese and American occupations of Korea—among many other factors. Such events prevented any successful engagement of traditional values with the values and policies forced upon the Asian nations by unwise foreign influence, and by the irrational forces of brute circumstance.

At the international level, both Asian Confucianism and American pragmatism have suffered from Eurocentrist devaluations derived from the rationalist sensibilities expressed by the European Enlightenment. Confucian thinking has been construed as little more than a sterile set of moral truisms and ethical conducts that offers nothing of real value to either the analytic or speculative extremes of Anglo-European thought. Though this has begun to change in recent years, it is still the case that the majority of professional philosophers in the Continental and British traditions have little interest in Asian philosophy.

The marginalization of Confucianism has continued within modernizing Asian societies. The new Confucian sensibility, insofar as it has active proponents within various of the Asian countries, has the ambiguous character of all conservative reforms. While it aims above all to maintain and reinforce the values of the society of which it is a part, it is nonetheless often in conflict with social and political forces leading the country in an alternative direction.

Confucianism adds a dimension to Asian national life that has been suppressed in recent times. Beyond its political and social import, Confucianism offers a distinctly *cultural* dynamic with a potentially transformative influence upon politics and civil society. Obviously, the forces of Western modernization are threatened by this dynamic. In China, for example, the sphere of culture has been traded back and forth between the individualism of the Western modernist impulse and the counter-discourse of Marxian revolutionary reform. Only of late has the voice of the tradition been heard with some clarity.

The voice of the Confucian, like the voice of the new American Pragmatist, is difficult to hear over the din of international business activities. The Confucian insistence that the rulers and ministers, as well as the leaders in business and finance, be moral exemplars seems futile in the face of the challenges of world competition. Reformist thinkers in Asia, confronted with the rise of capitalist influences in the late nineteenth and early twentieth centuries, have sought to maintain a balance among the needs of economics, politics, and culture. Capitalism and technology were promoted in order to augment the power of the Asian states vis-à-vis Western powers and one another. There was no attempt to abrogate the communitarian motives of Confucianism. Wealth was to be social and communal, not personal.

Carter Eckert makes this point effectively in his essay on the South Korean Bourgeoisie.[6] He insists that Confucian culture urges contemporary corporate capitalists in Korea to demonstrate that their motives are nationalistic and communitarian rather than simply personal. Nonetheless, the necessity to compete in international markets leads to compromises with both nationalist and individual morality. The individual CEO cannot easily maintain even the facade of morality when international business is so obviously cutthroat. For example, a recent head of Hyundai Corporation is cited as saying, "If a businessman acts like a religious man, how can he undertake the responsibilities of the overseas market, where competition is intense."[7]

To say that both American pragmatism and Asian Confucianism have been marginalized by modernizing forces is to say that, to the degree Asia and America are informed by Confucian and pragmatic values, respectively, both are ambiguously related to the modern, Western world.

The marginalization of Confucianism and pragmatism within the modern world seems incontrovertible. But it should be said that these sensibilities share more than just a common fate. With appropriate adjustments for the distinctive rhetorical expressions of each, there is a significant overlap of their respective core convictions. Moreover, for a variety of reasons, both Confucianism and pragmatism presently appear to be in a position to challenge their marginalized status and rise to the level of significant influence in their home cultures. This means that there are important reasons for supporting a dialogue between these sensibilities.

In fact, this dialogue has already begun. The American and Asian encounters with their respective traditional cultures have been occasioned, not only by the removal of the ideological and practical impediments that had interrupted such engagements, but also by their encounters with one another.

For example, the economic miracles in Asia have raised questions about whether modernization must mean *Westernization,* with the consequence that Confucian values are being reexamined. And in America, the question is raised among the more sensitive of those individuals engaged with Asian/Western encounters as to whether America has anything more to offer than economic and political models shored up by the bare bones credo of liberal democracy, capitalism, and technology.

This returns us to our thesis in a slightly more sophisticated form: There is real value in the potential conversation between Asian Confucianism and American pragmatism, not only because the similarities in their positions will ease the dialogue that must take place between Asia and America, but equally because such conversation will create an alliance permitting creative remonstrances directed to their respective political and economic institutions, as well as to the global social and economic context to which each contributes.

Shortly, we shall attempt to highlight specific commonalities between American pragmatism and Confucianism that could further stimulate an intercultural dialogue. We do not mean to underestimate the differences that could be outlined as well. Nor do we wish to overestimate the extent to which either Confucianism or pragmatism can be efficacious in bringing real changes to their respective societies. We do hope, however, to highlight some genuine possibilities for dialogue.

The Confucianism that at least marginally infuses Asian culture still today is, particularly in China and Korea, a *neo*-Confucianism reshaped by the mediation of Buddhist philosophy and practice. The systems of Zhu Xi (1130–1200) and Wang Yangming (1472–1529) in China, and of Yi Hwang (1501–1570) and Yi Yulgok (1527–1572) in Korea, are the principal sources of Confucian understandings. For a variety of reasons associated with distinct and well-known historical circumstances, Korea may be said to have maintained a more coherent connection with its particular forms of Confucianism than has China. This is important to note since, just as Korea served as a stimulus for the Chinese democracy movement in the pre-Tiananmen era, so it has now begun to serve as a model for the renewal of Confucianism there, as well.

Neo-Confucianism must be distinguished in part from the so-called "New Confucianism" being forwarded both in Asia and America as a program of cultural reconstruction. The important distinction is that the New Confucianists are less interested in the rather complex epistemological and metaphysical concerns associated in China with Buddhist-inspired Confucianism. The New Confucian sensibility is, to the extent that it can be thematically focused, a return to the simpler moral and aesthetic concerns of classical Confucianism. It is a return to the origins, to the cultural roots embedded in a soil long disturbed by war, political division, occupation, and the frantic pace of economic and social developments. This Confucianism is, in the minds of many of its proponents, a program of reconstruction and reform that will allow the emergence in the Asian world of modernized, but not necessarily *Westernized*, societies.

The term "New Pragmatism" has been used rather narrowly to refer to the philosophical position of Richard Rorty, whose work, beginning with his 1979 *Philosophy and the Mirror of Nature*, has drawn heavily upon the thought of John Dewey. But it is doubtless more appropriate to use that term in a much wider sense to refer to the general renewal of interest in pragmatic philosophy attendant upon the increasing substitution of a broad range of American cultural resources for European modes of thought. In any case, as the testimony of the most prominent of the New Pragmatists, Rorty, suggests: It is the thought of John Dewey that dominates any understanding of American pragmatism—old or new.[8]

## 3. Some Commonalities

The New Pragmatism and the New Confucianism are, each in its own fashion, concerned with intercultural dialogue between Asia and America and have recently begun to initiate serious conversations.[9] We wish to outline some specific areas of commonality between Confucianism and Pragmatism that promise to make this emerging conversation most worthwhile.

In each case, our comparison of pragmatism and Confucianism will cut two ways. We will suggest that there is an important resonance between pragmatism and Confucianism, and, at the same time, we will argue that there is a significant contrast between both pragmatic and Confucian understandings and the dominant senses of modernity and modernization. If we are at all persuasive, we shall make at least plausible the belief that an alliance of Confucian and pragmatic sensibilities may well provide resources for the development of models of democratization alternative to those that currently dominate the developed nations of the world.

## *Ethnocentrism and the Importance of Narrative*

First, as we have indicated in our discussion of John Dewey's theory of democracy, pragmatism is a fallibilist and historicist philosophy. The pragmatist makes no claim to absolute or final truth, nor does he hold his theoretical perspective to be an exclusive manner of thinking about things. The pragmatist's views are dependent upon the historical narrative of the community of which he or she is a member.

Both pragmatism and Confucianism entail the denial of essentialist categories of the sort that have, in the West, been associated with the European Enlightenment. Universal laws of nature, scientific principles, or logical categories, do not best serve to define us at the levels of personal, social, and political existence. Our cultural narratives tell us who we are. This particular element of pragmatism and of Confucianism argues, as well, against the cultural imperialism associated with the forced exportation of Western values.

Modernity is Eurocentric, not only in the obvious sense of ignoring the more exotic areas of the world, but in the less obvious, but far more pernicious, sense of masking ethnocentrism under the guise of universalism. The modern Westerner is encouraged by such universalist pretensions to believe that being human, and having a correct conception of the human person, means to think and act pretty much as Anglo-Europeans do.

Both Confucianism and pragmatism support a recognition of the uniqueness of cultural narrative. They both argue against the malignant ethnocentrism that would offer a contingent set of cultural values as universals for others. Each supports, rather, the "benign ethnocentrism" of the sort forwarded by Rorty who asserts (what should be obvious) that we begin our thinking, acting, and feeling from where we are.[10] There is no choice but, initially, to privilege our own experiences, our own narratives, as central in the determination of our selves. Only from such a center can we move outward, and through engagement with other ethnocentrics, win a broader "we-consciousness."[11]

## Social Engagement

A second area of agreement between pragmatism and Confucianism concerns the distinctly *social* character of each. The social character of pragmatism is captured in Dewey's understanding of experience as "participation and communication."[12] Experience thus construed is envisioned as language *in use.* Experience is communication, which presumes, of course, a communal context. The healthiest individual is one who lives in the healthiest society, which is, we recall, "a communicating community."

This particular stress of pragmatism leads to a concern over the forms of social engagement and interaction that optimize communication. Such investigations lead through a spectrum of interest in the character of communication from fundamentally evocative and aesthetic modes of expression to the institutional activities that promote or retard creative interactions. Pragmatism, as a philosophy of social engagement, is a *communitarian* philosophy.

In the *Analects,* Confucius claims that "a person who does not understand words has no way of knowing others."[13] By this he means more than a simple grasp of one's native tongue; he is indicating the need to master, insofar as possible, the tools of communication. In addition, Confucius claims that "following the proper way, I do not forge new paths,"[14] and further says of himself: "to quietly persevere in storing up what is learned, to continue studying without respite, to instruct others without growing weary—is this not me?"[15] Confucius is a transmitter, a teacher, a master communicator. It is this emphasis on virtuosic communication that leads to the central Confucian concern with the "proper use of names (*zhengming* 正名)."

Against the solitary *cogito* of Enlightenment rationality, both pragmatism and Confucianism see individuals as constituted by relationships that are realized and maintained through effective communication. Dewey's belief, cited in the last chapter, that integrated individuality is "the product of definite social relationships and publicly acknowledged functions,"[16] makes this point most effectively.

In Confucianism these relationships and functions are established and maintained through ritualized roles and behaviors (*li* 禮). The notion of ritual is very broad, embracing everything from manners to roles and relationships, from posture and personal gestures to social and political institutions. It is the determinate fabric of Confucian culture and further, is defining of sociopolitical order. It is the language through which the culture is expressed.

## Self-Cultivation

A third element in American pragmatism that resonates well with Confucian thinking concerns the emphasis in each upon *self-cultivation*. We discussed this issue in the last chapter with regard to Dewey's understanding of education. Those accustomed to the heavy-handed contrast of Western and Confucian interests in terms of the former's concern with *orthodoxy* and the latter's stress upon *orthopraxy* will not immediately appreciate the extent to which self-cultivation is a prominent theme in American thought. But on reflection, those familiar with the American intellectual tradition will not be surprised by this comparison, since a concern for the practical issues of self-cultivation goes back to the very beginnings of American thought with the Calvinist theologian Jonathan Edwards and the famous essayist, Ralph Waldo Emerson.

The stress upon self-discipline and self-actualization is deeply rooted in American soil. The substance of Emerson's essays on "Love," "Self-reliance," "Prudence," "Friendship," "Character," "Heroism," "Manners," and "Ability" helped to shape the content and direction of Dewey's numerous ethical works as well as his countless lectures on educational reform. Further, self-cultivation is thematized not only by Emerson's essays and Dewey's moral and educational theory, but finds interesting echoes in Rorty's discussions of philosophy as useful primarily for self-creation.[17]

For both Confucianism and pragmatism, self-cultivation, in the sense of education in morals and character, is central. Traditionally, the Confucian emphasis has been upon educating leaders in a direct manner, while American pragmatism has sought to generalize moral and aesthetic education as a means of producing the largest possible pool from which leaders may be drawn. Nonetheless, the distinctly *social* motives supporting Confucian and pragmatic understandings of the aims of education provide one of the most productive grounds for mutual dialogue.

## The Duty of Remonstrance

A principal characteristic of Confucianism as a political vision is its stress upon the duty of "remonstrance (*jian* 諫)."[18] The mutual obligations of rulers and ministers require that the latter are expected to behave not only as functionaries mediating decrees of the rulers, but as responsible advisors, as well. There are crucial periods in the historical narratives of Confucian Asia in which the duties of remonstrance played a central role. It is true that these duties were sometimes taken more seriously by the ministers than the rulers, with sometimes fatal consequences for the remonstrators, but it is nevertheless safe to say that without the role of ministers serving as guides for, and checks upon, governmental policies, Confucian societies would have been markedly less stable.

As Tu Wei-ming well notes, classical Confucianism defines the ruler/minister relationship not simply as that of father and son, but as a combination of that relationship and the friendship relation as well.[19] Indeed, in a well-known remark in the preface to the *Book of Songs*, it is said that the benefits of self-cultivation should be used both by the ruler to influence the people and by the people to remonstrate with the ruler.

The final two essays in Tu Wei-ming's *Way, Learning, and Politics* concern the hope for, and possibilities of, a renewal of Confucianist humanism that would not only reconstitute ancient Asian values but contribute to emerging international order as well.[20] American pragmatists seek a renewal of pragmatism as a vital supplement to the modernizing dynamics derived from the European Enlightenment. Such efforts as these are being made in the spirit of remonstrance associated with both Confucian and pragmatic philosophies.

In Western democracies, remonstrance has been associated ideally with the power of the *bourgeoisie* and intellectual classes to influence government through the exercise of the ballot, and through participation in the actions of educational and voluntary associations.

Practically, of course, powerful economic and political interests have often threatened the legitimate interests of the larger population.

In modern Asian societies in the process of democratization, the responsibilities of remonstrance have been shifting from aristocratic classes toward a newly developing *bourgeoisie*. The intellectual community, submerged for some time in a number of Asian societies, has begun to reemerge as a productive source of creative remonstrance.

Conversations among scholars, teachers, and governmental officials, in both Asian and American societies, can support an alliance of pragmatism and Confucianism based upon their common virtues and common cause. The same dynamic in Asian and American societies that recognizes the need for a middle class conditioned less by purely economic motivations and more by real communitarian concerns supports the requirement that potential remonstrators be culturally informed. That is to say, the spokesmen for reform within a society must be educated in, and sensitized to, values supporting the well-being of all members of the society. Scholars, teachers, and intellectuals within their respective societies, as well as members of the world community, may then take up the duty of remonstrance.

It will be helpful, perhaps, to note recent examples of the resort to remonstrance within both Asian and American societies. In a note to our Introduction, we mentioned a specific instance of creative remonstrance currently underway in South Korea which involves Asian, American, and European scholars in deliberations aimed at the construction of a model Confucian constitution for the Republic of Korea.

Though this project is not in any direct manner associated with the Korean government, it has not been conceived merely as an academic exercise. The publication of the constitution and the surrounding deliberations will be undertaken with the specific aim of appealing to Korean government officials, university administrators, business and civic leaders, to take into account the Confucian cultural context that willy-nilly provides the ground for economic and political institutions. Initial interest in the project on the part of the Korean public and media suggests that the effort may have some impact upon future political deliberations.

In America, the exercise of remonstrance has taken the form of a public "Call to Civil Society" by The Council on Civil Society, a joint project of the Institute for American Values and the University of Chicago Divinity School. The committee issuing the Call includes United States senators, clergymen, university presidents, and professors of politics, economics, philosophy, and religion.

The document published by the committee begins with the claim that "the core challenge facing our nation today is not primarily governmental or economic. Neither government action on its own, nor economic growth on its own, nor the two in tandem, can cure what ails us."[21] The chief problem affecting American society is the failure to recognize the importance of moral values as the groundwork of a democracy. America's problem is *cultural* at base.

The "Call to Civil Society" is directed to the American public, including the officials charged with overseeing the public sphere. This is clearly an exercise in remonstrance which has its roots deeply embedded in American soil.

These two brief illustrations of creative remonstrance urge a common direction for processes of democratization, one that leads away from the excesses of impersonal political and/or economic activity toward a greater appreciation of a morally grounded community.

## The Importance of Tradition

A fifth manner in which pragmatic thought overlaps with Confucianism is that, while responsive to the novelties issuing from the immediacies of interactive experience, the pragmatist is most positively oriented toward habit, custom, and tradition, since these serve as the "funded experiences" from which all problem-solving activity begins. The popular Western view is that the conformity associated with the maintenance of a continuity with the past is undesirable, because it leads to unproductive inertia and stagnating inflexibility. But, for pragmatism, conformity with the past is one means of maintaining connections with the sources of moral and aesthetic feelings that shape and maintain one's character.

The frantic obsession with technological novelties at the expense of tradition is largely responsible for the uprooted and alienated lives endured by all too many in economically privileged societies. Both pragmatists and Confucians would consider the question of how one might balance the demands of novelty with the claims of tradition to be one of the most significant social questions.

Pragmatism sees tradition as fundamental to the organization of society and the individual's proper engagements with it. It is equally fundamental to the very definition of what it means to be human. Charles Sanders Peirce characterized knowledge in terms of beliefs, which he saw as dispositional habits. For Rorty, the self is a complex of habits, a centerless web of beliefs and desires.[22] And, as we have already mentioned, Dewey claimed that "thinking is secreted in the interstices of habit."[23] This last statement, which alludes to Dewey's concept of "intelligence," is distinctly Confucian. In Chinese Confucianism, to be "reasonable" (*heli* 合理) is to think and act in accordance with the order of things as mediated through tradition.

*Li* 理 understood here as "pattern" or "coherence" is inclusive of the more narrowly defined *li* 禮 as ritual. It entails being aware of those constitutive relationships that condition each thing and which, through patterns of correlation, make the world meaningful and intelligible. All things evidence a degree of coherence as their claim to uniqueness and complexity, as well as their claim to continuity with the rest of their world.

In contrast to reasoning as the process of uncovering essences of which particulars are instances, the cognitive aspect of *li* involves tracing out correlated details forming the pattern of relationships that obtain among things and events. Thus "thinking" has as its goal a comprehensive and unobstructed awareness of interdependent items and their latent, vague possibilities. The meaning and value of each item is a function of the particular network of relationships that constitute it. Thinking, then, goes on in the interstices of the patterns of things and events. These patterns are derived from tradition.

## A Democratic Vision

A final commonality of pragmatism and Confucianism concerns the democratic disposition of each. Dewey's pragmatism is unqualifiedly *democratic*. His understanding of democracy is strikingly similar in many respects to that which has begun to emerge from Confucian theory.

Democracy, especially in its modern forms, is often thought to be a peculiarly Western invention. Confucian societies considered too au-

thoritarian and hierarchically structured to allow for true democratization. Samuel P. Huntington's recent, widely read work, *The Third
Wave: Democratization in the Late Twentieth Century,* sums up this opinion
in a single sentence: "Confucian Democracy is clearly a contradiction in
terms."[24]

Views such as Huntington's illustrate serious misunderstandings
both of Confucianism and of the most productive meanings of
"democracy." Such dogmatic views usually result from The Fallacy of
Misguided Comparison that urges the comparative thinker to contrast
the ideals of his society with the institutional practices of another.

Typically, there is an asymmetrical relationship set up in any comparison that bears the quality of critique. Social criticism is the most
profound illustration of this claim since the social critic so often attacks
the practices of one social grouping while appealing to the ideals and
theories meant to characterize her own. Alternatively, she compares the
wrongful practices of her country, contextualized by mitigating
circumstances, to the raw uninterpreted practices of her target. Responsible critique requires that we match ideals with ideals, and practices
with practices, and then compare a selection of precepts and practices
that are plausibly deemed to be efficaciously related.

Those who believe that "Confucian Democracy" is an oxymoron are
guilty of at least two principal misunderstandings: The first lies in a failure
to recognize that the Confucian idea of "authority" entails indispens-
able moral and aesthetic content. From its inception, Confucianism has
been concerned with the self-cultivation of individuals—preeminently
that of rulers and ministers. The Confucian sensibility enjoins the ruler
to rule by virtuous example. This can only be possible if the rulers are
themselves products rather than producers of culture. Moreover, the
Confucian doctrine of *zhengming* 正名, "the proper use of names," is
meant to prevent abuses of personal authority. A father who does not
act as a father ought not be called "father." A ruler who does not act as
a ruler is not deserving of the name.

In practice, of course, Confucianists often compromise their ideals
by investing de facto rulers with moral qualities in the absence of legitimate claims. One cannot rule effectively without presenting himself as a
*moral* leader. Cynical rulers and ministers often feel themselves forced

to erect a moral facade. Mao Zedong is a case in point. Claims made on his behalf to calligraphic skills, athletic prowess, statesmanship, poetic genius, and deep wisdom were ex post facto assertions that in reality offered rather empty justifications of his rule, which, particularly in his last years, was increasingly despotic.

In the face of such evidence of bad government in China, critics of China will hardly be mollified by our pointing to times when Confucian principles have been better served by their rulers. One should pause, however, to consider, along with the sinologist and philosopher Angus Graham, the consequences of the fact that China today presents "the unique spectacle of an empire surviving from the age of Egypt and Babylon. . . . China [has] discovered the secret of immortal empire, the unkillable social organism."[25] Such continuity could hardly be sustained by an unrelieved succession of despots.

It is commonly noticed that in Confucian societies, from classical times to the present, conflicts are settled through informal mechanisms for mediation and conciliation. Healthy Confucian societies are largely self-regulating and thus have required a minimum of government. It is this same communal harmony that defines and dispenses order at the most immediate level that is also relied upon to shape and express authoritative consensus in the absence of more obvious formal provisions for effecting popular sovereignty.

Part of the reason the appeal to moral authority has been as effective as it has been in China lies in the fact that Chinese society has traditionally been as much as 80 percent rural. Local traditions and familial connections have allowed informal mechanisms to operate in the relative absence of detailed legal codes. The demographics of China are changing rapidly, however, with a dramatic increase in the urban populations. One can expect that this fact will increasingly challenge the efficacy of moral authority in the maintenance of social harmony, leading to a greater dependence upon "the rule of law." We shall address the issue of law in somewhat greater detail in our discussion of the role of ritual in Confucian community in chapter 10 below.

A second misunderstanding of those who find a contradiction in the notion of Confucian democracy is based upon the belief that somehow hierarchy is irreconcilable with democracy. This latter misconception is most telling, for it identifies democracy altogether too closely with understandings predicated upon discrete individualism and the purely mathematical notion of equality that follows from it.

The aesthetic richness required for the realization of a communicating community as the ground of democratic society cannot be achieved within a context defined by simple equality. Not only Confucianism, but pragmatism as well, requires hierarchical relationships of parity rather than relations of abstract equality. A society in which individuals stand in relationships that reflect the unique characteristics of their relevant roles and functions is a democratic society.

In earlier times, democracy in America included the presumption of important inequalities with respect to knowledge, virtue, and the burdens of responsibility. Deference paid to teachers, the clergy, and public officials did not cancel the recognition of "equality before God and under the law." Persistent and widespread recourse to the attitude of deference in acknowledging excellence is one of the most effective means of preventing democratic community from suffering the bland sameness associated with merely mathematical equality.[26]

Equality, construed in individualistic terms, is a distinctly quantitative notion. Such an understanding promotes the conception of individuality as inviolate; it also mitigates the value of informal pressure and persuasion that can serve as alternatives to more coercive instruments for maintaining order. Autonomy stands in tension with the nonegalitarian institutions of family, union, and academy that promote goods-in-common. As we noted in our outline of rights-based liberalism in chapter 6, the definition of persons as autonomous individuals militates against the notion of goods held in common.

The Confucian project is to create community as an extended family. And family relationships are resolutely hierarchical. Ideally, the effects of hierarchy are meliorated by the processive conception of person. The performance of different roles and relationships enables persons to give and to receive comparable degrees of deference. Deference to my teachers will in due course place me in a similar relationship with my students. The roles of communal benefactor and beneficiary alternate over time. Hierarchy need not be as rigid and inflexible as it is often thought to be.

Having said this, in even the best of Confucian societies, as was historically true in ideal Western societies (for rather different reasons),
hierarchical assumptions have threatened the realization of equality for
all. The treatment of women and minorities is the most obvious illustration of such inequality. In chapter 9, we shall briefly consider the resources within Confucian society for the promotion of equality for
women and minorities. There we will find, surprisingly, that Confucianism offers important, largely unused, resources for overcoming gender
inequities. And though the news will not be quite so reassuring with
respect to the treatment of minorities, we shall offer some quasi-Confu-
cian suggestions on that matter as well.

At least with respect to the theoretical elements outlined above, it
cannot be said that Confucian democracy is a contradiction in terms. In
fact, Confucian models of democracy more closely approximate pragmatist understandings than do the ideals of currently popular forms of
Western liberalism.

As is usually the case in situations as complex as that which we have
been discussing, there is good news—and bad news. The *bad* news is
that the technological, political, and economic forces of globalization
seem to be moving the entire world inexorably in the direction of an
abstract amorality defined by the dynamics of international capitalism.
The requirement that the *bourgeoisie* must be culturally informed is
largely ignored by virtue of the marginalization of pragmatism and
Confucianism within their respective cultures. An equally negative consequence is the marginalization of all value issues within the sphere of
international politics and economics.

Nonetheless, not all the news is bad. The good news is that there are
important movements emerging from within individual societies, both
Western and Asian, that would challenge those amoral dynamics by appealing to distinctly cultural forces that express the unique values of
those societies. The even better news is that the cultural forces associated with Confucianism and pragmatism promise to revitalize interest
in the distinctive characters of their respective traditions, and will thus
militate against the growing movement toward sameness and unifor-
mity hidden in the seemingly benign phrase, "One World."

But the best news of all is that, however distinct Confucianism and American pragmatism continue to be, there is sufficient productive overlap in their core beliefs, and sufficient commonality in their senses of responsibility to their respective cultures and to the world beyond, that a real alliance is possible in which each sensibility can reinforce the other in ways that lead the world along at least a slightly better path.

The reemergence of Asian Confucianism and American pragmatism in the contemporary world challenges all those who identify with either sensibility to take up together the duties of creative remonstrance, and thus to assist those in power in making decisions that benefit not just a relatively few fortunate individuals, but the interests of all of us in forming a stable, rewarding, and enriching community life.

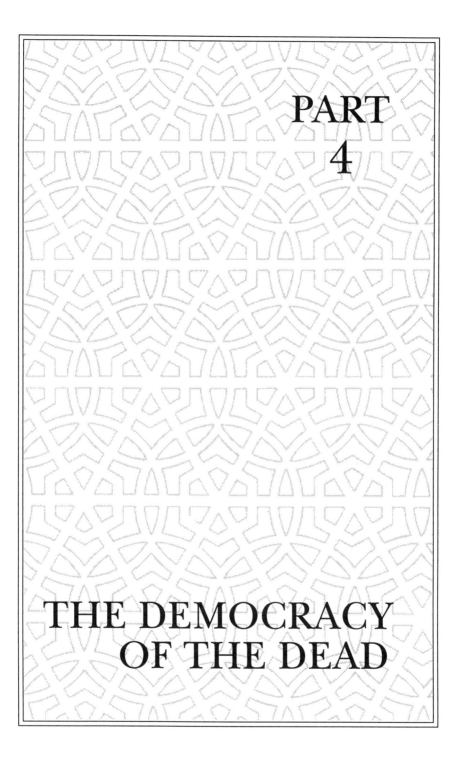

# PART 4

# THE DEMOCRACY OF THE DEAD

# Confucian Democracy: A Contradiction in Terms?

Typically, Westerners who pride themselves on their democratic institutions see China as a straightforward example of a totalitarian state. A bit more sympathetic, if equally condescending view is that the Chinese are a people "brought up by long habit to hug their chains."[1] Most of those who approach China with the idea of promoting democracy, usually with unimpeachable sincerity, begin by flogging Chinese governmental institutions and practices with rhetoric born either from interests distinctly more economic than democratic, or from the vaguely idealistic, and wildly irrelevant ideologies of contemporary rights-based liberalism.

Were we to shift our perspective slightly, by reckoning that capitalism frustrates rather than promotes a viable democracy; that the nineteenth-century brand of individualism is anathema to any recipe for a truly democratic community; that claims to human rights do not have to be written in the heavens in order to be a reality on earth; that democracy, as the ideal of community life, follows different rhythms and time schedules in different cultural environments; and if, above all, we were to reject the Fallacy of the Wholesale Judgment which would offer the Chinese a democratic baby only on the condition that they accept, as well, its befouled bath water—that is to say, were we to look at China with John Dewey's democracy in mind, our vision might be transformed.

The title of this book was inspired by words of G. K. Chesterton: "Tradition means giving votes to the most obscure of all classes, our ancestors. It is the democracy of the dead."[2] We now intend to take a look at China's "democracy of the dead" through the eyes of John Dewey and communitarian thought. What we shall see might be as surprising to some readers as it has been to us, for as the ironic genius of history would have it, China is in many ways closer to Dewey's communitarian ideal of democracy than is his own native land. And in any future engagements, it may well be the influence of China that brings the United States and other North Atlantic democracies closer to Dewey's democratic vision.

# 1. Dynamics of Democratization

In our consideration of a Confucian model of democracy, we are not centrally concerned with politics or government per se, but with the idea of a democratic community. We believe, as did Dewey, that the chief barrier to the implementation of democracy lies in the confusion of the democratic ideal with some political institution hypocritically claiming to embody it. Though governments are always involved in processes of democratization, they are seldom the leaders of the march toward democracy. And when they are, the ad hoc "democracy" thus conceived is soon aborted.

We should perhaps offer some reason to believe that a discussion of "Confucian democracy" is not an exercise in utopian thinking. Our conviction that it is not lies in the belief that our present international environment is sufficiently volatile to permit the movement toward democracy in China. This makes democratization of China at least *possible*. After a brief consideration of the conditions permitting this possibility, we will offer some reasons why this movement toward democracy is a plausible hope.

Roberto Unger has identified three principal sources of change in world politics: (1) the rise of mass politics, (2) the emergence of "world history," and (3) enlarged economic rationality.[3] The phenomenon of mass politics entails the assumption that some variant of "the popular will," either through elected representatives or an oligarchic party system, authorizes the power of the state. The shifts of power possible under such conditions are threatening to both current representatives and their policies. The severity of the 1989 crackdown of the Tiananmen square protests testifies to the Chinese government's recognition that the rise of mass politics in China is a persistent possibility.

As for the dynamic of world history, Unger plausibly notes that "every custom and dogma may be changed through deliberate policy, under the shadow of foreign threat, or by mass conversion, at the touch of foreign example."[4] Certainly the presumed Marxian structure of China, stimulated by "the touch of foreign example" is an apt illustration of this dynamic. How deep such changes go is a matter of dispute. China presently faces far more important "threats" or "examples" in the form of the modernizing impulses of rights-based liberalism, free enterprise capitalism, and global technologies.

The third dynamic, that of enlarged economic rationality, depends upon a society's capacity to "rearrange relationships, techniques, and organizations, according to productive opportunity or economic reward."[5] Such rationality would preclude the possibility that the rewards of the division of labor—or of the control of capital— become a vested right. The massive ad hoc reorganization occurring throughout contemporary China, with its Special Economic Zones and its "floating" population of migrant workers, promotes greater economic rationality, in Unger's sense of the term, than is currently possible in more stable capitalist countries.

Present international conditions lead many to expect significant social, economic, and political changes within China. And though missionizing capitalists and liberal democratic reformers in Western nations may think that the changes ought to be along the lines of rights-based liberalism, there is no inherent reason why this must be so.

There are resources within Confucianism for the development of distinctly Asian forms of democracy. In developing this idea, we shall not be merely touting a democracy with "Asian characteristics." We believe that the development of a Confucian model of democracy will benefit not only Asian proponents of democratization, but Western proponents of communitarian democracy as well. It is the possibility of mutual benefit that raises the hope for Chinese democracy from a *possible* to a *plausible* expectation.

In chapter 4 we alluded to the fact that Confucian values might be employed to address Daniel Bell's "contradictions of capitalism." As

Asian supporters of democracy begin to recognize the relevance of Chinese understandings of community beyond specifically Asian contexts, one can expect an increasing sense of parity with the West. This will render the idea of democracy far more palatable.

## 2. Classical Sources of Democracy in China

We now intend to explore classical Confucian assumptions about a politically viable community, and to suggest that there is much in this tradition that is consistent with the communitarian's prescription for American democracy.

The communitarian Michael Sandel, writing in the spirit of John Dewey, traces the reconfiguration of American democracy in the latter part of this century.[6] Small "r" republican liberty provided the opportunity to participate in those deliberations that collectively define the common good. Such freedom required a formative civil society in which the qualities of character necessary for self-government were actively cultivated and the sense of belonging encouraged. Liberty was expressed as full participation in shared self-government.

This sense of liberty is far removed from merely "the absence of constraints." In a communitarian democracy, "freedom for an individual means growth, ready change when modification is required."[7] The ability to change when "modification is required" is the very essence of self-governance.

Such a conception of liberty no longer drives American democracy. With the expansion both of corporate culture and of national government, there has been an erosion of the institutions that mediated individual and government. Institutions such as the family, neighborhood, school, union, social club, and parish have traditionally educated the citizenry in civil virtues. In the place of civil liberty, freedom has become simply the capacity of citizens to choose their own ends.

American democracy has become increasingly procedural and neutral: It guarantees a framework of rights enabling persons to choose their own values and ends. In principle, the government neither encourages nor discourages any particular conception of the good life.

This conception of freedom leaves the society with a vacuum that is quickly filled by the unbridled proliferation of every kind of marginal, intolerant, moralism: militias, Christian fundamentalists, militant pro-lifers, neo-Nazis, white supremacists, organized pedophiles, and so on.

Sandel identifies two arguments that are often posited against reha-bilitating the civic notion of freedom. First, it is said that the world has become so complex that the ideal of local self-government is no longer feasible. Secondly, the claim is made that the cultivation of civil values requires a trade-off on individual freedoms that often appears coercive.

Sandel responds to the argument that life is becoming increasingly complex by suggesting a return to the local arena:

> [T]he politics of neighborhood matters more, not less. People will not pledge allegiance to vast and distant entities, whatever their importance, unless those institutions are somehow connected to politi-cal arrangements that reflect the identity of the participants.[8]

Sandel assumes that the reigning American conception of liberal de-mocracy is not viable in the long term. His prescription for America recalls Dewey's insistence that democracy is expressed in attitudes rather than institutions, and that democratic attitudes are both gradu-ally formed by and reinforced through education. Sandel advocates the promotion of personal identities that are educated locally. These iden-tities can be secured in a noncoercive and self-governing community and then extended into more complex areas of life.

Sandel observes that "the image of persons as free and independent selves, unbound by moral or communal ties they have not chosen, is a liberating, even exhilarating, ideal."[9] But the pursuit of just such an ideal has in fact arrested and is now retarding American social progress. Some are beginning to see that the seemingly "undemocratic" notions we associate with Confucian philosophy—ritualized roles and relation-ships, hierarchy, deference, interdependence, and so on—might not be entirely pernicious. Given the interdependence of the world's cultures, appeal to Confucian resources suggests a possible direction for a new and more viable American democracy. At the very least, the contempo-rary American problem might serve as a caution to those Asian cultures inclined to abandon a Confucian legacy without exploring its possible contribution to an Asian-style democracy.

If we turn now to China, we may wish to recall the discussions of chapter 2 which addressed some of the transformations currently taking place in China under the influence of accelerated economic activity. With these forces in mind, we can understand how the counterdiscourse of American pragmatism may serve to balance the economic and political consequences of the rights-based liberalism now setting the terms of Chinese/Western conversations. This is a most promising possibility since, as we shall now attempt to show, the cultural resources within China that would support democratization are clearly inconsistent with individualistic forms of democracy.

A typical strategy for making the case for the compatibility of Confucian thought and democracy is to search the classical texts for passages that resonate with contemporary democratic commitments. There is a problem with this approach, of course, since ex post facto explanations can be offered to account for almost any present state of affairs. It is always true that countless other causal forces, usually those of a far less obvious kind, are involved in the institutionalization of this or that form of life. Indeed, though far more positively inclined toward the efficacy of cultural influence than is the political scientist, Edward Friedman, we can certainly endorse his following statement: "All cultures are rich in conflicting political potentialities. Had China democratized before Europe, historians could have found that China's cultural heritage was uniquely democratic."[10]

Having endorsed this caveat, it is nonetheless important to note the presence of such resources in the Chinese tradition supportive of democratization since, at the very least, they can be helpful in translating democratic concepts derived from external sources into terms more closely congruent with Chinese traditions. Of equal importance, they provide significant support for proponents of democratization in their arguments with more conservative and authoritarian opponents of democracy within their own societies.

In the *Book of Documents*, dating from the Western Zhou dynasty (*circa* eighth century BCE), we read: "The masses ought to be cherished, not oppressed, for it is only the masses who are the root of the state, and where this root is firm, the state will be stable."[11] And in a well known passage from the *Mencius* (fourth century BCE), we find, "*Tian* 天 ("Heaven") sees and hears as the people see and hear."[12]

An additional resource that could promote the aim of popular government is one that has more often than not been construed as perpetuating elitism. Bureaucratic examinations, a mainstay of the Confucian tradition, promote an educated set of political administrators. Further, Confucius is clear about the need for equal access to education: "In instruction, there is no such thing as social classes."[13]

Equal access to education does not, of course, guarantee equality of success. Most candidates failed their exams and lost, thereby, their opportunity to become part of governmental service. Further the meritocracy built into the Confucian understanding of the rewards of education is in tension with at least the more simplistic notions of democratic equality. But the meritocratic principle is inconsistent with a viable democracy only if it opposes the wishes of the relevant voting population, or threatens the legitimate interests of all citizens. Even in the most individualistic of liberal democracies, widespread support for the employment of individuals and the assignment of their duties by appeal to the principle of merit is hardly controversial.

As we noted in chapter 7, the duty of both familial and political remonstrance, long a part of the Confucian tradition, enjoins a criticism of governmental excesses. Mencius is adamant that rulers are legitimated by popular support, and there is a duty not only to oppose, but also to *depose*, any unjust ruler.

The Confucian stress upon the priority of morality over penal law is a bedrock value in any viable form of communitarian democracy. As we shall discuss at some length in subsequent chapters, the efficacy of tradition in a Confucian society argues for the priority of morality over law as the principal means of insuring social harmony. Confucius said, " In hearing cases, I am the same as anyone. What we must strive to do is to rid the courts of cases altogether."[14]

This view is not in the least inconsistent with the rule of law, though the Confucian does wish to balance the concern for litigation by enjoining recourse to informal mechanisms of conciliation and moral suasion prior to legal resort. It is hardly conceivable that the harmony of even the most litigious society should not be primarily grounded upon moral habit, and only secondarily upon law and sanctions. The question is one of the degree to which legal recourse is necessary to protect the welfare of members of a society. Daniel Bell's claim cited earlier, that late capitalism has resolved the tension between law and morality in favor of law, would definitely not apply to the realities of Chinese society where persistently "the rule of man"—meaning the morally sound ruler or minister—is held up as the ideal.

Clearly, Confucius is on the side of minimalist government and a self-ordering community. It was his wish to have rulers achieve sociopolitical order while remaining essentially inactive (*wuwei* 無爲). "Governing with excellence (*de* 德) can be compared to being the North Star: the North Star dwells in its place, and the multitude of stars pay it tribute."[15]

In traditional China, as in other Asian societies, there are dynamisms that urge a harmonious blending of Confucianism, Daoism, and Buddhism into a rich tradition that does not finally subvert any of its constitutive strands. In addition to offering some grounds for the development of patterns of tolerance and deference that do not require the radical separation of political and spiritual culture, this "values synthesis" permits appeal to Daoist and Buddhist elements without undermining the predominantly Confucian sensibility. Chinese, even today, often describe themselves as combinations of all three visions ("I wear a Confucian hat, Buddhist robe, and Daoist sandals. In public life I am Confucian; when I retire to my home, I am a Buddhist; strolling about in Nature, I am a Daoist.")

Daoism provides a celebration of freedom and spontaneity along with a critical perspective on the mainstream culture. Buddhism offers an egalitarian dynamic to the mix, which qualifies somewhat the Confucian notions of hierarchical relations patterned after the family as center.

Beyond the sensibilities comprising the principal elements of the Confucian synthesis, there are other philosophical movements, in greater or lesser tension with mainstream Confucianism, that offer doctrines supporting democratic ideas. For example, the Legalist school promoted the notion of equality before the law. And even more than Buddhism, the consequences of Mohist doctrines were decidedly egalitarian.

There are more than enough themes within Confucian, and broader classical Chinese, thought consistent with democratic institutions to qualify any skepticism concerning the possibility of a Confucian democracy in the Deweyan sense thereof. This is particularly so if we presume a communitarian model. But we certainly need to spell out some of these hints and suggestions in greater detail if we are to make the case that a Confucian democracy is not only *possible*, but presently *plausible.*

We might begin from a representative passage in the Confucian *Analects*:

> Lead the people with administrative injunctions (*zheng* 政) and keep them orderly with penal law (*xing* 刑), and they will avoid punishments but will be without a sense of shame (*chi* 恥). Lead them with excellence (*de* 德) and keep them orderly through observing ritual propriety (*li* 禮) and they will develop a sense of shame, and moreover, will order themselves."[16]

Confucius, like any good pragmatist, is committed to the fundamental importance of proximate, self-invested relationships. He sees a thriving, self-governing community, achieved through mediating institutions such as family and neighborhood, as the optimum guarantee of a personal liberty and the best opportunity for full participation in a shared vision of community. The Confucian model depends upon the powerful informal pressures of shame (*chi*) and the personalization of deferential roles and relations (*li*) as its motive forces. Coercion is explicitly rejected as an effective means of sustaining communal order. Self-ordering is the stated goal.

Confucian philosophy is a doctrine of personal cultivation and articulation elaborated within the context of the extended family. Perhaps the *locus classicus* for the assumption that personal, familial, communal, political, and cosmic realization are coterminous and mutually entailing is the core text of the *Great Learning* 大學, a brief yet often cited document that has defined orthodoxy in the tradition from medieval times to the present:

> Those in ancient times who wanted their pure and excellent character to shine in the world would first bring proper government to the empire; desiring to bring proper government to the empire, they would first bring proper order to their families; desiring to bring proper order to their families, they would first cultivate their persons; desiring to cultivate their persons, they would first attune their hearts-

and-minds; desiring to attune their hearts-and-minds, they would first make their purposes sincere; desiring to make their purposes sincere, they would first extend their understanding to the utmost; and desiring to extend their understanding to the utmost, they would first investigate things and events.

Traditionally, as we have said, the family is the model of social organization. Personal identity is realized first and foremost through the cultivation of those roles and relationships that locate one within the family and the community more broadly construed. As the *Great Learning* continues: "All alike from emperor to the common people should take self-cultivation (*xiushen* 修身) as their root." The state, then, is conceived as an enlarged family that emerges out of the process of self-cultivation, where the "self" of "self-cultivation" is radically embedded in communal roles and relations. The centrality of this familial model has significant consequences for the shape of Confucian democracy, since it determines an interpretation of "citizen" or "public individual" that readily contrasts with the liberal democratic tradition.

Since Aristotle's reflections of this subject, the democratic citizen has more often than not been construed as one who is nurtured in the family until adulthood, and who then takes leave of his family for public life. The contrast between life in the family and life in civil society is one of the fundamental manners in which the limits of the private and public spheres are fixed in Western societies.

In Confucian societies, one never leaves the family. To do so would be, *quite literally*, to give up one's identity. Thus the notion of the public person, indeed the distinction between public and private spheres would have to be conceptualized differently in Confucian context. We shall discuss the meanings of "public" and "private" in chapter 10. There we shall see that John Dewey provides some hints for construing public life in a manner consistent with (communitarian) democratic institutions.

## 3. Dewey and Confucius on Community

In rights-based liberalism, social and political theory has in large measure revolved around questions such as the relation of the individual to society, the realms of private and public activity, the status of natural and positive law, the character of rights and duties, the sanctioning powers of the state (legitimate authority), the meaning of justice, and so forth. By contrast, concerns relevant to discussion of Chinese social and political thought would include the cultivation of personal and communal life, the function of tradition-based ritual activity (*li* 禮) in reproducing sociopolitical harmony, the definition and attunement of social and political roles through the proper ordering of names (*zhengming* 正名), the efficacy of cultural modeling, modes of justifiable remonstrance, and so on.

Our discussion of Deweyan democracy has provided us a means of understanding the term "Confucian democracy." For Dewey, democracy is a communicating community. If communitarian concerns are central within a society there will be an important check upon the pursuance of novelty of beliefs and opinions simply for their own sake. This must be so since the central desire is the promotion of a sufficient commonality to insure significant communication. Normatively, constraints will not be imposed from outside either through legislation nor oppressive "public opinion." If the desire for communication is truly operative, there will be increased tolerance of differences as well as a concern not to destroy the potential for communicative interactions through the insistence upon mere empty novelty.

This raises one of the most difficult of the issues relevant to the erection of a Confucian democracy—namely, the issue of *pluralism*. What is the role of the pluralism of ideas and beliefs in a society that has always so obviously prized cultural continuity?

The first thing to say is that there is, of course, a significant degree of pluralism in Chinese society. To doubt this fact would be to carry the stereotype of Asian cultural homogeneity to ridiculous extremes. On the other hand, there is as much and sometimes arguably more ethnic and linguistic homogeneity in China than in America and many European societies. And, all things considered, it is perhaps easier to achieve something like true "consensus" in China than in most Western societies.

Part of the difficulty in understanding how Confucianism might accommodate a healthy pluralism lies in a failure to recognize the shift in meanings of terms such as "consensus" and "pluralism" as we move from Western to Chinese society. For example, the claim of the traditional Chinese individual that he is not only a Confucian, but a Daoist and Buddhist as well, is confusing to most Westerners who equate philosophic or religious allegiances with consciously entertained doctrines or beliefs.

The interweaving of distinct sensibilities such as Confucianism, Daoism, and Buddhism into a viable harmony both within a single culture and, importantly, within a single personality, raises the issue of pluralism in Chinese society in the appropriate terms. For, in a Confucian society, as in a Deweyan democracy, consensus is often achieved at the aesthetic and practical levels rather than with regard to the claims of reason. The aesthetic orientation of Confucianism and Deweyan pragmatism militates against the presumption that "right thinking" is assent to formal and often exclusive doctrines or credos.

Randy Peerenboom discusses a pertinent contrast between the Western liberal commitment to many voices and the traditional Chinese concern for consensus as a social good: "Freedom of thought lies at the very core of contemporary Western liberal democracies. The ability to think our own thoughts is our most cherished and fundamental right, the cornerstone of all other rights."[17] The commitment to freedom of thought calls into questions any appearance of rigid conservatism and orthodoxy of opinion in the name of a healthy pluralism of beliefs.

In defining this contrast between Confucian "right thinking" and the liberal commitment to "the right to think," Peerenboom begins from the familiar reading by many Western critics of the Chinese record:

> How are we to account for the striking difference between the rhetoric (and reality) of unification of thought in China and freedom of thought in Western liberal democracies? The easy answer, of course, is that the repeated attempts to unify thought around the correct line of the leadership are simply totalitarian socialism at its most despotic— Orwellian Big Brother reaching into the minds of individuals to strangle creativity, crush dissent, and compel adherence to the party line.[18]

The extent to which Chinese socialism is committed to orthodoxy is evidenced in the practice of establishing and reformulating *tifa* 提法, the "correct" vocabulary for articulating social goals prescribed by the central government.[19] Peerenboom points out, however, that the *tifa* are a persisting extension of the imperially sanctioned canon and commentaries that anchored orthodoxy and paved the way to an official career for the greater part of Chinese history.

> [M]ost Chinese political theorists have never accepted the inevitability of pluralism. The dominant belief has been that all interests, including the interests of the state and the individual, are reconcilable. For Confucians (and Daoists), social, even cosmic, harmony was attainable as long as moral rulers were on the throne.[20]

The phrase "harmony was attainable as long as moral rulers were on the throne" certainly does not mean that harmony is imposed from above. Ideally, the process of achieving communal harmony was through moral consensus: not an agreement about how individuals ought to behave, but a consensus at the level of aesthetic feeling and common practice.

It is important to note that the term "harmony (*he* 和)" as it is understood in the Confucian tradition strongly and explicitly suggests contrasting elements that must be harmonized.

> Achieving harmony (*he* 和) is the most valuable function of observing ritual propriety (*li* 禮). In the ways of the Former Kings, this achievement of harmony made them elegant, and was a guiding standard in all things large and small. But when things are not going well, to realize harmony just for its own sake without regulating the situation through observing propriety will not work.[21]

The Confucian quest for social harmony entails, therefore, a tacit recognition of diverse elements in need of harmonizing. And, whereas on the model of rational consensus, sameness of belief is suggested, on the aesthetic model, criteria of intensity and contrast are presupposed.

In any consideration of the distinction between the "right to think" and "right thinking" one needs to keep in mind a fundamentally important difference between Chinese and Western problematics. That difference is associated with the Chinese refusal to entertain ideas and actions as disjunctively related. The mutually entailing relations among ideas, dispositions, and actions in the Chinese tradition contrasts dramatically with the positing of thinking, acting, and feeling as distinct functions among by the dominant ideologies of the Western tradition.

In chapter 2 of our *Thinking From the Han: Self, Truth, and Transcendence in Chinese and Western Culture,*[22] we discussed the contrast between the dominant philosophical concern of the emergent literati class in classical China, and that of the traditional Western philosopher. There we cited Angus Graham's comment that the question of the literati was "not the Western Philosopher's 'What is the Truth?,' but 'Where is the Way?'"[23] Graham's statement contrasts succinctly the problematics of Western and Chinese cultures with respect to the issue of how one might orient oneself within the natural and social worlds.

The basic question of the ancient Greek thinkers, the *cosmological* question that shaped subsequent speculations in the West, was "What kinds of things are there?" "What is the world made of?" or simply, "What *is* this?" Such questions have resulted in a catalog of facts and principles, which assist one in taking an inventory of the world about us. The classical Chinese "how" question, on the other hand, led to the attempt to identify the appropriate models of conduct that provide one with a cultural bearing and thus enable one to build upon a "way" (*dao* 道) of living productively in one's world.

It is often remarked that the breakdown of moral and political order at the very period in which reflective thinking began in China caused the Chinese to be concerned with social harmony. It is said that they were preeminently concerned with continuing a moral path that would guarantee a sufficient degree of social stability. Thus they were primarily seekers after the Way *(dao)*. By contrast, so this interpretation goes, the ancient Greeks were somehow free to go off on a dispassionate search for truth. This rather simplistic explanation of the contrast between Truth-Seekers and Way-Seekers is altogether misleading since it suggests that social and political harmony were somehow more important to Chinese than to Western culture.

Surely the chief concern manifest in both Chinese and Western societies, however, was that of maintaining social stability. In ethnically and linguistically diverse societies, such as existed in the world of the ancient Greeks, it is more difficult to chart a concrete and specific way among the many ways suggested by diverse languages, myths, customs, and rituals. Harmony must be sought through ascent to abstract and ultimately universalizable principles and standards. The quest for capital "T" Truth serves the aims of social and political stability in both positive and negative manners. Positively, it promises, down the road, a standard of common assent that can ground common values and practices. Negatively, it suggests the necessity of a certain tolerant circumspection in the treatment of those who do not share our present truths.[24] Clearly, both of these implications are compatible with the development of democratic institutions.

The implication of this contrast between Truth-seekers and Way-Seekers is that it is easier to promote cognitive pluralism in a society that distinguishes ideas from moral actions. Freedom to think as one wishes is an incomplete freedom if one cannot act upon one's ideas. In a tradition such as China's that does not distinguish between idea and action, ideas are already dispositions to act. It is our theory/practice distinction that permits us to have the right to think as we please. If we were to regard ideas as already dispositions to act, we should not as readily enjoy the freedoms that we do.

There are obviously advantages to be found in attempting to maintain a strong separation between thinking and acting. Freedom to think as we please is one of the advantages. But there is a downside to this effort to dichotomize theory and practice. First, it allows us to separate perhaps too easily our ideas and principles from the responsibility to realize them in practice. There is hypocrisy in saying more than we are able to authenticate in our actions. Second, the very idea that ideas may be maintained in disjunctive relationships from feelings of actions is likely just bad psychology. Proponents of the censorship of TV violence probably have a point. We cannot avoid the practical consequences of the ideas and images we entertain, or allow to entertain us.

Two further implications of the contrasting meanings of consensus between China and the West need to be considered here. First, consensus in Western societies tends to be more conscious and conceptual than in China by virtue of the need to find abstract or general principles to accommodate differences among diverse populations. Chinese models of consensus can presume a greater degree of tacit commonality as background for any disputes.

Second, conscious, doctrinal, consensus is usually preferred by liberal democracies predicated upon the priority of the individual as social unit. Associations of any kind—including those based upon the espousal of common doctrines or beliefs—are associations of individuals presumed to have the rights of *dissociation*. Thus, the consensual model argues for the realization of a general commonality of commitments on broad issues while affirming the right to dissent.

In a democratic society of the size and complexity of the United States, national consensus is presumed to be rather thin compared to the kind of consensus that might be achieved in more local and specialized voluntary associations. This thinness applies to consensus both at the tacit, *aesthetic*, level, as well as at the conscious level of concepts and doctrines. How much consensus is necessary for the realization of a viable society is hardly a question that concerns a society structured around consciously entertained doctrines or beliefs. It is the unspoken consensus that binds us, if for no other reason than once we raise our commitments to the level of consciousness, we find altogether too many ways to disagree—and our stability is threatened. The greater the tacit quality of the consensus the more effective it appears to be.

Daniel Bell has claimed that the United States was once held together by a consensus comprised by three unspoken assumptions: "that the values of the individual were to be maximized, that rising material wealth would dissolve all strains arising from inequality, and that the continuity of experience would provide solutions for all future problems."

Clearly, as Bell contends, this consensus has broken down. In addition to the communitarian critics of liberal democracy who promote specific *community* values, there has been the emergence of multiculturalism that promotes the balkanization of cultural or ideological groupings within a context that allows each to promote its own agenda. Furthermore, increased wealth has not led to a concomitant rise in the standard of living of all people. In many ways, inequality is a greater problem today than ever before. And finally, dependence upon continuity of experience has run aground of novel and complex technological problems for which the past offers no precedent.

Bell argues for the promotion of a new public philosophy to articulate new candidates for consensual beliefs. Quite apart from the fact that a spoken consensus lacks the efficacy of the unspoken, it is not clear that one can offer such a consensus without getting bogged down in tedious hair-splitting scholarly debates.

There is a slightly different approach to the problem of consensus implicit in both American pragmatism and the Confucian sensibility. Eschewing both the individualistic and multicultural approaches to pluralism, we find in Dewey's insistence upon the importance of art and aesthetic activity in establishing grounds of social togetherness a means of responding to democratic pluralism. Pragmatic approaches to pluralism celebrate the greatest sustainable differences on primarily aesthetic grounds. That is, differences of values and beliefs that, logically or rationally, are seriously inconsistent may nonetheless be sustained on aesthetic criteria of intensity and contrast. Such a model is presupposed by pronouncements such as "I disagree with what you say, but will defend to the death your right to say it." In general, communitarians will promote the idea of a community that manages to harmonize the greatest degrees of difference. Difference itself becomes a value to be prized.

Pragmatic pluralism does not promote associations based on ethnic or linguistic homogeneity. Indeed, Dewey was adamant that such associations could easily undermine democratic society. Primary social groupings were to be local and voluntary and the nation as a whole was to be seen as a complex association of these smaller associations. Consensus at the national level was to be exceedingly thin—in order to downplay the importance of national identity. Citizens could agree upon such values as good health, sound education, general welfare, and peace. Their differences were to be adjudicated within the context of a broad intellectual tolerance and the essentially aesthetic recognition of the value of difference in guaranteeing the greatest richness of experience for all.

Applying these insights to Chinese society would require a recognition of the rather distinct form of social organization it represents. Because of the relatively high degree of ethnic and linguistic homogeneity in China, supported as it is by the myth of Han unity, a widespread unspoken consensus has been important in maintaining social harmony. The promotion of Han identity attempts to insure that this consensus is ethnically and linguistically based.

As we have indicated, the 8 percent minority populations of China are balkanized among themselves and isolated from the Han majority. Thus, with respect to minorities, at least, the fact of pluralism has not been confronted in any significant manner.

Nonetheless, there are some significant signs of a healthy pluralism in traditional Chinese society. It is in evidence in those elements of China that have inherited the traditional Confucian synthesis. That synthesis, as we have noted, combines Confucian, Daoist, and Buddhist elements. The harmony of these traditions is a function of unspoken consensus.

A second pluralistic feature, newly important in a developing China, is that of local identities mentioned in chapter 2. The means of accommodating these differences within China has traditionally been to maintain a sense of one's origin as primary focus in terms of which to play variations upon the theme of Han unity. This notion of "focal" identity is important and will be considered in more detail in the following chapter.

The hope for Confucian democracy hinges in large measure upon the ability of the Chinese people to engage the pluralism of belief and action that always accompanies democracy—even and especially in its communitarian forms—by recourse to a model something like that of pragmatic pluralism.

Fortunately, Confucianism is not wholly without resources for accomplishing this feat. Stress upon a tacit, affective consensus celebrated through ritualized roles and practices that do not require raising difference to the level of consciousness, promotes authentic social harmony. The concern for living the moral *way* rather than discovering cognitive *truth* precludes the concern for too readily placing one's sentiments in the form of consciously entertained propositions. Consensus is primarily unspoken. The essentially *aesthetic* dimension of ritual practice promotes communication at a level precluding the necessity of debate.

None of these factors promoting the harmony of contrasting elements overcomes the fact that the consequences of pluralism are significantly more problematic once there is widespread recourse to elections and referendums which require individuals to vote this way or that. Economic and political differences are then articulated in ways that otherwise may not have been the case. Further, minorities integrated into the *demos* increase the tensions that can lead to serious imbalances in traditional harmonies. The racial problems of American society bear sad testimony to this fact.

Doubtless, an emerging pluralism of ideas and beliefs will present serious challenges to the persistence of Confucian traditions within China. And possibly, Confucianism may not be able to meet the challenge. Indeed, the question is raised daily within American society whether our civic culture will in fact survive. In spite of all the difficulties China will face in the following decades in its attempts to meet the challenges of modernization, it is clear to us that, on balance, there is no real choice but to meet those challenges with the most powerful resources of its indigenous tradition.

If Confucianism is to serve as a resource for reflections on democracy, we must avoid one of the most pervasive and persistent *misreadings* of the tradition. This all too familiar misreading presumes that the interests of the Confucian individual must be sacrificed for the good of the community. According to Donald Munro:

> Selflessness . . . is one of the oldest values in China, present in various forms in Taoism and Buddhism, but especially in Confucianism. The selfless person is always willing to subordinate his own interests, or that of some small group (like a village) to which he belongs, to the interest of a larger social group.[25]

R. Randle Edwards reinforces Munro's interpretation:

> Most Chinese view society as an organic whole or seamless web. Strands in a web must all be of a certain length, diameter, and consistency, and must all be fitted together in accordance with a preordained pattern. . . . The hope is that each individual will function as properly as a cog in an ever more efficient social machine.[26]

Both Munro and Edwards construe Confucian society as a kind of collectivism in which personal interests are insignificant except and to the extent that they are of service to those of the group.

Ann Kent continues this perception by construing the relationship between person and social context as one of means and ends:

> The view of society as an organic whole whose collective rights prevail over the individual, the idea that man exists for the state rather than vice versa, and that rights, rather than having an absolute value, derive from the state, have been themes prevailing in old as well as new China.[27]

It is certainly true that the Chinese tradition promotes a relational definition of person. It must be further allowed that there appears to be no adequate philosophical basis to justify self as a locus of interests independent of and prior to society. Under the sway of this relational understanding of human being, the mutuality and interdependence of personal, familial, societal, and political realization in the classical Chinese model must be conceded. But there is no reason to believe that a relational understanding of the individual entails the necessity of self-abnegation. Indeed, the above assumptions are shared by all communitarian interpretations of democracy.

The consequence of claiming that selflessness is an ideal of Chinese society is to sneak in both the public/private and the individual/society distinctions by the back door. To be "selfless" requires that individual selves first exist, and that they then be sacrificed for some higher public interest. And the suggestion that there are "higher interests" on the part of either person or society covertly establishes a boundary between them that justifies the adversarial relationship of individual and society. This interpretation of the Chinese individual does not support the claim that the person is irreducibly social. Ironically, it vitiates it.

The "selfless" ideal ultimately suggests the culture-specific struggle between advocates of group interests over individual interests that has separated Western collectivists from rights-based liberals. This conflict has little relevance to the Chinese tradition. While self-realization among the Chinese does not require a high degree of individual autonomy, the alternative to autonomy is hardly capitulation to the general will. Becoming a Confucian person, much like becoming a Deweyan individual, involves benefiting and being benefited by membership in a world of reciprocal loyalties and obligations which stimulate one, and help to define one's own worth.

The relationship between person and community presumed in the Chinese model contrasts with the liberal Western concern to limit state powers as a means of preserving individual autonomy. On the other hand, traditional assumptions about the mutuality of personal and communal ends are in many ways comparable to the Deweyan vision wherein communal bonds are constitutive of personal identity.

For both Confucius and Dewey, the person is *person-in-context.* The notion of "individuals" has as little relevance for American pragmatism as for Chinese culture. Rather than the "means-end" distinction characteristic of the liberal democratic model (society as a means to individual ends) and the collective model (individual as a means to societal ends), the Confucian assumption is essentially consistent with that of John Dewey—namely, the broader purposes of the community emerge from personal and communal goals. In Confucianism, the privileges and duties entailed within familial living are seamless, and extend beyond the family to become the basis for proper government.

> It is a rare thing for persons who have a sense of filial and fraternal responsibility (*xiaodi* 孝弟) to have a taste for defying authority. And it is unheard of for those who have no taste for defying authority to be keen on initiating rebellion. Exemplary persons (*junzi* 君子) concentrate their efforts on the root, for the root having taken hold, the way (*dao* 道) will grow therefrom. As for filial and fraternal responsibility, it is, I suspect, the root of becoming authoritative in one's conduct (*ren* 仁).[28]

The Confucian notion of a ritual-constituted community does not presume a totally secular society. Rituals have an enduring human-centered spiritual significance. Thus, in assaying Chinese religious experience, we must look to ritually constituted community as the primary locus for spiritual self-cultivation.

Confucian ritualized roles and relationships do not have a transcendent reference. Rather, they point to a cultural legacy invested in these communal life forms as the resource for continuing spiritual development and religious experience. *Tian* 天, conventionally translated "Heaven," and *dao* 道, "the way," are not the primary categories of Chinese spirituality. The ritualized roles and relationships (*li* 禮) that unite the community in pursuit of a common good serve that function. In fact, rituals are the specific content of both *tian* and *dao* as these ideas are relevant to the human community. These notions, so constituted, express the aggregate spirituality inherited from a continuous historical lineage.

John Dewey expresses a similar vision:

> The community of causes and consequences in which we, together with those not born, are enmeshed is the widest and deepest symbol of the mysterious totality of being the imagination calls the universe. It is the embodiment of sense and thought of that encompassing scope of existence the intellect cannot grasp. . . . It is the source that the moral imagination projects as directive criteria and as shaping purposes.[29]

For the pragmatist and the Confucian, cultural values are the cumulative achievement of a community over time. It is unwarranted to presume some supernatural realm meant to house these values. The values prized in those religions that have ideal elements are idealizations of things characteristic of natural association, which have been projected into a supernatural realm for safekeeping.[30]

There is an analogy between the commitment that Chinese have to their traditional culture and the intensity with which Christians feel about their relationship with God. It is in this sense that the Confucian model of democracy, with deference directed at ancestors and cultural heroes, is truly a "democracy of the dead." Though a community which includes those now deceased, this "democracy of the dead," is still very much alive. Thus, when Zigong, one of Confucius's closest protégés is asked to identify Confucius's teacher, he replies:

> The way (*dao* 道) of Kings Wen and Wu has not collapsed utterly—it lives in the people. Those of superior character (*xian* 賢) have grasped the greater part, while those of lesser parts have grasped a bit of it. Everyone has something of Wen and Wu's way in them. Who then does the Master not learn from? Again, how could there be a single constant teacher for him?[31]

As long as a person and the values that he or she has authored are remembered, he or she has a place and a life. The emphasis on genealogical continuity, the ethic of filiality, the cultural requisite of returning the body to the ancestors intact, the elaborate structure of Chinese funerary rites, and the role of ancestor reverence as the primary religious observance, are all an expression of this living social memory.

There is much in traditional Confucian attitudes toward communal living that promotes a robust and sustainable, even religiously fortified, conception of democracy. In the recent literature, Lee Seung-hwan has argued that we need not choose between liberal and "Confucian style" sensibilities, but rather we should seek to combine them.[32] Lee's sentiment is on target, of course. If Chinese/Western engagements are to be productive for both parties, mutual influence is to be expected. But we have argued that the rights-based democratic vision characterizes both the individual and society in terms that cannot be reconciled with the communitarian vision, either Chinese or Western. Our hope, therefore, is that the combination of Chinese and Western values and beliefs that emerges from future conversations will consist of elements of Chinese Confucianism and Western pragmatism.

In the following chapters we shall be considering three principal concepts underlying a model of Confucian democracy—the *individual*, the *community*, and *human rights*. Using these notions as the axis of our discussions, we shall be able to enter into more detailed discussions of some allied issues involved in the prospect of institutionalizing Confucian democracy—specifically, gender and minority issues, the role of the "public sphere," and the rule of law.

# The Chinese Individual

Throughout this work we have stressed the fact that there are several important sources of individualism in the West, all of which support the general assumption that the modern self is a discrete and autonomous individual. The self as subjective consciousness has its origins in the Platonic conception of the soul, ramified by Christian theology. The soul is a self-contained unit, capable of performing its rational functions without recourse to any other soul or consciousness.

An alternative vision of the self as radically individual is found in the atomistic tradition that traces back to classical roots, receiving its initial modern expression in the writings of Thomas Hobbes. The person as a social atom, or as the isolated terminus of pleasure or pain, is a highly influential understanding of the asocial self, finally socializable through the manipulations of rewards and punishments.

A third source of the individuated self, which we have identified as the *assertive* self, has the most recent origin. The speculations of the third- and fourth-century Stoics, culminating in the systematic constructions of St. Augustine in the fifth century, led to the first articulations of the distinctive faculty of the human will. The self-assertive individual became fully autonomous when endowed with an independent volitional faculty. This volitional element has the potential of placing the individual over against his environment and other wills.

Through the notions of the human being as self-conscious, or as self-assertive agent, or as isolated desiring machine, we have arrived at conceptions of individuality that entail a strong commitment to human equality, and contribute in various manners to the liberal doctrine of human rights. This vision subordinates human differences to secondary status.

The counterdiscourse of pragmatism, expressed in its most cogent form by John Dewey, provides an alternative characterization of the self. In contrast to the extreme individualism of the dominant Western views, Dewey stresses the notions of sociality expressed through mutual interaction and communication. The life of the individual is *life together*. Individuals are unique by virtue of their participation and communication with others, which serves to enrich their own and others' experiences. This Deweyan understanding grounds the American "Call to Civil Society" cited in the Introduction and chapter 7:

> We humans, at least in the U.S., are autonomous units of desires, rights, and legitimate values of our own choosing. . . . [Ours is] a philosophy of expressive individualism, or a belief in the sovereignty of the self—a kind of modern democratic equivalent of the divine right of kings. We view this understanding of the individual as fundamentally flawed. . . . We understand human beings as intrinsically social beings . . . . We humans only live in communities, through which we are talked into talking and loved into loving. Only through such connectedness can we approach authentic self-realization.[1]

Though this language used to articulate the meaning of the self or individual might seem initially somewhat strange, the understandings of the human being that have held sway in the Chinese tradition are based upon assumptions quite similar to these. The major difference is that the philosophical underpinnings of the Confucian tradition directly entail "field" notions of the self or individual while pragmatic communitarianism must be articulated in tension with the dominant philosophical dynamics, which entail the various models of the discrete individual alluded to above.

The discussions of the following section will *initially* be of little interest to those more practical-minded individuals who are less concerned with the question of the philosophical origins of ideas or values than with their present meaning or function. We hope that they, and others disinclined to such considerations, will bear with us. We shall try to demonstrate that the dominance within the Chinese tradition of field notions grounded in the presumption of continuity presents powerful evidence for the inhospitality of Chinese culture to Western style understandings of the discrete individual. If true, this conclusion has significant implications for efforts to institutionalize a conception of the discrete, autonomous individual in Chinese society.[2]

# 1. Classical Roots of the Communal Person

The Chinese commitment to the processional and transformative nature of experience renders the "ten thousand things (*wanwu* 萬物 or *wanyou* 萬有)" which make up the world at once continuous with one another and unique. The primary philosophical problem emerging from these assumptions is how to correlate these unique particulars in such a manner as to preserve continuity and foster productive harmony.

The classical Chinese tradition presumes that the human being is something that one *does* rather than *is*. The individual is *how* one behaves within the context of the human community. Principal sources of this understanding of human becoming are found in the meanings of two important Chinese terms—*qi* 氣 and *xin* 心.

*Qi* is a highly difficult term to contextualize within Western conceptual frameworks. It is variously rendered, "hylozoistic vapors," "psychophysical stuff," "the activating fluids in the atmosphere and body," and, perhaps most appropriately, "vital energizing field." In the earliest texts, before the notion came to be adapted to the speculative constructions of the Han cosmologists, it had a significance not unlike the Greek *pneuma*—viz., "breath, "animating fluid." In the cosmological speculations of the Han dynasty (202 BCE–220 CE), *qi* came to be understood as the vital stuff constitutive of all things, and was characterized in terms of the active and passive dynamics of *yin* and *yang.*

The problematic status of *qi* for the Westerner may be illustrated by the alternative careers of the notions of *qi* and *pneuma,* and their cognates in Chinese and Western cultures. Western categories came to be associated with cosmological interpretations built up from discrete "parts," while *qi* requires notions of continuity. Thus, Plato's tripartite soul is constructed from Homeric understandings of alternative interpretations of the individual as living *(psyche)*, perceiving (*noos*), and feeling (*thymos*). These Homeric notions which Plato expressed in terms of thinking (*logistikon*), acting (*thymoeides*), and feeling (*epithymetikon*), required a separation between the rational and nonrational aspects of the person. The latter aspect came to be identified with the material body. The majority of subsequent interpretations of the vital and spiritual character of things had to struggle with a physical/spiritual dichotomy.

Thus, the animating principle was largely distinguishable from the things animated.

In China the animating fluid seems to approximate what we would today call an "energy field." This field not only pervades all things, but also in some sense is the means or process of the constitution of all things. That is to say, there are no separable "things" to be animated; there is only the field and its focal manifestations. Later in the Han period, the notions of *yin* and *yang* were used to characterize the transformations that constituted the field of *qi*.

The energizing field is the reality of things. This fact precludes the efficacy of categories or principles that advertise the existence of "natural kinds." Discriminations in the field of *qi* are made in terms of conventional classifications associated with diurnal and seasonal changes, directions, colors, body parts, and so forth. Processes associated with these correlative classifications are then charted in accordance with the rhythms of the *yang* and *yin*, or active and recessive forces.

*Qi* is both field and focus, both environs and individual. The most productive understanding of the self from a traditional Chinese perspective would involve recourse to a focus/field model in which the individual is not considered a part of the society to which he or she belongs, but a productive *focus* of the experiences and interactions constituting that society. Such an interpretation, adumbrated in our consideration of Dewey's philosophy, contrasts rather dramatically with the part/whole interpretations dominating Western theory.

The notion of *xin* 心 will clarify the focus/field model of the individual. *Xin* could be translated simply as "heart," but since it is the seat of thinking and judgment, the notion of "mind" must be included as well. Indeed, what we often think of as "will" or "intention" is, likewise, included in the notion of *xin*. In the West, questions of the distinguishability of mind and matter, and of reason, volition, and emotion, and the relations that obtain among them, are issues central to the understanding of the meaning of persons. These topics are of little interest to mainstream Chinese thought.

Like the notion of *qi*, the concept of *xin* precludes any distinction between thinking and feeling, or idea and affect. In the classical period, the heart (*xin*) as the seat of thinking was held to be an organ similar to the other sensing organs, but with the advantage of being able to think:

"Organs such as those of hearing and of sight, being unable to think, can be misled by external things. . . . But the heart does think. Only by thinking will the answer be found."[3]

The interpenetration of idea, intention, and affect expressed in this notion of *xin* entails the conclusion that thinking is never a dispassionate speculative enterprise. Thinking always involves normative judgments that assess the relative merit of the sensations, inclinations, and appetites. Since appetites and ideas are always clothed with emotion, they are to be understood, more often than not, as *dispositions to act.*

Another implication of the unity of feeling and thinking is the practical orientation of most of Chinese thought. If ideas are dispositions to act, "theories" are little more than wholesale practical recommendations. Thus it is most difficult among the Chinese to find contexts within which the separation of theoretical and practical activities would prevail.

Thinking and learning are, within the Chinese tradition, oriented to the practical ends of the moral life. As Mencius observes: "For a person to realize fully one's heart-and-mind is to realize fully one's nature and character."[4] When Confucius said, "from fifteen, my heart-and-mind was set upon learning,"[5] he was indicating his commitment to an ethical regimen aimed at self-realization.

We are accustomed to think of efforts aimed at moral perfection to involve a struggle between the reason and passion, or between what we believe we ought to do, and an obstreperous will that frustrates our appropriate actions. Thus, we say with St. Paul, "The good that I would do I do not do, and the evil that I would not do, that I do." In the Chinese tradition there is little such internal conflict involved in ethical development. Given the unpartitioned self characterized by *xin,* it is unlikely that we would find Hamlets or St. Pauls prominent among the Chinese.

If, however, the conflict associated with self-realization is not waged within one's breast between heart and mind, reason and passion, then what are the dynamics of moral development? If the problematic of unrealized selfhood does not entail the self divided against itself, what *is* the source and nature of the disturbance that the moral discipline is meant to overcome? It can only be a disturbance in the relationships that constitute the self in its interactions with those "external" things which provide its relational context. "The stillness of the sage is not a matter of his saying: 'It is good to be still!' and thus he is still. He is still because none of the myriad things are able to agitate his heart-and-mind."[6]

It is through mirroring the things of the world as they are in their relatedness to us that we reach a state in which "none of the myriad things are able to agitate [our] heart(s)-and-mind(s)." In other words, we defer to the integrity of those things that contextualize us, attempting to sustain a noncoercive and thus productive relationship with them.

The ideas of *qi* and *xin* are helpful in allowing us to understand the dominant Chinese model of the individual. These are important background notions that contextualize what in Western culture would be the relations of person and world, as well as the psychological dynamic internal to the self. The decidedly field-oriented character of these relations must be taken into account in any treatment of the Chinese conception of selfhood or individuality.

## 2. The Individual and Social Harmony

The presumption of continuity displayed in notions such as *qi* and *xin* is a fundamental factor in understanding the Chinese notion of world as "the ten thousand things (*wanwu* 萬物)." This presumption renders the notion of harmony (*he* 和) most important in the Chinese cultural sensibility. Cultural conventions are ways of realizing harmonious patterns of correlation among the things of the world.

Ancestor reverence as the defining religious sensibility, family as the primary human unit, co-humanity (*ren* 仁) and filiality (*xiao* 孝) as primary human values, ritualized roles, relationships, and practices (*li* 禮) as a communal discourse, are all strategies for achieving and sustaining communal harmony. As is stated repeatedly in the *Analects*:

> Exemplary persons (*junzi* 君子) seek harmony not sameness; petty persons, then, are the opposite.
>
> Exemplary persons associating openly with others are not partisan; petty persons being partisan do not associate openly with others.
>
> Exemplary persons are self-possessed but not contentious; they gather together with others, but do not form cliques.[7]

For the Chinese, harmony is still the guiding standard. And this harmony is not that achieved through the mutual adjustment of otherwise isolated particulars, but is the realization that individuals are foci in a field of relations. Further, the harmony of the field is achieved through the appropriate focus.

When we consult the Chinese dictionary in an effort to understand such a world, we discover that terms are not defined univocally by appeal to literal meanings, but are brought into focus "paronomastically" by semantic and phonetic associations. "Exemplary person" (*junzi* 君子), for example, is defined by its cognate and phonetically similar, "to gather" (*qun* 群), with the assumption that "people gather round and defer to exemplary persons." As the *Analects* insists: "Excellent persons (*de* 德) do not dwell alone; they are sure to have neighbors."[8]

The Chinese penchant for achieving harmony involves a person in a set of associations that provides an aesthetic ground for what otherwise might be considered moral or ethical relations. The term *yi* 義, "appropriateness," illustrates this quite well. When translated as "right" or "righteous," as it often is, the term suggests conformity to some external standard. From this understanding, a deontological ethics is imported into the Chinese tradition suggesting that the individual has a *duty* to comply with ritual *obligations*. This is to entirely miss the point of *yi* and its central role in permitting the achievement of harmony.

"Appropriate" is a far better translation of *yi* since it construes the term as a kind of *aesthetic* rightness, which calls attention to the successful placement of one detail of a particular context, within that context. In social terms, *yi* addresses the appropriate placement of the individual within his or her community.

Morality is contextual. Acting in such a manner as to achieve harmony involves *ars contextualis,* the art of contextualization, in which one's understanding and embodiment of ritual propriety is based, ideally, not upon duty or obligation, but upon the desire to achieve the most harmonious circumstances. "To truly love it is better than to just understand it, and to enjoy it is better than to simply love it."[9]

When we extrapolate from the understanding of words such as *yi* to the understanding of persons, we find that individuals are to be understood by exploring relevant associations that constitute their specific patterns of harmonious relationships. Persons are not perceived as agents independent of their actions, but are rather ongoing *events* defined functionally by constitutive roles and relationships.

Familiar in the mainstream West is the self-conscious self related to its social environs through the entertainment of principles, laws, and institutional patterns which define the natural and social worlds, as well as the self. The self-assertive self is so related by patterns of conflict and consent in which administrative agents of a presumed "community will" seek to adjudicate disputes and redress imbalances. The self as *homo economicus* is related to society through needs and desires that are mediated through economic structures disciplined by political institutions. The creative self is institutionally alienated from its society since its identity is to be found in its exceptional, idiosyncratic, or *avant garde* character.

The irrelevance of Western individualism to the Chinese context is better understood by reflecting upon the fact that it is expressed in its preeminently political form by appeal to the individual's adversarial relationship with government. The Chinese understanding of the individual's relationship to authority is distinctly nonadversarial, rooted as it is in the metaphor of family. If one presumes a "Han identity" based upon a reasonable degree of local linguistic and ethnic unity, then it is easy enough to see how the understanding of the individual in China would not develop in the same manner as in the individualistic West.

In Anglo-European societies, strong central authorities, both political and ecclesiastical, determined institutions. Under such circumstances there is a tendency to characterize freedom as an ultimate value over against central controlling powers. Liberty is then freedom from governmental or ecclesiastical constraints.

As Dewey recognized, the origin of Western individualism derives not only from the assertion of individual liberties over against political authorities, but also with opposition to the forms of authority which would hamper economic freedom. Thus, the theory of the discrete individual was ramified by appeal to distinctly economic factors.

> Fear of government and the desire to limit its operations, because they were hostile to the new agencies of production and distribution of services and commodities, received powerful reinforcement. . . . The economic movement was perhaps the more influential because it

operated, not in the name of the individual and his inherent rights, but in the name of Nature. Economic "laws" . . . were set in opposition to political laws as artificial man-made affairs.[10]

Individualism was expressed not only in terms of political action and economic production and consumption; it received its capstone articulation through appeals to freedom of thought vis-à-vis principally ecclesiastical authority. These appeals were directly occasioned by the increased prominence of scientific reflection. Philosophers of widely divergent orientations introduced theories of the rationally autonomous individual.

> Nothing better exhibits the scope of the movement [of individualism] than that philosophic theories of knowledge made the same appeal to the self, or ego, in the form of personal consciousness identified with the mind itself, that political theory made to the natural individual, as the court of ultimate resort. The schools of Locke and Descartes, however much they were opposed in other respects, agreed in this, differing only as to whether the sentient or the rational nature of the individual was the fundamental thing. From philosophy the idea crept into psychology which became a solitary and introverted account of isolated and ultimate private consciousness.[11]

In sum, understanding persons as discrete individuals expressed in terms of individual liberty derives in part from the existence of an adversarial relationship with authority expressed through appeals to the autonomy of rational thought, political action, and economic production and consumption. There is no significant area of social life in which persons are characterized primarily in terms of association.

The classical Confucian position suggests that, because self-realization is fundamentally a social undertaking, selfish concerns are to be rejected as an impediment to one's own growth and self-realization. A perennial issue in Chinese philosophy, repeatedly referenced as early as the *Analects,* has been the likelihood of conflict between the pursuit of selfish advantage (*li* 利), and the negotiation of that which is appropriate and meaningful (*yi* 義) to all concerned. As expressed in the *Analects:* "Exemplary persons (*junzi* 君子) understand what is appropriate (*yi* 義); petty persons understand what is of personal advantage (*li* 利)."[12]

# 3. The Focus/Field Model of Persons

In Confucianism, personal order and the order of society are mutually entailing. This is consistent with Dewey's understanding of the individual as dependent upon "definite social relationships and publicly acknowledged functions."[13] An effective manner of appreciating this Confucian and Deweyan assumption is by appeal to a focus/field understanding of the relations between the individual and society. When the society succumbs to disorder, the exemplary person returns to the more immediate and substantive precincts of home and community to begin again to shape an appropriate order.[14]

On being asked by a rather unsympathetic second party why he did not have a formal position in government, Confucius replied that the achievement of order in the home is itself the basis on which any broader attainment of social and political order depends.[15] The central doctrine of graduated love and ritually ordered community is predicated on the priority of participation in the immediate and concrete. Even when a higher order of social or political organization is deferred to, it is given definition and represented in the concrete embodiment of a particular person—a specific individual with whom one can assume a personal relationship. The importance of the local and focal in Confucianism is, of course, shared by Deweyan pragmatism.

The contrasts between Confucian and dominant Western understandings of the self as individual can be summarized in the contrast between part/whole and focus/field models of self and environs. Thus, if we understand by the term "individual" something like "particular focus," we are in a position to translate understandings of the relation of the individual and society into Confucian (and pragmatic) terms.

The term "individual" can refer to a single, separate, indivisible thing that, by virtue of some essential property or properties, qualifies as a member of a class and which, by virtue of that membership is "equal before the law," "entitled to equal opportunity," "a locus of unalienable rights," and so on. If one employs the focus/field model, however, "individual" will mean *particular focus*. This sense of individuality lies in the achieved quality of a person's relationships. A person becomes "recognized," "distinguished," or "renowned" by virtue of the quality of his or her relations. Much of the effort in coming to an understanding of the traditional Chinese conception of self has to do with clarifying this distinction, and reinstating the unique individual. While the definition of self as irreducibly social certainly precludes autonomous individuality, it does not rule out a second, less familiar, notion of unique individuality as particular focus.

The particularity of the individual is realized in the observance of ritualized roles and practices. These roles locate one, and form a kind of social syntax that generates meaning through coordinating patterns of deference. The process of extending and deepening these roles is accompanied by a feeling of profound significance.

The fact that personalization comes through specific modes of ritual action means the emergent community will in some important respect always be local. It will be Dewey's communicating community, conditioned by the expectations and the imagination of its specific cultural leaders and the circumstances of its time and place. It thus falls to those who are the most active participants of a community to assist in shaping a future for their particular community.

Like Dewey's understanding of the individual, the Confucian conception is dynamic, entailing a complex of social roles. It is the quality of these roles that focuses one's identity, and which is constitutive of one's self. Not just role playing, but *appropriate* role playing, creates a self.

The conception of person as a specific matrix of roles will not tolerate any assertion of natural equality. Persons so understood stand in irrevocably hierarchical relationships that reflect fundamental differences among them. Having said that, ritual practice serves the notion of qualitative parity in several ways. First, the dynamic nature of roles means that privileges and duties within one's community tend to even up across a lifetime. One's duties as a child are balanced by one's privileges as a parent; one's role as benefactor during the middle years gives way to beneficiary as one grows old. A dynamic field of relationships over time produces a degree of parity in what is perceived as the most vital source of humanity—one's human relations.

Dewey's understanding as well expresses an indifference to natural equality:

> Equality [says Dewey] does not signify that kind of mathematical or physical equivalence in virtue of which any one element may be substituted for another. It denotes effective regard for whatever is unique

and distinctive in each... [Equality] is not a natural possession, but is the fruit of the community when its action is directed by its character as a community.[16]

Liberal critics of this communitarian vision of equality are likely to worry about defining equality in terms of "unique and distinctive" qualities. For it is always the case that one must identify these qualities if they are to be appreciated. This requires active and empathic engagement of individuals with one another. This begins to sound altogether utopian. The liberal understanding of "equality before the law" avoids this difficulty, at least in principle, by offering the same legal comforts to all individuals. In practice, liberal societies often provide unequal access to legal guarantees associated primarily with differences in power or economic status.

We must candidly acknowledge that the gap between principles and practice is likely to be as great in communitarian as in liberal societies. The real point, however, is the nature of the failings represented by both positions. In Confucianism, for example, the failures are primarily associated with institutionalized roles and relationships that characterize in advance what is presumed distinctive in each person. "Father," "son," "daughter" are, in fact, primarily names for roles and relations.

Now a democratic society envisioned from a communitarian perspective has plenty of room for qualitative differences and the understanding of "equality" that takes these differences into account. But it is less able to accommodate inflexible hierarchies of the sort found in traditional Confucianism. A modernized Confucianism in the form of a "Confucian democracy" will doubtless have to begin to find ways of construing roles and relationships in a more flexible fashion. Before yielding too easily to the quick fix of attacking inequalities by strictly legal means that abstract from any qualitative differences, the proponent of Confucian democracy might wish to determine whether there are legitimate resources within Confucianism itself to meet this most serious challenge.

This will be one of the issues that democratizing Asian societies will have to deal with for some years to come, and we will not presume to offer any final resolutions in this context. We do wish, however, to address briefly the more serious aspects of the problem of Confucianism's structured hierarchies as they concern the status of minorities and women.[17]

Anyone with first-hand experience of Confucian societies recognizes their pervasive masculist character. Indeed, one quickly learns to expect a strong skepticism among Asian women with respect to the idea of Confucian democracy. Having spent their lives in the subordinate roles of daughter and wife, and having undertaken countless hours of burdensome service to the ancestral rites, many Asian women would, understandably, wish to escape from Confucius in any guise. If they are at all interested in democracy, it is clearly not in the form they presume Confucian democracy would take.

On the other hand, it must also be acknowledged that the cost of achieving equality by strictly legal means, even if possible, would be enormous to the Confucian societies. Turning one's back upon one's own culture, however questionable parts of it may be, takes its toll in the forms of alienation and confused senses of identity. The negative effects of modernization and democratization may be ameliorated somewhat if a means of transition may be found that maintains some grounding in indigenous cultural resources.

In liberal rights-based democracies, equality of the sexes is sought not only by providing equal access to legal guarantees affecting family, occupation, and general social relationships, there is some effort at moral suasion that reshapes public opinion. Clearly, legal recourse will be required as well in Confucian societies if anything like a viable equality is to be achieved. But, to be consistent with the character of a Confucian society, the balance between moral suasion and legal recourse must be weighted in favor of the former. Second, as we have seen, the understanding of equality is quite different in Confucian societies as compared to liberal ones. Equality for the Confucianist and pragmatist, as well, is a qualitative rather than a quantitative notion.

In Western cultures, sexual differences are expressed in broadly dualistic categories. These same categories tend to ground the gender distinction. This is but to say that the disjunction of male and female is often carried over into the construction of principal masculine and feminine characteristics. Male dominance has led to the definition of the truly human person in terms that, by and large, privilege masculine gender traits. Self-actualization is implicitly construed as the realization of maleness. Escape from the dominance of the male sex does not mean escape from the dominance of masculine gender. That is, the female is not free to realize herself by appeal to feminine traits, but rather, like the male, she must realize herself by appealing to the masculine model.

Ideally, in Confucian societies, a broad continuum of human traits are divided into complementary characteristics that together suggest the range of possibilities for one's self-cultivation. In traditional China, self-realized individuals are defined in terms of a dynamic balance of *yin* and *yang* characteristics.

At the practical level, both politically and in moral terms, male dominance has de facto led in important degree to the exclusion of females from the project of becoming fully human. Thus, only the male has been free to pursue the task of realizing fully his individuality.

The distinctive feature of the Chinese conception of gender is that were, *per impossibile*, the female to be allowed freedom to pursue the same project of self-actualization as the male, she too could seek a harmony of the same range of human traits that the male employs as his standard. Chinese sexism, which traditionally has denied to the female the possibility of becoming fully human, is certainly no more excusable than its Western variety. However, the gender model to which appeal must be made in order to democratize male/female relationships might conceivably be more humane than is the Western model. Presently, the general status of women in Western cultures is presumed to be better than that obtaining in most Asian societies. Nonetheless, the Western means of becoming truly human perpetuates the old male prerogative: To be (fully) human you must be (largely) male. Surprisingly perhaps, Confucianism has something to teach us about how to achieve real equality of the sexes.

The situation with regard to women is far more hopeful than is the case with minorities. In this respect, the Asian and Western experiences have distinct parallels. As we indicated in chapter 2, China's treatment of minorities is shaped by its appeal to Han ethnic and cultural identity as the defining feature of China. Minorities are isolated and encouraged to maintain their own cultural identities. It is true that minority representation in governmental positions is legally guaranteed as is some opportunity for participation in the more prestigious, Han-dominated, universities. But, in practice, these guarantees are not implemented as evenhandedly as is publicly claimed.

An important difference between Han/minority relations in China and the Anglo-European treatment of minorities is the degree to which ethnic and cultural identity is foregrounded in China. For example, a Han Chinese introducing a member of a minority population to a foreigner will, more likely than not, make a point of identifying the individual by appeal to his ethnic or cultural status. There is, rather than an effort to attenuate ethnic or cultural differences, an attempt to *celebrate* them. It is clear, of course, to the minority individual, the *hanren*, and the foreigner alike, who benefits most from such celebration.

The difficulty is that, unlike the issue of sex and gender inequities, there is no obvious model in Chinese culture that might support the democratization of both Han and non-Han populations. This difficulty is exacerbated by the fact that, relatively speaking, the minority population of China as compared, for example, to that of the U.S., is rather small. There is little internal pressure for change, and the external pressures upon China instituted by countries such as the U.S. have relatively little effect since we so obviously have our own problems dealing with minority issues.

The Confucian principle that has the greatest potential effect in changing things for the better is the principle of *merit*. Those best qualified should be drawn from both Han and non-Han populations—and, in principle, this is the case. The problem in practice is that governmental interest in maintaining the linguistic and cultural identity of minorities precludes their having equitable access to the means whereby merit is demonstrated. Perhaps the best one can hope for in China, at least in the short run, is increased fairness of treatment under the current balkanization policy. As the long history of failures to resolve minority problems in America testifies, it is likely that a solution will be neither easily discovered nor quickly implemented.

The realization of a qualitative equality that does in fact recognize the unique and distinctive features of individuals requires, with respect both to gender construction and the treatment of minorities, a kind of imagination and courage that is seldom found among politicians. There are features of Confucianism that *ideally* would permit precisely this. Insofar as the transition to democracy in Confucian societies involves more than the inexorabilities of political and economic processes, one can plausibly hope that these features will be taken into account. Otherwise we shall be left with the default position of a merely quantitative equality grounded in the sameness of discrete individuals.

An obvious weakness of the doctrine of discrete individuality lies in the presumed priority of individual freedoms and privileges over communal and environmental duties. Taken to the extreme, it becomes the tyranny of the shameless individual, consuming precisely those communal resources that are necessary for the promotion of strong families, robust communities, and adequate education, while inflicting unrelenting violence upon those who protect him, and the environment that provides him shelter and sustenance.

The testimony of both Confucianism and pragmatism is that individual autonomy does not necessarily conduce to human dignity. In fact, if dignity is felt worth, and if worth or value is a function of invested interest, the exaggeration of individuality might be anathema to the ultimate project of protecting and fostering human dignity. The communitarian concept of person shared by the Confucianists and pragmatists might well be useful in renewing the commitment of all of us to the promotion of self-fulfillment.

There is much in the relational definition of human being found in the Confucian tradition that may be favorably compared to the major tenets of Dewey's understanding of the democratic individual. Both pragmatism and Confucianism promote a rethinking of the dominant Western notion of autonomous individuality.

# The Role of Ritual in a Communicating Community

## 1. The Aesthetic Organization of Community

Confucianism is commonly misconceived as a dull, unimaginative, and profoundly conservative sensibility primarily concerned with the most mundane aspects of the sphere of practical affairs. Given this general misconception, our insistence that Confucianism is grounded upon aesthetic premises cannot but seem rather odd. After all, Dewey claimed that "the function of art has always been to break through the crust of conventionalized and routine consciousness."[1] And given the ritualized, seemingly tradition-bound character of Chinese society, what is to be found there but a society literally encrusted by convention? We shall argue that an understanding of the role of ritual activity (*li* 禮) in the promotion and maintenance of a Chinese community will allow us to discern the paradoxical vitality of a *democracy of the dead.*

The notion of ritual as a communal discourse embraces all of those various roles, relationships, and institutions that bind and foster community. It involves the performance of any formalized, meaning-invested conduct that organizes particular human beings in community. Thus, ritual spans everything from table manners to court ceremony, from living familial relations to observances for the dead.

At the personal level, rituals give shape to the various formal media through which we communicate personal experience. These include bodily comportment, clothing, gesture, language, and calligraphic style. At the communal level, rituals encompass social and political institutions, from family to government. Rituals are the language through which Chinese culture is expressed.² It should be noted that the performative, perlocutionary function of language is most effective in societies that are stabilized through the observance of ritual propriety.

Though ritual practices initially lure the performer into social relationships by virtue of the stability of their authorized forms, they are more than given standards of appropriateness sedimented within a cultural tradition. Ritual practices also have a creative personal dimension. In this sense, they are more exhortative than prohibitive. Beyond any formal social patterning, there is an open texture of ritual that is personalized and reformulated to accommodate the uniqueness and the quality of each participant. From this perspective, ritual is a pliant body of practices for registering, developing, and displaying one's own sense of cultural importances. It is a vehicle for reifying the insights of the cultivating person, enabling one to reform the community from one's own unique perspective. Rituals authorize those who participate in the life forms of community, and the community is in turn authored by them.

Because of this participatory emphasis, rituals cannot be construed as mere passive deference to external patterns or norms. Ritual action is an ongoing re-creation of community requiring the investment of oneself, one's judgment, and one's own sense of cultural importance. The Chinese vision of community defined by ritual activity has an immediate resonance with Dewey's insistence upon the importance of aesthetic activity in forging democracy. Dewey says:

> When the liberating of human capacity operates as a socially creative force, art will not be a luxury, a stranger to the daily occupations of making a living. Making a living economically speaking, will be at one with making a life that is worth living.³

The satisfaction of making a life worth living involves a making of a community worth abiding in.

In China, community has in large measure been self-regulating, and thus has required a minimum of formally constituted government. The same communal harmony that defines and dispenses order at the most immediate level is relied upon to focus authoritative consensus.

For example, in modern China, political directives have appeared to take the form of broad and abstract slogans promulgated by the public institutions and the press. What is not apparent is the degree to which such directives require interpretation and application as they ramify throughout society.

Members of individualistic societies often believe that pursuing a conscious continuity with tradition is undesirable since it promotes an unthinking assent to the past. The idea of a "democracy of the dead" would be a perplexing notion to such individuals. But by giving a pragmatist's endorsement to Søren Kierkegaard's aphorism, "We live forward, but we understand backward,"[4] William James emphasized that understanding in its most practical sense is always constituted by reflections upon the living past. The Chinese side with James and Dewey on this issue.

Tradition is mediated through rituals that constitute the *ethos* and coherence of any given community. As such, rituals cannot be thought independent of a particular context. In the absence of transcendent appeal, there is only an ongoing process of correlation and negotiation within the business of the day. In a society defined by constitutive relations, individuals are continuous with one another, and thus are interdependent conditions for one another's lives.

The failures of ritualistic societies in practice are often rehearsed. They are principally two: The first is that ritualized societies perpetuate the *status quo*. Fixed hierarchies associated with predefined roles and relationships are not easily altered. This is a serious criticism since it addresses not merely the failures of specific rituals, but the inertial character of ritualized practices per se. The second criticism is that ritual practices stifle spontaneity and creativity. This complaint is perhaps somewhat less defensible.

With regard to the conservative character of ritual: It is true that rituals perform primarily a conservative function, and this is particularly challenging to societies such as China's confronted as it is with enormous pressure to accommodate the changed conditions associated with its emergence onto the world scene. The brief discussion of minorities and women in the last chapter offered more than enough evidence that the traditions of Chinese society must be reshaped to accommodate the desired equality of women and minorities within Chinese society.

As we have suggested before, we can expect that China will have increased recourse to legal mechanisms in order to maintain social stability. It is also the case that for a society so accustomed to maintaining social harmony by appeal to ritual actions, attempts to shift from moral suasion associated with custom and tradition to the specifically legal guarantees could be equally destabilizing. The individualist presuppositions underlying Western liberalism have no roots in Chinese society. Moreover, they cannot easily be transplanted.

The second general criticism of ritual societies suggests that spontaneous and creative actions are somehow suppressed by ritual. This criticism is most often made by those who equate such actions with the model of artist and innovator as rebel against established norms. In this case, the conservatism of ritual seems automatically to preclude creativity. Such a criticism turns out to be less compelling, however, when one reflects on how dependent creativity is upon the kinds of rituals we associate with technique and method.

Most novel discoveries depend upon and are achieved through the proper exercise of ritual. The discovery of the scientific method, if that method is not too rigidly defined, constituted the liberation of the scientific imagination. And it is a truism that artistic technique is equally liberating for the artist. To ignore these conditions of the artist's project when assessing the value of ritual action is to ignore an important aspect of spontaneity and creative expression.

Those ritual forms—aesthetic methods, methods of science, techniques of commercial exchange—that provide means for their own revision are what is required if ritual action is to offer a viable basis for the social organization of our modern, pluralistic age. It is always true that ritual forms accommodate a great deal more novelty than seems to be allowed by the external ritual forms. And it is equally true that there is far less novelty in Western societies than is suggested by the constant claims to originality made by would-be innovators.

There may appear to be something altogether utopian in arguing for the importance of communitarian ritual in a world increasingly shaped by modernizing impulses associated with the individualistic

West. If so, we may recall the criticisms could be leveled against John Dewey who might well be echoing Confucius when he claimed that "conformity is enduringly effective when it is a spontaneous and largely unconscious expression of agreements that spring from genuinely communal life."[5]

The ideal of Chinese community is the maintenance of just such a disciplined spontaneity played out within the security and stability of communal forms. This allies Confucianism with Dewey's insistence, quoted earlier, that "thinking goes on in the interstices of habit." It is far more likely that important aspects of ritual community will be maintained in China, however great the transforming pressures, than in Dewey's home culture. It is important, nonetheless, to note the value of such community in both contexts.

## 2. Neither Individualism nor Collectivism

In Western political theory the contrast between the absoluteness of either the individual or of the social realm has set the context for the discussion of the extremes of individualism and collectivism. Strictly idealist readings of Hegel provide us with the model of the subsumption of the human being to the collective in which "the state is the only individual." Atomistic theories of Hobbesian variety construe society as a complex of distinct individuals. And most sociopolitical theories attempt to balance these extremes.

Dewey took the presumed antithesis between the individual and society to be a consequence of an unwarranted assumption. The fact that, in a rights-based society, an individual has the right to dissociate herself from any particular grouping may suggest to the unthinking person that individuals may exist apart from any association whatsoever. But common sense instructs one that the antithesis of the individual and society is a false dichotomy. The right to dissociate ourselves from all groupings is the "right" to cease having any meaningful existence as a human being.

It would be difficult to claim that Chinese society, even under Marxism, is collective or socialistic in the sense of rendering personal realization subservient to some higher collective good. The problem is that when we speak of the relations of an individual to society we tend to use the abstractive, quantitative, and atomistic language of part and whole. In discussing China, however, as we have argued above, it is more appropriate to speak of the relation of a focus to the field it focuses. Thus, the constitutive continuity between person and family suggests the particular human being is a focus and the family is the field. "This culture of ours" is the field. Exemplary cultural models such as the Sage Kings, Confucius, Laozi, and so forth, are foci.

Although the family, the community, the state, and the tradition itself as the most extended context, is vague as *a grouping*, this vagueness is focused and made immediate through its embodiment by a particular father, a communal exemplar, a ruler, an historical model. This is but to say that the meaning of the group is made present in its exemplary personalities: one's own father, one's own teacher, one's own Confucius, and one's own Mao Zedong.

The Confucian sense of social order assumes that personal and communal realization are mutually interdependent, and as such, cannot be understood in terms of classical forms of either individualism or collectivism. The principal ideas undergirding either of these views in the West have had little influence in China.

The defect of individualism from the Confucian perspective is its challenge to a ritually ordered society in which the boundaries of one's person may be only vaguely delineated. The Confucian "self" is not superordinated or individuated, but is rather a complex of roles and functions associated with one's obligations to the various groupings to which one belongs. A particular person is invested in personalized relationships: *this* son, *this* daughter, *this* father, *this* brother, *this* husband, *this* wife, *this* citizen, *this* teacher. In the absence of the performance of these roles, nothing constituting a coherent personality remains: no soul, no mind, no ego, not even an "I know not what."

The identification of the person with roles is not in any sense a collectivist understanding. It is not a philosophy of self-abnegation in which "selflessness" is taken as a primary virtue. On the contrary, there is a palpable sense of not only personal identity, but self-realization, albeit one distinctly at variance with dominant Western views. The roles defining the person are ritually enacted. Again the resonance of Confucianism is not with classical Western views but with the pragmatic vision which holds that individuals in a community realize their greatest productivity through their distinctive roles and relationships.

The phenomenon of the individuated self is a rather late development within our tradition. In the beginnings of Greek culture, the tribal character of social organization effectively precluded a strong sense of otherness.[6] This sense increased markedly with the growth of cosmopolitan cities. In fact, as the word itself suggests, "civilization" was a process of "citification."

Attendant upon the rise of cities and of the commercial relations that sustained these urban centers, the Greeks enforced a strong distinction between the private and the public spheres. This separation of the intimate relations of the family from the more impersonal relations of public life further enhanced the possibility of a sense of self-identity. The family became a training ground for the public life.

Things went quite differently in China. Ancient China overcame the threat of the tensions and conflicts attendant upon ethnic and cultural pluralism by recourse to *language,* rather than the process of urbanization, as the medium for the transmission of culture. A class of Confucian literati emerged as official counsel to the imperial throne; a canon of classical works was instituted along with a commentarial tradition to promote Confucian doctrine as a national ideology; an examination system based upon these texts was introduced by the literati in the early Han. Throughout the two thousand years of imperial rule, a centralized and hierarchical bureaucracy perpetuated itself as a social and political infrastructure.[7] Further, the Chinese never stressed a distinction between private and public realms. Since the family was the model of all types of relationships, including the "nonfamilial" relations obtaining among subjects, and between ruler and subjects, there was no effective public sphere.

The notion of "public" is problematic in Chinese society insofar as one wishes to contrast it with a distinct sphere of "private life." However, there is a sense in which we might speak of the public sphere in China in much the same fashion as John Dewey defined it. For Dewey, the public consists of "all those who are affected by the indirect consequences of transactions to the extent that it is deemed necessary for those consequences to be systematically cared for."⁸ Government consists in institutionally organized actions of those officers charged with the responsibility of overseeing these indirect consequences.

In pluralistic societies the public sphere is quite significant since there will be an indefinite complex set of interactions accruing indirect consequences with respect to which there must be concern. This may not be so in a more homogeneous, tradition-oriented society—particularly a ritually organized society such as that of China.

China has always constituted a political paradox. On the one hand, it has traditionally possessed a strong central government. On the other hand, the majority of the population expresses the rather casual attitude that "the skies are high, and the Emperor is far away." We may resolve this seeming paradox by further articulating the rather attenuated sense of "public life."

The ritually organized community is shaped by custom understood as "widespread uniformities of habit."⁹ Rituals articulate these customs without requiring members of the community to develop individual habits. Insofar as one wishes to speak of a collective mind it is, as Dewey asserts, "a custom brought at some point to explicit, emphatic, consciousness, emotional or intellectual."¹⁰

In more individualistic societies, customs are not ends in themselves, but serve as the conditions under which individuals form their individual habits. In societies in which customs are less articulated through individual habits, the chances are greater that, under the pressure of novel events, collective consciousness will be manifest. This can lead to mob action.

> [In] a political democracy . . . thought is submerged in habit. In the crowd and mob it is submerged in undefined emotion. China and Japan exhibit crowd psychology more often than do Western democratic countries . . . because of a nearer background of rigid and solid customs conjoined with a period of transition. The introduction of many novel stimuli creates occasions where habits afford no ballast.¹¹

The Cultural Revolution was perhaps the greatest manifestation of "crowd psychology" in recent Chinese history. And the severity of the government's response to the 1989 Tiananmen protest was predicated upon the fear of a reversion to mob action. The presence of a strong central government in China is a consequence of recognizing the potential for serious collapses of ritually sustained order during periods of transition. China's xenophobia is not so surprising in the light of the potential consequences of immediate and direct foreign influence. If its transition to democracy is to be successful, the Chinese government will likely have to guide the process in a manner not unlike that which is taking place in Korea. Western critics might wish to moderate their criticisms of China's presumed authoritarianism with respect to the issue of democratization, lest they render even more fragile an already delicate situation.

Before leaving this discussion of individualism and collectivism we need to ask after the relevance of the recent "crisis of Marxism" in Eastern Europe to the Chinese situation since that crisis has been construed as a rejection of collectivist societies and a movement toward the individualism sustained by liberal democracies.

The first thing to be said is that the consequences of such a crisis in China are likely to be dramatically different from those we are witnessing in the European world. Indeed, the 1989 events at Tiananmen Square were in part defined by students and teachers demanding greater respect for intellectuals. Had this demand been met there would have been a movement away from both Marxist and capitalist forms of egalitarianism, in the direction of a revitalized Confucianism.

The relatively transitory impact of Marxism on China reveals the inertia of the Chinese tradition. When the leadership of China decided to import Marxism, counsel was solicited from the Soviet Union that had just gone through its own communist revolution. Russian advisors, appalled by the absence of a proletarian class in China, in effect told the Chinese to call on them again when they had developed a proletariat. Undaunted by the absence of the "essential conditions" for the success of Marxism, Mao Zedong organized the peasantry, adopting the Marxist ideology in a form that over time moved increasingly closer to the realities of Chinese society and culture, and away from Marxist principles.

For example, Mao's customized version of dialectical materialism rejected the absolute determinism of economic principle, and instead asserted an interdependence between economic conditions and the cultural superstructure. The theoretical pretentions of Marxism gave way to localizing historicist and particularist sensibilities familiar in our discussion of Confucianism. Further, by selectively promoting those elements of Marxism that condemned the disharmonious effects of competition and private property, he actually increased the weight of basic Confucian values. And, however much the nuclear family was affected by Marxian ideas, the family as a model of the larger society, and the paternalistic character of rule which follows from this model, remained intact.

There is little evidence to suggest that contemporary China has abandoned any significant elements of its Confucian orthodoxy. The leadership of contemporary China maintains many of the same characteristics that have dominated Chinese government since the Han dynasty—namely, the nation understood as a family, the filial respect for the ruler as father, and the consequent sense of rule as a *personal* exercise.[12]

With respect to the personal character of rule, it continues to be the case in China that to object to the policies that articulate the existing order is in fact to condemn the ruler's person. Good rulers promulgate good policies. As John Fairbank observes:

> Here the American observer is again baffled by a Chinese tradition that equates undesirable policy with bad morals. . . . Once this tradition became established, one could not make the Western distinction between policy and morality. On the contrary, a policy is part of an official's conduct. If his policy becomes disesteemed, then his moral character is similarly impugned. . . . One result of this concept is that it is impossible to have a 'loyal opposition,' because a person who is opposed to one's policies is ipso facto opposed to one's character and one's self.[13]

Fairbank goes on to register the continuity that this relationship between policy and morality has with Confucian China:

> In Mao's China political deviance had been a treasonous crime far more serious than theft or homicide. It was not possible to separate policy from patriotism and tolerate a loyal opposition. Today the old Confucian tenets seem embedded in the CCP system: that one rules by virtue of wisdom and rectitude; that theory and practice are a unity,

policies a form of conduct manifesting one's character, and attacks on policy therefore attacks on the ruling power.[14]

We can add to Fairbank's insights the unabated concern over official corruption as the most pernicious contamination of government, echoing as it does the pervasive Confucian worry over the dissembling "village worthy" as "excellence (*de* 德) under false pretenses."[15]

In China, the "crisis of Marxism" can only lead to an accentuation of those Confucian values that have in fact served to define Chinese society throughout the so-called socialist period.

# 3. Law, Constitution, and Community

In China, social order has been construed as a harmony achieved through personal participation in a ritually constituted community. Thus the ideal of social order could not be realized by following an objective set of laws or customs. Appeal to law, far from being respected as a legitimate resource for adjudicating social conflicts, has been seen as an admission of communal failure.

The emphasis upon social harmony achieved through personalized ritualized roles and relationships dramatically distinguishes the Chinese *ritual community* from the Western *society of laws*. Perhaps the most significant contrast between ritually shaped order and the more rule-based order is the personal cultivation of a sense of shame, and the self-rectification of the community that ensues from it. Confucius, in comparing these two alternative models of communal order,[16] claimed that, because of the self-attuning harmony within the Chinese community itself, "the Yi and Di barbarian tribes with their rulers are not as viable as the various Chinese states without them."[17]

No one doubts that a modernizing China will find it necessary to continue to institute the "rule of law" in certain areas of its society. Commerce with the West has forced the Chinese to accede to the importance of formally contractual relations. This factor alone has led to an enormous increase in the number of lawyers in China. As always, the question is how one might secure the dominance of moral suasion as the primary means of securing harmonious community life.

Unfortunately, China cannot simply import the Western interpretation of the "rule of law" without placing a tremendous strain upon the fragile balance of the dynamics of law and morality in Chinese society. Some sensitivity to the alternative histories of the two cultures is necessary if China is to benefit from the importation of Western-style legal mechanisms.

In Anglo-European cultures, the rule of law developed within societies already characterized essentially as collections of individuals. Conceived as a defense against the exercise of despotic power, the rule of law quite rapidly developed in the direction of the protection of individual human rights associated with the limitation of governmental powers. The essential elements currently associated with the rule of law are constitutional guarantees for civil liberties (due process, equal protection), guarantees of the orderly transition of power through fair elections, and the separation of governmental powers. Together these comprise the fundamentals of a contractual relationship between rulers and citizens that prevents the latter from suffering abuses by the former.

The rule of law developed *pari passu* with the rights-based liberal ideology. As we have noted, liberalism envisions the state as a neutral framework within which citizens may pursue their individual conceptions of the good life with a minimum of state interference. Such a framework is required, so the liberal argues, because of the pluralism of modern societies in which agreements on the meaning of "the good life" cannot be expected. With the development of the modern conception of the state, the rule of law is deemed essential because unchecked power always threatens to become despotic. Also, even in the best governed society, pluralism requires that governments remain neutral with respect to the promotion of goods in common. Laws such as those guaranteeing the separation of Church and State are deemed essential to protect citizens against the state (as well as the minority against the majority).

China's rather different historical development precludes easy translation of the rule of law into a Confucian context. China advertises neither an adversarial relationship between rulers and citizens nor a plurality of individual conceptions of the good life. The principal preconditions of the distinctive understanding of the rule of law in the West were not present in China. In China, law (*fa* 法) developed as a supplement to ritual action (*li* 禮) aimed primarily as the stipulation of administrative duties. Law developed alongside the development of the complex bureaucratic structure that served as the primary means of stabilizing Chinese society from the Han dynasty to the beginning of the twentieth century. With respect to what we in the West would term civil and criminal law, these increased in number and application in periods in Chinese history when the ritual actions lost some of their efficacy as a binding force. Moreover, such laws were for the protection not of the citizen but the rulers—and the "social order" they were enjoined to maintain. The relative absence of a concern for due process removes any doubt that the origin of appeals to *fa* in both traditional and modern Chinese societies has little in common with the Western appeal to the rule of law.[18]

In China, the preference for the rule of the virtuous man over impersonal law establishes an enormous chasm between Western and Chinese political sensibilities. Given their deep and abiding suspicions of governmental power, Westerners cannot think of the "rule of man" as anything other than an invitation to despotism. But to give that notion its best argument one has only to reflect upon the different origins and functions of law in Chinese society. In the West, law originates as a response to despotic power. The rule of law functions to protect the individual citizen against the state, and against the tyranny of the majority. In Confucian China, law develops to articulate administrative duties and to overcome the deficiencies of ritual in maintaining social stability. "The evolution of law in China may be described as a *devolution* of ritual (*li*) into law (*fa*) and of law into punishment (*xing*)."[19]

A principal implication of the contrasting roles of law is that the unthinking importation of Western legal mechanisms into contemporary China may occasion significant disruption in the sense of social obligations that bind the community. In particular, the Western contractual understanding of law—interpreted by appeal to the model of social contract or of commercial contracts—has traditionally made little sense to the Chinese.

In general, law is positively valued in the West because of its association with the protection of rights. In Confucian China, law (in any sense other than administrative rules) is denigrated as a sign of the failure of ritual to achieve social harmony—essentially a *moral* failure.

We have been rehearsing some of the more important tensions between elements of the modernist impulse and the traditional character of Chinese society. In so doing, we have stressed the implications of a liberal democratic vision grounded in individual rights and freedoms. We shall continue that emphasis with a brief discussion of the manner in which constitutional government, a strong implication of a liberal democratic society, has translated into the Chinese context. In so doing we will be characterizing contemporary Chinese constitutional experience, and the documents that purport to define it, as an extension of a traditional ritually constituted community.

Andrew Nathan, whose work on the Chinese constitution figures prominently in our analysis, observes that a comparison of the American and Chinese constitutions reveals the "challenging combination of broad rhetorical similarities with deep differences in values and practices."[20] If these deep differences discernable in the constitutions can be traced to the contrast between a Chinese dependency upon ritual practice and a Western reliance upon legal contract, we should be permitted to suggest that the Chinese are still in some important measure looking to ritualized community to do the work reserved in our society for the norms and sanctions guaranteeing human rights.

A first indication that "constitution" means something decidedly different in the Chinese context is the fact that, since the turn of the last century, China has promulgated nothing short of twelve official constitutions and numerous constitutional drafts of one kind or another.[21] Since in the Chinese tradition, neither "human nature" nor the social order it defines is static, constitutions must remain open and be adaptable documents. In addition, we must hope that the changing economic and political structures of a modernizing China may be accommodated by a suitably flexible attitude toward constitutional change.

Chinese constitutions not only define a presently existing sociopolitical order, but also offer blueprints for further achieve-

ments.[22] Like ritual practice, they do not merely codify existing practices but suggest novel configurations and concrete refinements. Any
constitution can thus be regarded as only the most recent manifesto of
party policies and aspirations. Chinese constitutions function like
American "party platforms."

In China's ritual community, constitutional guarantees do not, as in
the American case, fix a boundary on the enactment of laws ("No law
shall be enacted that . . . "). Rather, the changing social order requires
that law and party policy have a free hand in articulating the changing
rights and duties of the community.

The Chinese constitution is more a social than a political document.
Its primary function is to promote social harmony. Jerome Cohen in his
discussion of the 1978 PRC constitution, asserts that in China a constitution hardly conforms to what we mean by the term. It is "a formalization
of existing power configuration rather than an authentic institutional
framework for adjusting political forces that compete for power."[23]

While the American constitution is a source for the establishment of
laws, the Chinese constitution primarily formalizes status, privilege, and
obligation on the assumption of coterminous interests among persons
and community. There is no assumption that strengthening the authority of the community weakens the options of the particular persons that
constitute it.

Because the constitution is primarily a compact of cooperation for-
mulated on a premise of trust between person and community rather
than a contract between potential adversaries, there are no independent provisions for the formal enforcement of claims against the state.
The assumption is that order will be effected and guaranteed by informal pressures that are more immediate to the circumstances. As a last
resort, the constitution does provide for appeal to state organs, but like
appeal to law in traditional China, this is a no-win course of action. Resort to legal appeal is, by Chinese tradition, an admission of a failure to
maintain communal harmony.

A final characteristic of the Chinese constitution is that rights derive
solely from one's ongoing membership in society. While in our tradition the concept of the individual and his attendant rights serves to
ground the notion of his social and political relations, in the Chinese
context, humanity exists solely within the bounds of community. Rights

are socially derived proprieties rather than individual possessions. These proprieties are primarily articulated as social welfare entitlements rather than individual political rights.

Given that only *social* beings are *human* beings, it is conceivable in the Chinese case to disqualify oneself from rights considerations by withdrawing from community participation. This radically social definition of person is reflected in the inseparability of rights and duties in Chinese constitutions. In these documents, even a positive right such as the right to education is both a personal right and a social duty.

One of our greatest difficulties in appreciating ritual activity is the recognition that we have insufficient analogies within our contemporary Western cultures to make legitimate comparisons. In an individualistic society, rituals are seldom seen as fundamental to self-realization but are regarded with some real impatience as someone else's formal demands that we must reluctantly observe. From the vantage point of the informalities of American society, it is difficult indeed to understand the power of ritual as a strategy for constituting community.

A second problem in appreciating the Chinese version of the "communicating community" is the extent to which informal mechanisms such as "shame" do the work of enforcement. The expression "no rights without remedy" is usually understood to mean that rights must be enforced by appeal to judicial means. In a ritual community, it is a developed sense of shame that serves as the primary guardian of entitlements and dignity. Law is perceived as a secondary, usually only temporarily effective, means of securing order.

Thirdly, a "Chinese democracy" constructed in Confucian terms might be "government of the people" and "government for the people," but it is not yet perceived as government "by the people." But even on the legal front there is some evidence that China is moving formally in the direction of government by the people. The recent institution of village elections throughout the greater part of Han China has been promoted as a first step in the full-scale transition to nation-wide elections. Given the decidedly rural character of the Chinese population, it is important that elections expected to be reasonably democratic begin at this level. In the best of circumstances, control over one's local community is far more beneficial to the individual than having a say in what goes on at the national level.

In addition to this move toward Chinese self-governance, rituals serve as a conduit through which all members of a ritual community participate in governing themselves. To the extent that a ritual community aspires to be self-ordering, the governance derived from ritualized roles and relationships is internal to it. Again, an exaggerated confidence in the rule of law and an unrelenting suspicion of informal mechanisms for social order might make it difficult for us to appreciate this alternative Confucian model.

# Communal Sources of Human Rights

## 1. Rights or Rites?

Before assaying the Confucian approach to issues of "human rights," it will be helpful to highlight a typical liberal democratic interpretation of that perspective. Jack Donnelly has written broadly and intelligently on the issue of human rights in a comparative Asian/Western context. His particular slant makes of him a fair representative of the rights-based liberal perspective on this issue.[1]

Setting aside all cultural, historical, and ethnographic differences, Donnelly affirms an unconditional, universalistic, and in the strict sense, *transcendent* claim for human rights.

> To claim that there are human rights is to claim that all human beings, simply because they are human, have rights in this sense. Such rights are universal, held by all human beings. They are equal: One is or is not human, and thus has or does not have (the same) human rights, equally. And they are inalienable: One can no more lose these rights than one can stop being a human being.[2]

Donnelly allows that this liberal conception of rights emerges out of the specific economic and political conditions of seventeenth-century Europe. He claims, nonetheless, that it could have begun its journey in Asia just as well.[3]

Donnelly is aware that the concepts of rights defined as existing prior to and independent of social obligations is anathema to many of the Asian cultures that have chosen to define the human being as irreducibly social. From the Asian perspective: "'Western' rights and their exercise often conflict with traditional duty-based values and practices and appear wildly, even destructively, individualistic."[4] Donnelly considers alternatives to his position presented from an Asian perspective and disqualifies them, one and all, because they do not satisfy the stipulated conditions that he takes to be essential to any plausible conception of rights—namely, that they must be individual, innate, inviolate, equal, and so on.

For Donnelly, the Western understanding of rights is not only universal; it is the only game in town. He says:

> I am skeptical of projects for an Asian third way. . . . To compare exist-
> ing Western practices with a vague, never-yet-implemented ideal is un-
> fair and unilluminating—as is underscored by the deviation between
> Western ideals and practice on which so much Asian criticism is based.[5]

Donnelly is allowing that Western human rights practices are of limited success. Yet he dismisses the possibility of a compromise position informed by the specificities of non-Western culture that might serve as a means of reformulating and improving upon our own Western theory and practices. He further assumes the substantial difference between us and what we call "other cultures" is reducible to the difference between modern and premodern practices:

> A different form of political naivete can be seen in the assumption of
> the continuing relevance of traditional practices in modern conditions.
> . . . I am especially skeptical of such claims because most of the argu-
> ments being made about Asian differences could have been made
> equally well in eighteenth-century Europe.[6]

Despite the significant participation of Non-Governmental Organizations (NGOs) in the sentiments expressed about cultural differences, stages of economic development, priorities to be accorded individual, economic, social and cultural rights, and so on,[7] Donnelly assumes resistance to Western notions of human rights is largely the voice of oriental despots bent on rationalizing totalitarian oppression.[8] In short, Donnelly suggests that there is only one plausible conception of human rights, and that "We've got it, and they don't." Disagreement with this position is dismissed as the self-justification and perpetuation of totalitarian regimes.

Like most defenders of rights-based liberalism, Donnelly ignores the negative consequences of a belief in universal human rights. In this regard, R. J. Vincent has warned against "the tendency to call our rights natural rights or human rights which others should also benefit from or conform to, when they have their own pattern of preferences in this regard (and no doubt their own tendency to universalize them)."⁹

From a Chinese perspective, the smugness of arguments such as Donnelly's recalls the infamous Rites Controversy in China, finally resolved in the eighteenth century. Against the best advice of their own "accommodationist" colleagues, the Jesuits on taking Christianity to China, ultimately insisted upon the universality and exclusivity of their religion. The decision that observing rites in honor of the ancestors (so-called "ancestor worship") was antithetical to the doctrines of the One True Church effectively meant that accepting Christianity would require the Chinese to give up their cultural identity.

From Rome's point of view, the universality of the Judeo-Christian God means that Rome's religion is everyone's, and for the Chinese to forsake this religion is to forsake religion altogether. Some four centuries later, unpersuaded by an unrelenting program of Christian proselytizing, accompanied by much money and more good intentions, a meager fraction of China's population has committed to this decidedly foreign religion.

With so little success in foisting universalistic religion on China, and so ample proof of China's resistance to universal pretenses, we might want to think of a different strategy for achieving a sincere commitment of China's government and people to greater protections for first-generation human rights. That strategy at the very least requires that we understand the manner in which "rites" serve the function of promoting "rights" in a Chinese context.

Ritual practice is present in all cultures, but its prominence as an apparatus for ordering society and its dominance over formal legal institutions gives ritual activity a unique role in defining social order in China. The *History of the Han*'s "Treatise on Ritual and Music," describes the dynamics of ritual as the center, the medium through which the cultural tradition is inherited, revised, and transmitted.

> To realize the real meaning of ritual and music is to be able to create; to understand the culture which inheres in ritual and music is to be able to carry on the tradition. One who creates is called sagacious; one who carries on the tradition is called enlightened.¹⁰

Ritually defined place and role has some force in staking out the privileges and obligations of a person in community. By knitting one into a pattern of relationships, ritual serves to mitigate the extent to which any vested authority can proclaim its decisions and implement its will over against others.

The community constituted by ritual relations involves a gathering around a central authority. This notion of centripetal center is made explicit in the language that defines community, both classical and modern. The term for "society," *shehui* 社會, taken literally conjures forth the image of "a deferential assembly gathering around the sacred pole erected in the center of the community." Nishijima Sadao tells us:

> Such community life, based on the hamlet, had its religious center in the altar (*she* [社]) where the local deity was enshrined. In the same way there was an altar for the state community (*kuo-she* [*guoshe* 國社]), and each county and district also had its own altar. The religious festivals which took place at the hamlet altar (*li-she* [里社]), at which meat was distributed to the participants, helped to strengthen the community spirit.[11]

Family, as the Chinese model of order, is an instance of the graduated, centripetal harmony.

The contemporary sociologist, Ambrose King, argues persuasively that in the Chinese world, all relationships are familial:

> Among the five cardinal relations, three belong to the kinship realm. The remaining two, though not family relationships, are conceived in terms of the family. The relationship between the ruler and the ruled is conceived of in terms of father (*chun-fu* [*junfu* 君父]) and son (*tzu-min* [*zimin* 子民]), and the relationship between friend and friend is stated in terms of elder brother (*wu-hsiung* [*wuxiong* 吾兄]) and younger brother (*wu-ti* [*wudi* 吾弟]).[12]

The family as the "in-group," is determinate and focused at the center, but becomes increasingly vague as it stretches out both diachronically in the direction of one's lineage, and synchronically as a society full of uncles and aunties.

Conveniently, this sense of relatedness is embedded in a cluster of cognate characters: It is articulated in terms of "relationships (*lun* 倫)," a ritual "wheel (*lun* 輪)" of social relations that "ripple out (*lun* 淪)"

through patterns of "discourse (*lun* 論)" to define the person as a network of roles. For China to abandon its traditional model of ritually constituted person and society and embrace a liberal democratic vision would take nothing less than a revolution in Chinese ways of thinking and living.

Most certainly, the Confucian model of ritual relatedness lacks several prerequisites for the realization of a first-generation rights-based social order. There is, for example, no belief in a discrete individual, no sense of strict identity as the basis for social equality, and no celebration of human autonomy. Small wonder that theories of human rights influenced by the Confucian sensibility should be found unsatisfactory by proponents of rights-based liberalism. Having said that, however, it is equally true that communitarian understandings of the sort represented by John Dewey would fall under the same strictures.

We might recall that Dewey refused to entertain the idea that the individual has any identity apart from the society to which she belongs.

> The idea of a natural individual in his isolation possessed of full-fledged wants, of energies to be expended according to his own volition, and of a ready-made faculty of foresight and prudent calculation, is as much a fiction in psychology as the doctrine of the individual in possession of antecedent political rights is one in politics."[13]

It is the persistence of that fiction in the minds of rights-based liberals that prevents their recognition of the value of rites-based Confucianism as a model of social order.

# 2. China on Human Rights in America

The subject of "human rights" is certainly one of the most controversial of the topics addressed in Chinese/Western dialogues. At present, the liberal democratic, rights-based, ideology of Western democracies confronts the communitarian discourse of the Chinese, and the result has been, until recently, an almost complete breakdown of communication.

Before discussing the commonalties of Confucianism and pragmatism on the subject of human rights, it will be of some benefit to see how the Chinese/Western discussions of this topic are presently shaped. Most Westerners would be shocked to discover how unimpressed are many Chinese concerning the vaunted achievements of Western societies, particularly America, in protecting human rights. This is not only the opinion of the Chinese government, but of many of the best educated of the Chinese people as well: They have just about as negative an opinion of us as do we of them. The reason for this has a great deal to do with what the Chinese see as the untoward consequences of our individualistic form of social organization.

One way of assaying the attitude of the Chinese government toward America is by looking at a truly remarkable document entitled "Human Rights in America," published in March of 1996 in Beijing.[14] That the Chinese government should sponsor research into the question of human rights in America might seem surprising, for how could China not but be extremely embarrassed by the contrast between the Chinese and American record on human rights?

The striking fact is that, employing U.S. Justice Department statistics, this publication manages to produce a rather frightening picture of American society with regard to the very issue upon which the U.S. government is given to preach to the Chinese on an almost daily basis. This picture, be it noted, is not a novel one from the Chinese perspective. Conversations with Chinese citizens from all walks of life would likely persuade one that the attitude expressed in this document is shared by many of the general public. A summary of the claims included in "Human Rights in America" will indicate straight away why the American government's attempts to engage the Chinese on the issue of human rights have had so little success.

In providing this summary, we are certainly not endorsing the Chinese claims about their own rights record. We only mean to argue that the picture the Chinese have of the United States concerning violent crime, imprisonment, voting patterns, narcotics abuse, and so on, is of a country in which few Chinese would wish to live—at least outside of the various "Chinatowns."

Among twenty-four specific indictments against the U.S., the report on "Human Rights in America" contains the following notable claims:

Rapes and other violent crimes against women are eighteen times (per capita) greater in the U.S. than in China. In spite of the continued coverage in the Western press about the numbers of individuals imprisoned in China, the per capita rate of imprisonment in the U.S. is five times that of China. In addition, recidivism rates in America have stayed above 40 percent in recent years, while the recidivism rate of China is about 8 percent. Chinese officials assert that their government has far greater concern for the rehabilitation of its criminals than does the U.S.

The report indicates that there are 220 million firearms in the U.S. and notes that this country is one of the few nations without strict gun control laws. There are approximately one million criminal shooting incidents a year in America. Thirty-three women a day are raped at gunpoint, and forty children are killed or wounded by firearms. The authors of this report note that "China does not regard the right to own a gun as a guarantee of human rights."

Again appealing to Justice Department figures, the report notes that in America approximately 20 million people use marijuana, six million use cocaine, and 500,000 use heroin. Further, 60 percent of prisoners in the U.S. are imprisoned for drug-related crimes. China, it is said, "has been effectively cracking down on crimes relating to drugs" and, in any case "the situation in China is far less serious than that in the U.S."

Even constitutional guarantees are said to be lacking in the United States. Whereas China's constitution grants rights of economic, social, and cultural self-actualization (so-called "second-generation" rights), the U.S. constitution does not guarantee rights of economic security and self-development. The report expresses chagrin that the U.S. constitution does not recognize as basic human rights the right to have enough to eat and to be provided shelter.

The report expresses particular concern with the fact that the rate of millionaires in the United States Congress is thirty times that of the country as a whole. Quoting statistics familiar to most Americans concerning the gap between the richest and poorest elements of U.S. society, the authors of the report conclude that the government is controlled by monetary interests, which suggests that the right to equality for U.S. citizens cannot be guaranteed.

Concerning the issue of democracy and democratization, the report claims, surprisingly, that voter turnout in China is far greater than in the U.S. As already noted, 360 million Chinese voted in recent village elections in China—with turnout averaging well over 80 percent. Though the Chinese do not as yet have elections in the cities, or for national leaders, democracy is said to be alive and well in the villages.

This is significant, if true. For, contrary to the urbanized United States, the vast majority of the population (over 70 percent) live in rural areas.

Talk concerning China's political conditions can only proceed responsibly if consistently negative observations are tempered by an awareness of a strangely provocative fact: Chinese apologists argue that there are some important senses in which their country is more democratic than the U.S.A.

With respect to issues of gender equity: In China, female deputies take up 21 percent of its current National Peoples' Congress, while the figure for America was (in 1992) 10 percent of the U.S. Congress.

Under the rather gruesome heading, "Experiments on Human Bodies," the report discusses the numbers of individuals unknowingly exposed to radiation and harmful chemicals in U.S. government experiments. In addition to experiments with its own population, notably in the military, the report states that "The United States conducted experiments upon human bodies in some African, Asian, and European countries, which brought about all kinds of 'strange illnesses.'" This section concludes with the rather questionable statement: "Such inhuman things have never happened in the Peoples' Republic of China."

Finally, a remarkable feature of this document is paragraph 23 entitled "The Encroachment on Human Rights of Other Countries." Here we find noted the fact that "the United States has launched some 70 wars and invasions against other countries in the 200 years since its founding, causing countless casualties among foreign civilians." For a country known for its isolationism, and its relative indisposition toward colonization and military conquest outside its immediate vicinity, this fact cannot but make a most negative impression on the Chinese people.

"Human Rights in America" concludes:

> Full enjoyment of human rights requires all countries in the world to devote painstaking efforts before they can reach this noble objective. Virtually no country in the world can style itself as being perfect in terms of human rights conditions. Due to limitations in historical and economic development, China has a long way to go before it realizes the goal of fully enjoying human rights. However, it is a basic fact that China has been doing much better than the U.S. in terms of equally

enjoying and universally guaranteeing basic human rights and freedoms. The U.S., on the other hand, should make greater efforts to improve its domestic human rights conditions. The U.S. is not qualified at all to feed its own arrogance and make indiscreet remarks or criticisms against China on this matter.

There is no doubt that this document serves primarily as government propaganda. However, it would be naive not to note that, however accurate the Chinese claims regarding their own rights record, the publication points to very real problems indigenous to any highly individualistic society. And, though there is more than enough evidence of Chinese failures with regard to human rights, replying to their criticisms of the U.S. with a series of counter-charges would not be productive. Detailing China's unconscionable treatment of minorities and political dissidents, for example, must proceed *pari passu* with recognition of our own severe shortcomings with respect to the protection of the rights of minorities and the poor. Otherwise, we shall only make things worse.

Few would be persuaded by "Human Rights in America" to believe that the people of China are somehow better off than are Americans. We are enjoined, however, to take seriously the fact there are plausible reasons why many Chinese, most of whom live at some distance from the arm of governmental power, might believe this to be the case.

Until recently, the Chinese government saw the topic of human rights as one raised by the imperialistic West to criticize, blame, and humiliate China. But since the Bangkok Declaration of 1993 which urges respect for cultural diversity in the formulation and implementation of human rights, China has done an about-face with regard to its willingness to engage in conversations on human rights. Over the past five years, the Chinese government has appeared to welcome such discussion as an opportunity to make a case for the importance of cultural difference. There has been an avalanche of Chinese language publications, official and otherwise, purporting to give voice to an internal perspective on the subject of human rights.[15]

There are at least two reasons for encouraging the continuation of the present conversation. The Chinese people will certainly benefit from their government's increased commitment to civil and political human rights. And if the American democracy is to be changed in any sustained relationship with China, an understanding and critical appreciation of the Chinese experience might make it a change for the better.

It would certainly be a stretch to expect that Americans will begin thinking of themselves as beneficiaries of a Confucian world view, but, at the very least, a growing appreciation of Confucian values might well animate increased interest in the indigenous communitarian alternatives to excessive individualism. The question that needs to be addressed is: What strategy should we embrace in order to maximize the chances of productive conversations on human rights?

Experience tells us that the only way to persuade is to be open to persuasion. Thus, it is necessary that we attempt to gain a better understanding of traditional Chinese values and, whenever possible, to justify human rights to China on terms that are consistent with her own traditional values. This is not to say that we should be at all reticent in forwarding our own views. Nor should we be surprised that China might wish to find fault with these views. And when we discover, as we have in our considerations of pragmatism, that we have our own home-grown critics who effectively side with the Chinese against the unqualified promotion of rights-based democracy, we should not assume an overly defensive stance.

## 3. Human Rights in a Communitarian Context

Proponents of rights-based liberalism presume that individuals are willing to accept the costs of violent crime and social and economic inequities as the price they pay for individual freedom and autonomy. In a communitarian society such as China, however, this preference for freedom over both personal safety and economic equity seems extreme. Thus, improvements in the protections of human rights in China, if they proceed along Chinese lines, will not likely lead to the development of a society that looks much like ours.

Liberal democratic theory contrasts with any understanding that would find the individual to be emergent from, and continually dependent upon, his or her relations with others. Thus, terms such as "freedom" and "autonomy" are central to liberal discourse, while the communitarian thinks in terms of "cooperation" and "responsibility." The voluntarist notion of the individual presumed by rights-based liberalism is essentially that of the *homo economicus* of eighteenth- and nineteenth-century economics. On this view, self-interest is presumed to dominate over sympathy or fellow feeling. But this understanding of the human being is a most controversial one, especially among communitarians who reject the idea of individuals defined in abstraction from their social relations.

The priority of right over good presumed in liberal democratic theory insures the predominance of individual autonomy over community-based values. Rights are accorded to individuals; goods tend more often to be considered goods-in-common. A fundamental problem with rights-based understandings of democracy is that they have few mechanisms that prevent individuals from becoming alienated from communities by virtue of the fact that the rights that are considered the fundamental signs and rewards of a just society are more often than not enjoyed in private.

The Chinese have traditionally held, consistent with the pragmatic view, that "rights" are granted by society. Further these rights are promoted through the sort of education meant to sensitize individuals to their importance both to individuals and to the overall harmony of society. Thus, in traditional China there is less of a tendency to stress the strictly legal enforcement of rights. In fact, reliance upon the application of law, far from being a means of realizing human dignity, is fundamentally dehumanizing since it leads to the impoverishment of mutual accommodation, and compromises the particular responsibilities of the community to define what would be appropriate conduct.

It is also important to realize that the Chinese communitarian understanding of rights tends to lead to the promotion of social *interests* over individual *rights*. The distinction between rights and interests mirrors the liberal distinction between the right and the good. The distinction provides some protection against collectivist arguments that would lead to the coercion of the individual in the name of some social good.

Rights are defined categorically in terms of moral principles. Interests, on the other hand, are associated with utility and social welfare. The moment social welfare is appealed to, the interests of the majority is sustained over those of the minority. Rights sometimes function to protect the individual against the majority. Appeal to interests tends not to allow for such protection. The goal in an interest-based society is not the protection of the individual, but the integration of individual interests with those of the group. This is a real roadblock to the development of a Confucian conception of human rights. By making social harmony the goal, Confucianism does not seem readily consistent with a vision of human rights that would protect the individual against the majority.

> Translating rights into the language of interests generally produces outcomes favoring state action and impinging upon individual protections. When one weighs the interests of the individual against the interest of the many individuals, the community, the state, the many usually win.[16]

In a communitarian society, when social harmony collapses the consequences are indeed most grave. For in the absence of legal mechanisms promoting social stability, and protecting the individual against the state and the majority, authoritarian actions by the government are all that remain. The present rapid transitions in China, therefore, are peculiarly troublesome since it seems inevitable that China will suffer from excess reliance upon actions of the central government. In spite of the imminence of this crisis, a careful and sympathetic look at the Chinese model might suggest that long-term solutions do not lie in the direction of increased legal resort to resolve conflicts, but to alternative nonlegal mechanisms.

The reason for our skepticism with regard to increased legal guarantees is that, as we shall discuss momentarily, the practical consequences of such guarantees are decidedly unimpressive if not grounded upon a significant degree of "social empathy"—the feeling that others are as deserving of legal protections as oneself. Honest reflection upon the status of minorities and the poor in liberal societies suggest that legal guarantees are hardly enough. Sadly, social empathy is inversely related to the implementation of legal mechanisms.

We must attend to rights-based liberals when they caution that considerations of social welfare over individual rights might lead to the submergence of the individual into the collective. This is, after all, a possibility. Precisely this has happened often enough in the course of the history of modern political associations. But it would be going too far to suggest that it is inevitable. And offering this caution in the absence of any acknowledgment of the defects of rights-based liberalism is a bit self-serving. The fact of the matter seems to be that, beyond the other profound philosophical differences that separate liberals and communitarians, there is at the heart of their disagreements a fundamental antinomy that has always resisted, and will continue to resist, any satisfactory resolution. It is the basic contrast of *individual absoluteness* and *individual relativity*.

The dominant strains of Confucianism suggest that almost all of the actual rights and duties recognized within a sociopolitical order are sustained by extralegal institutions and practices, and are enforced by social pressures. The Chinese government and, with few exceptions, the Chinese people as well, do not recognize anything like inalienable rights. In the series of constitutions promulgated during this century, citizens have been deemed to possess only those rights granted by China's various governing bodies.

It is assumed that rights, far from being an acultural and ahistorical condition of humanity, are earned through participation in and contribution to a specific cultural world. And as the cultural constitution of this society is reconfigured over time, an ongoing revision of those documents meant to codify human rights is required.

Even such fundamental rights as the right of free speech has not existed in China. And it is arguably the case that the absence of freedom of speech is not the consequence of a totalitarian government overriding the popular weal, but is due, rather, to an assumption integral to the centuries-long Confucian tradition. As we indicated in our discussion of pluralism of belief and action in chapter 8, the Chinese have never recognized a severe theory/practice distinction, and have thus always considered not only "saying" but "thinking," as well, as a kind of "doing." Thus the inhibition of free speech is not a modern invention of repressive Chinese communists, but a persistent feature of a Confucian society in which ideas have always been regarded as dispositions to act.

We in the West deplore censorship and believe free and open inquiry will result in consensus upon what is true about the needs and desires of the majority of human beings. But many forms of censorship are widely accepted by the members of a Confucian society. This is because it is felt that the government has a responsibility to prevent disrupting influences from damaging the social fabric.

Chinese society cannot be interpreted as a complex of distinct and autonomous individuals who hold sovereignty over their own interiority, and whose togetherness is most significantly regulated by codes of law. Nor is such a society an organization wherein personal autonomy is to be protected by natural rights.

One confronts dramatic evidence for the absence of this concept of autonomous individual in the Chinese context when attempting to translate the rhetoric of liberal democracy into the Chinese language. The English sentence, "Liberalism rests on individualism under the supremacy of law," would in the first instance have read to the Chinese something like this: "The doctrine of spontaneous license (*ziyouzhuyi* 自由主義) rests on the doctrine of self-centeredness (*gerenzhuyi* 個人主義) under the supremacy of administrative regulation (*falü* 法律)."[17]

Our tacit assumption in the West is that the meaning of persons requires an appeal to transcendent, or objective, truth. Without such truth guaranteeing the identity of the individual, we believe that notions of liberty, equality, and fraternity would not be secure. Under such conditions all human relations perforce become external and mechanistic.

Contemporary China remains, even under socialism, a ritually constituted society, without even a rhetorical appeal to the belief in objective principles associated with Reason or Natural Law. This does not mean, however, that the Chinese are left with a mechanical society of external relationships. The pervasive Confucian assumption that there is "a continuity between *tian* (heaven) and humankind" provides the sense of an ever-enlarging field of meaning and relationships within which one's particular actions may be focused. The order of contemporary Chinese society is defined by the sagely exemplars resident in its historical tradition. The members of the society are themselves possessed of their humanity neither as a gift from God nor by virtue of a common genetic inheritance, but as created by ritual enactment.

The real irony of the liberal approach to human rights is that even if it were wholly defensible, the exclusive rhetoric of its presentation precludes Chinese investment in its ideas and implications. After all, the consequences of Western universalism for China have thus far been hegemonic and humiliating. And given the communal commitments entailed by the indigenous Chinese notion of person, the values aspired to by liberal democracy are not perceived as an ideal. On the contrary, they are held to constitute a pathology.

Many Chinese historians have chronicled the atrocities of the Cultural Revolution. Reflecting on their graphic stories, the real possibility of personal betrayal made taking other people, even family members, into one's confidence, imprudent and sometimes dangerous. At Peking University alone, over seventy professors and staff perished during this ten-year ordeal. This decade of orchestrated national insanity forced Chinese persons into the mold of self-sufficient, independent individuals. Within this Chinese experience, individuality, albeit in a skewed and aberrant form, was not a worthy ideal. Rather, it was the consequence of repression. Liberation from this social malaise came with the possibility of giving up the privation of privacy, to once again live shared, interdependent, and richly communal lives.

# 4. A New Discourse

One of the saddest features of contemporary debates on human rights is the amount of energy expended in trying to certify the precise status and/or content of rights. There are some universalist thinkers who seem determined not to rest until everyone agrees that rights are inscribed in Nature by the Hand of God. The more modest rights-theorists like Jack Donnelly cited above argue that rights are deductions made from the reasonable requirements of associated living that should be persuasive to all thinking people. The task is the same in both cases: to ground the notion of human rights—both with regard to their status and their content—in objective, rationally defensible, principles. A second preoccupation of the rights-theorists is to create and argue over a complete catalog of rights to be consulted by all governments and their citizens, with less energy left to deal with the issue of how we are to insure opportunities for the exercise of these rights. In spite of the fact that most of us would allow that Martin Luther King, Jr.'s effectiveness as a champion of civil rights for African-Americans was a function of his appeal to values that are defining of us as Americans, there is little concern to justify human rights to China on its own terms.

So much of the liberal rhetoric concerning human rights amounts to little more than abstract theorizing about the need for every individual to be granted this or that right, with the communitarians' appeals to cultivating thick social practices being dismissed impatiently as pollyannic utopianism. Dewey recognized this theoretical bias as a central problem of human rights discussions. It was his view that the more attention we pay to the implementation of rights, and the less to abstract speculations concerning their status and content, the better off we would be. Wryly alluding to the French wag who observed that "the law prohibits both the rich and the poor from stealing bread," Dewey suggests that we see the problem of human rights as having "changed from that of seeking individual rights themselves to one of seeking the opportunity to exercise those rights."[18]

> Political theory has to be reoriented to inquire into ways in which the individual can get property, so that he can exercise the right of property ownership, instead of continuing to theorize in empty abstractions about the need for every man to be granted the right to own property.[19]

Dewey's distinctly communitarian concerns are most clearly expressed here. Rights-based liberalism must be less concerned with the implementation of rights than the communitarian. Worrying over the fact that the have-nots de facto have less *effective* rights than the haves would tempt one to believe with the communitarian that second-generation rights, such as economic welfare, may actually precede the implementation of equitable first-generation rights. And no self-respecting rights-based liberal wishes to be so tempted. It is for this reason that communitarians find the hard and fast distinction between rights and interests to be both naive and pernicious.

Pragmatic discourse on human rights has been updated recently by Richard Rorty in a manner that addresses precisely the issue that concerned Dewey.[20] While Rorty accepts the majority of liberal beliefs concerning the content of rights, he believes any attempt to write such rights large into the Transcendent Beyond is senseless and counter-productive. This renders his thinking both like, and distinctly unlike, the approach of John Dewey. For, on the one hand, while Rorty up-holds the individualistic emphases of liberal democracy, he is as ada-mant as Dewey himself that the grounds for justifying rights must be found in the historical community in which the rights are to be exercised. And while Rorty is distinctly non-Deweyan in his apprecia-tion of a firm disjunction between the public and the private, he is ex-ceedingly close to Dewey in the manner in which he stresses the impor-tance of the community as the context within which the humanity of an individual is either threatened or promoted.

Rorty and Dewey share a concern to reject any presumed metaphysi-cal foundations for human rights. Rorty claims that "as long as we think that there is an ahistorical truth, or rationality—we shall not be able to put foundationalism behind us."[21] Echoing Dewey, Rorty's basic point is that the issue is not how to devise a list of appropriate rights undergirded by transcendent appeals to objectivity and truth, but sim-ply whether acting in a certain way—treating one's fellows as equals, for example—is, on balance, a more productive manner of acting than rel-evant alternative modes of behavior. If so, one might well wish to sug-gest that this manner of behaving might be offered as a model for oth-ers to follow.

In offering one's own provincial mode of behavior as a model for others, one need not seek rational arguments for the superiority of one's own values. It is far more helpful if one seeks merely to point to the concrete consequences of behaving in the suggested manner—or of the failure so to behave.

Rorty's claim is simply that appeals to any objective standards—the Divine Mind, a Realm of Eternal Values, Universal Reason, and so on—are examples of provincial narratives, the sort of stories people tell when they are trying to secure their own values in a Larger Beyond.

Rorty prefers other narratives, "sentimental" ones, that appeal to our emotions rather than our understanding. As he says: "Sentimental education . . . gets people of different kinds sufficiently well-acquainted with one another that they are less tempted to think of those different from themselves as only quasi-human."[22]

Rorty clearly believes that spelling out human rights is of no value unless we are willing to "expand the reference of the terms 'our kind of people' or 'people like us'"[23] as broadly as possible. Otherwise, we will accord rights only to those who fit within rather restricted definitions of the truly human. Rorty's blunt suggestion that members of a particular culture are more likely than not to exclude individuals of other cultural sensibilities from full membership in the truly human community resonates in an interesting manner with Confucian understandings.

The Confucian notion of *ren* 仁 —the achievement of becoming human in the best sense—refers to those who participate effectively in the ritualized roles and relationships that characterize traditional norms of social living in Chinese society. Even in a Marxist influenced China, the understanding of human being is still implicitly culturally Confucian. Anyone outside that culture, therefore, has a rather questionable hold on the cultural honorific, "human being." This fact is a direct consequence of an historicist and culturalist reading of what it means to be human, a reading shared by both the Confucian and the pragmatist.

This consequence is strange only to the essentialist thinker who believes in ahistorical essences defining the truth of all matters, and who is further sure that such beliefs are a necessary guarantee of truth. But if you believe as the Confucian and the pragmatist that "nothing relevant to moral choice separates human beings from the animals except historically contingent facts of the world,"[24] then this conclusion is hardly odd.

Though not necessarily odd, the conclusion that human beings are "folks like us" is certainly challenging. Asian and Western cultures have lived in relative isolation from one another until the last century. There is more than enough evidence from both perspectives to suggest that neither Asians nor Westerners have accorded full humanity to the other. Historical reflection on the Opium Wars, the Treaty of Versailles, the use of Chinese labor in the building of railroads in nineteenth-century America, and probably most perniciously, the absolute silence that has prevailed on the Asian American's participation in the construction of American culture, cannot but suggest that Westerners have not accorded full humanity to the Chinese. This in spite of an Enlightenment rhetoric that accords equal status to all putatively belonging to the human race. And though there is perhaps less historical evidence that the Chinese have treated Westerners as nonhumans, the Tibetan people well understand what it means not to be considered human. The rhetoric of Confucian culture is clearly on the side of reckoning only those who are *ren* to be fully human beings.

We need to take this argument quite seriously. Few believers in the universality of human rights would deny the honorific "human being" to women, African-Americans, or Asians. And yet, by whatever measure we wish to employ, there are sound and persistent reasons for believing that the treatment of these groups by the dominant Western establishment suggests, at least, that they are somewhat *less* human. To think otherwise by appeal to a principle that offers the guarantee of humanity without successfully enjoining actions in support of that guarantee is a simple commission of the Good Principles Fallacy.

We have argued throughout this work that, in conversations between Chinese and Western cultures, we in the West need to recognize the value of pragmatic discourse in furthering mutual understanding. The continued insistence that we employ an individualist, rights-based ideology in our engagements with China, based upon the expectation that China will simply yield its traditional culture and "go Modern," is a risky strategy at best. And given the enormity of the consequences of miscalculation, we believe that it certainly behooves us to test other, more viable, alternatives.

We have suggested that pragmatism can provide a far more relevant discourse with which to engage China, and other Asian cultures. With respect to the meanings of the individual and the character of the culture of human rights, pragmatism and Confucianism can find productive common ground. We Westerners, and we Chinese, have a choice. We can continue along the present line of mutual recrimination and moral preachment, or we can take up the task of building a world community that presumes parity for both Asians and Westerners.

However, conversations between China and the West are likely to lead to a mutual extension of "we-consciousness" only to the extent that the communitarian interests of both sides are foregrounded. And only through a richer sense of "we" can there be the mutual recognition of full humanity. In many ways our entire essay may be understood as an attempt to encourage both Chinese and Westerners to include one another in the term "we." The languages of Confucianism and pragmatism overlap sufficiently to facilitate that task.

# NOTES

## Introduction

1. Institute for American Values (1998):3. See also the discussion of America's moral malaise in White (1998).
2. Havel (1995):82.
3. Graham (1986).
4. It is through such combinations of the academic and the practical, the thoughtful and the pragmatic—that the seeming inexorabilities of political and economic forces may be most effectively countered. One example of our more practical pursuits involves our participation, along with Asian and European political scientists, sociologists, economists and philosophers, in a multi-year project aimed at the development of a model constitution for South Korea informed by both democratic and Confucian values.
5. Our philosophical work may be seen as complementary to books and essays written from a political and socioeconomic perspective. See Bell (1995) and Friedman (1994) for two excellent examples of such works.

## Chapter 1. The 'Myth' of Han Identity

1. For discussions of the place of mythical narratives in classical Chinese thought, see Girardot (1983) and Allan (1991) and Porter (1996).
2. See Hall (1978) and (1982), and Hall and Ames (1995).
3. Major (1993):5–11.
4. See Li Zehou (1987):38–81. We have made the same argument in Hall and Ames (1995).
5. See Alitto (1979).

6. The titles of these scholars' works tell the story. See, for example, Joseph Levenson (1959), "The Suggestiveness of Vestiges: Confucianism and Monarchy at the Last" and Myron Cohen (1991), "Being Chinese: The Peripheralization of Traditional Identity." As Marjory Wolf (1994):253 observes: "The Confucian principles defining the propriety of hierarchical authority structures and the orderliness of the patriarchal family system seem anachronistic in this age of multinational corporations in Fujian, and young people from Shanghai acquiring Stanford MBAs."

7. Dirlik (1995):238. He goes on to identify the activity of reviving Confucianism as "a particularly egregious instance of collaboration between state and intellectual discourse" (p. 242).

8. See Hall and Ames (1995) for a comparison of dualistic and correlative thinking.

9. See Hall and Ames (1987):110–27; Ames and Rosemont (1998): Introduction.

10. Yü Ying-shih (1993):145.

11. See Lin Tongqi, Henry Rosemont, Jr., and Roger T. Ames (1995).

12. Yü Ying-shih (1994):161.

13. See Levenson (1968).

14. See Metzger (1977).

15. Chang Hao (1987).

16. Benjamin Schwartz follows Donald Munro in challenging the suitability of Joseph Needham's use of the organic metaphor, preferring the family metaphor—ancestor, mother, womb, and so on—that we find as the vocabulary of the early cosmologies, and in the specifically genealogical cosmogonies. See Munro (1985):passim, and Schwartz (1985):200, 416–18.

17. *Zhuangzi* 4/2/33 and *Analects* 15.29.

18. *Analects* 8.9.

# Chapter 2. Challenges to the Myth of the Han

1. See *Analects* 4.15 and 15.3.

2. See Dru Gladney (1994).

3. See Levathes (1994). Levathes tells the fascinating story of the rise and fall of the Chinese navy in great detail.

4. See Van Kemenade (1997):223–34.

5. See Zhou (1996) and Croll (1994).

6. Van Kamenade (1997):264.

7. The role of the peasants in China has interesting resonances with the Jeffersonian vision of democracy as grounded in a localized farming class. It is here that many of the ironies associated with the subject of the prospects of democracy in China find their focus.

8. Van Kamenade (1997):401.

9. Croll(1994):13.

10. An English translation of the entire script of "River Elegy" can be found in the periodical *Chinese Sociology and Anthropology* 24, no. 2 (Winter 1991–92). Two subsequent issues, 24, no. 4 (Summer 1992), and 25, no. 1(Fall 1992), contain commentaries and review articles on the documentary.

11. "River Elegy" (1991–92, 24:2):84.

12. "River Elegy" (1991–92, 24:2):89.

13. "River Elegy" (1991–92, 24:2):83.

# Chapter 3. 'Modernity' as a Western Invention

1. Friedman (1994):4, 5.

2. See Huntington(1987) and (1997).

3. The following argument is developed in a more elaborate form in the first chapter of Hall (1994).

4. Smith (1952): p. 52.

5. Berman (1984):118–19.

6. Baudelaire (1974):403.

7. Baudelaire (1974):403.

8. Works such as Nussbaum (1986) and Raphals (1992) continue a line of thought that begins in the nineteenth century with Friedrich Nietzsche and includes such studies as Dodds (1951), Snell (1960), and Adkins (1970), among others. These books, as various as they may be in their specific foci, constitute a significant counterdiscourse to the rationalistic interpretations of Greek culture exemplified by the classic works of John Burnet and F. M. Cornford.

# Chapter 4. Accommodating Modernity

1. Lin Tongqi, Rosemont, and Ames (1995).

2. Cohen (1984)

3. See Solomon (1993).

4. Bell (1996).

# Chapter 5. The Irrelevance of Rights-Based Liberalism

1. Ryan (1995):367.
2. Walzer (1995).
3. See Rawls (1971):*passim*, and (1993):173–211.
4. Rawls (1971):114.
5. Rosemont (1998:55) expresses profound skepticism concerning the value of the foundational view of human beings as free, autonomous individual on which the theories of "first-generation" political human rights are constructed. Not only is such a definition of human being inconsistent with the aspirations of second- and third-generation human rights (economic, social, cultural rights), it serves to underwrite and justify the maldistribution of the world's resources.
6. Rawls (1985) and (1993).

# Chapter 6. John Dewey's Democracy

1. The complete works of John Dewey are now available in a uniform edition of thirty-seven volumes: see bibliography.

Richard Rorty's work has helped to stimulate a revival of interest in John Dewey and other pragmatists. Rorty's principal contributions to pragmatism to date include *Philosophy and the Mirror of Nature* (1979), *Consequences of Pragmatism* (1982), *Contingency, Irony, Solidarity* (1989), and *Philosophical Papers*, vols. 1 and 2 (1991), and vol. 3 (1998).

A number of significant works on Dewey have been written in the last few years, of which we shall mention only the following: Alan Ryan, *John Dewey and the High Tide of American Liberalism* (1995); Steven Rockefeller, *John Dewey: Religious Faith and Democratic Humanism* (1991); Robert B. Westbrook, *John Dewey and American Democracy* (1991).

An increasing number of books have also been written on figures such as Emerson, James, Peirce, and Mead, as well—altogether signaling a rather dramatic renascence of American philosophy.

2. Unger (1987):85.

3. Dewey (1963):173. Dewey's historicism is not as strong as that of Richard Rorty who carries that position to its greatest extreme. The difference between Rorty and Dewey on this issue lies in the fact that Dewey's notion of "intelligent action" is rooted in a model of scientific activity, while Rorty tends to stress a narrative approach to the interpretation of history. Dewey's "naturalism" (what there is of it) thus disciplines his historicist tendencies. Having said that, it seems to be the case that Dewey's shift in his later works away from the notion

of "experience" and toward that of "culture," tended to move him increasingly away from any form of naturalism and toward an essentially historicist position.

4. Dewey (1962):81.
5. Dewey (1962):81.
6. Fukuyama (1992).
7. Dewey (1963):10.
8. Dewey (1948):210.
9. Dewey (1927):148.
10. Dewey (1958):22–23.
11. Dewey (1958):244.
12. Dewey (1958):335.
13. Dewey (1981–90), 1:274.
14. Richard Rorty has recently picked up this implication of Dewey's pragmatism in his version of the "New Pragmatism," thereby aligning it with the concerns of late twentieth-century philosophers. For a discussion of Rorty's relationship to Dewey on this point, see Hall (1994):80–89. Though the issue is too complex to enter into here, we believe Rorty's elaboration of Dewey's understanding of experience in terms of language is one of the greatest potential contributions to the dialogue between Confucianism and pragmatism.
15. Dewey (1962):53.
16. Dewey (1962):57.
17. Dewey (1963):42, 41.
18. Dewey (1927):210.
19. Quoted in Dewey (1927):59–60; see James (1950), vol. 1: 121.
20. Dewey (1927):161–62.
21. Dewey (1973):87.
22. Dewey (1973):188.
23. Dewey (1958):45.
24. Dewey (1963):173.
25. Dewey (1963):48.
26. See Whitehead (1933):vii.
27. Dewey (1962):75.

# Chapter 7. Confucianism and Pragmatism

1. For discussions of Dewey's influence upon Chinese culture, see the "Introduction" to Dewey (1973), Hu Shih (1962), and Berry (1960).

2. Three works of John Dewey that demonstrate strong commonalities with Confucian thought are: *Art as Experience, Individualism Old and New,* and *The Public and Its Problems.*

3. American interest in the New Confucianism is well represented by the following important works of Tu Wei-ming: *Humanity and Self-Cultivation: Essays in Confucian Thought* (1979); *Confucian Thought: Selfhood as Creative Transformation* (1985); *Centrality and Commonality: An Essay on Confucian Religiousness* (1989); *Way, Learning, and Politics: Essays on the Confucian Intellectual* (1993). See also Tu's entry on "Self-Cultivation in Chinese Philosophy" in *The Routledge Encyclopedia of Philosophy* (1998).

We have thus far contributed the following works to this movement: *Thinking Through Confucius* (1987), *Anticipating China: Thinking Through the Narratives of Chinese and Western Culture* (1995), and *Thinking from the Han: Self, Truth and Transcendence in Chinese and Western Culture* (1998).

4. Nothing we say in the following argument should be taken to mean that we would in any way undervalue the importance of Anglo-European philosophy. Descartes, Locke, Kant, Hume, and Hegel—and a host of other European thinkers, from Nietzsche and Heidegger to Bertrand Russell and Wittgenstein—are undeniably important for understanding the modern Western world. But to consider these thinkers more relevant to an understanding of the distinctly American experience, and the pragmatic philosophy which interprets that experience, than are Jonathan Edwards, Ralph Waldo Emerson, Charles Sanders Peirce, William James, John Dewey, or Richard Rorty, is to make a serious mistake. And yet, until quite recently, the indigenous strain of American thought, which had reached its most sophisticated level of interpretation with the reflections of John Dewey in the early part of the twentieth century, has been largely ignored by both European and American intellectuals. On the whole, British, German, and French philosophies have dominated American, as well as European, intellectual culture.

5. In his *One World, Ready or Not: The Manic Logic of Global Capitalism*, William Greider has provided a passionate discussion of, among other things, the relations of democractic institutions to presumed economic determinants. Though he does not, as we recall, mention any of the pragmatic thinkers, his argument is largely consistent with the vision of philosophical pragmatism.

6. Eckert (1993):95–130.

7. Cited in Eckert (1993):120. In contemporary American society, still rhetorically shaped by the notions of competition and "rugged individualism," shored up by the forms of social atomism related to Locke and Adam Smith, there is greater tolerance for the idea that individual effort can be based on "enlightened self-interest." While it is doubtless the case that there is a greater tension between Confucian values and the form of modern societies, it is none-

theless true, as we have insisted, that a real tension exists between pragmatic philosophy and mainstream modern American society, as well.

8. The New Pragmatism is a much broader movement in America than is often understood. We have stressed Deweyan interpretations, because they are both more representative of the broad range of New Pragmatic thinking in contemporary American society and more consistent with Confucian understandings. With respect to some of the elements of pragmatism we shall be discussing—its concern for social engagement and its communitarian interpretation of democracy—Rorty's thinking could be interpreted as somewhat at odds with the emphases of Dewey's thought. Having said this, however, we would contend that there is a broad continuity between Rorty's thinking and that of Dewey and classical pragmatism.

9. In addition to numerous conferences and workshops held in Asian and American venues, a significant amount of published material is devoted to this interchange. The writings of Tu Wei-ming mentioned above, as well as our own collaborative work, are examples of these efforts. In particular, the three-year international project on "Liberal, Social and Confucian Democracy" mentioned earlier offers significant possibilities for Confucian/Pragmatic dialogue.

10. See Rorty (1991), "The Priority of Democracy to Philosophy" and "On Ethnocentrism: A Reply to Clifford Geertz."

11. The term "we-consciousness" is Rorty's.

12. Dewey (1958):22–23.

13. *Analects* 20.3; Ames and Rosemont (1998).

14. *Analects* 7.1; Ames and Rosemont (1998).

15. *Analects* 7.34; Ames and Rosemont (1998).

16. Dewey (1962):53. We might note here that Rorty's definition of the self as "a centerless web of beliefs and desires," though less distinctively oriented to the communitarian assumptions of Deweyan thought, remains consistent with the mainstream pragmatists' view that the self is a complex of habits. Thus, in both pragmatism and Confucianism, it would be vain to ask what remains of the person after the removal of her roles as a wife, daughter, mother, citizen, and so on. We human beings are first and foremost constituted by our roles and relationships.

17. For a discussion of this aspect of Rorty's thinking see Hall (1994):230ff and *passim*.

18. See for example *Analects* 4.18, 18.1, and 19.10.

19. See Tu Wei-ming (1985):138.

20. Tu Wei-ming (1993). The titles of these essays are: "Towards a Third Epoch of Confucian Humanism" and "The Modern Chinese Intellectual Quest."

21. Institute for American Values (1998):4.

22. For his discussion of the "self" as a web of beliefs, see Rorty (1991), vol. 2:143–63, "Freud and Moral Reflection."

23. Dewey (1927):151.

24. Huntington (1993):307. We may note in passing that an equally unfair claim made more than half-seriously by many Asian scholars has it that "American culture" is *clearly* a contradiction in terms. For a broad-ranging set of discussions of Asian democratization, see Friedman (1994). This is a most valuable collection. We must say, however, that none of the essays in the volume takes seriously the contributions of Confucianism, or any other cultural factor for that matter, to democritization in Asia. The opposite opinion has been expressed by the President of South Korea, Kim Dae Jung (1994). Referring to the classical Confucian and Buddhist traditions, he says: "Clearly Asia has democratic philosophies as profound as those of the West."

25. Graham (1986):5.

26. We shall return to the discussion of hierarchy and equality in our discussion of the Chinese individual in chapter 9.

# Chapter 8. Confucian Democracy: A Contradiction in Terms?

1. Dewey (1963):10. He is not here referring to China.

2. Chesterton (1970):176.

3. Unger (1987):52–60.

4. Unger (1987):57.

5. Unger (1987):59.

6. Sandel (1996).

7. Dewey (1948):207.

8. Sandel (1996):343

9. Sandel (1996):66.

10. Friedman (1994):27.

11. Legge (1960), vol. 3:158.

12. *Mencius* 5A5.

13. *Analects* 15.39; Ames and Rosemont (1998).

14. *Analects* 12.13; Ames and Rosemont (1998).

15. *Analects* 2.1; Ames and Rosemont (1998).

16. *Analects* 2.3; Ames and Rosemont (1998).

17. Peerenboom (1998):234.

18. Peerenboom (1998):235.

19. See Schoenhals (1992).

20. Peerenboom (1998):239.

21. *Analects* 1.12; Ames and Rosemont (1998).

22. Hall and Ames (1998). We refer the reader to that chapter for a detailed discussion of the problem of the meanings of "truth" in the Chinese tradition.

23. Graham (1989):3.

24. For a fuller discussion of the contrast between Truth-Seekers and Way-Seekers, see Hall and Ames (1998): chapter 2, "The Way and the Truth."

25. Munro (1979):40.

26. See Edwards (1986):44. This position is widely held. Compare in the same volume Louis Henkin, "The Human Rights Idea in Contemporary China: A Comparative Perspective," p. 39, and Andrew J. Nathan, "Sources of Chinese Rights Thinking," pp. 141–47.

27. Kent (1993):30–31.

28. *Analects* 1.2; Ames and Rosemont (1998).

29. Dewey (1934):85.

30. Dewey (1934):70.

31. *Analects* 19.22; Ames and Rosemont (1998).

32. See Lee Seung-hwan (1996):367–79.

# Chapter 9. The Confucian Individual

1. Institute for American Values (1998):16.

2. One of the more interesting implications of the dominance of field notions in ancient Chinese culture is the surprising absence of anything like atomistic understandings of nature or of persons. For a discussion of the absence of any form of atomism in the Chinese tradition, see Jean-Paul Redding (1998): "Words for Atoms—Atoms for Words: Comparative Considerations on the Origin of Atomism in Ancient Greece and the Absence of Atomism in Ancient China."

3. *Mencius* 6a/15. Such a characterization is, of course, not unique to the Chinese. The classical Hebrews also believed the heart to be a seat of thought and action.

4. *Mencius* 7A/1.

5. *Analects* 2.4; Ames and Rosemont (1998).

6. *Zhuangzi* 33/13/2.

7. *Analects* 13.23, 2.14, and 15.22; Ames and Rosemont (1998).

8. *Analects* 4.24; Ames and Rosemont (1998).

9. *Analects* 6.20; Ames and Rosemont (1998).

10. Dewey (1927):90.

11. Dewey (1927):88.

12. *Analects* 4.16; Ames and Rosemont (1998).

13. Dewey (1962):53.

14. See for example *Analects* 5.2, 5.21, 8.13, 14.1, and 15.7.

15. *Analects* 2.21.

16. Dewey (1927):150–51.

17. We have considered the issue of sexual inequalities and gender construction in China at some length in Hall and Ames(1998):79–100. The following paragraphs summarize part of that discussion.

# Chapter 10.  The Role of Ritual in a Communicating Community

1. Dewey (1948):211.

2. Given the centrality of communication to the concept of ritual action, it is not surprising that much of the classical philosophical vocabulary indicates directly the centrality of communication: "to know, to realize, wisdom (*zhi* 知)," "exemplary person (*junzi* 君子)," "naming (*ming* 名)," "deference (*shu* 恕)," "sage (*shengren* 聖人)," and "harmony (*he* 和)," all include the "mouth (*kou* 口)" radical; "to make good on one's word (*xin* 信)" are persons standing by what they say; "integrity (*cheng* 誠)" is consummating what is said; "shame (*chi* 恥)" includes the "ear (*er* 耳)" radical, and so on.

3. Dewey (1927):183–84.

4. James (1975):107.

5. Dewey (1962):86.

6. See Gouldner (1969):104ff for a discussion of the development of the Greek notion of the self.

7. This examination system persisted in China for two thousand years. Although it was abolished in 1905, one could well argue that the Communist regime which came to power in 1949 reestablished the familiar imperial structure, complete with supreme personality, national ideology, and hierarchical bureaucracy.

8. Dewey (1927):15–16.

9. Dewey (1957):58.

10. Dewey (1957):60.

11. Dewey (1957):61.

12. See Fairbank (1987):83–94.

13. Fairbank (1987):92.

14. Fairbank (1987):209.
15. *Analects* 17.11; Ames and Rosemont (1998).
16. *Analects* 2.3.
17. *Analects* 3.5; Ames and Rosemont (1998).
18. See Cohen (1968):5–8 and *passim.*
19. Ching (1998)24.
20. Nathan (1986a):79.
21. Nathan (1986a):82–83.
22. See, for example, Articles 14 and 19 of the PRC 1982 constitution.
23. Cited in Edwards (1986):48.

# Chapter 11. Communal Sources of Human Rights

1. See Donnelly (1989) and (1993).

2. Jack Donnelly, "Human Rights and Asian Values" in Bauer and Bell (forthcoming), ms. p. 2.

3. Joanne Bauer (1996) points out Donnelly's inconsistency in claiming that human rights are at once universal and, at the same time, a response to specific conditions, such as the growth of capitalism and the market system, of premodern Europe.

4. Donnelly (1989):23.

5. Donnelly (1989):27.

6. Donnelly (forthcoming), ms. 27–28.

7. See Yash Ghai (1994).

8. Even what we might take to be repressive regimes might have their own legitimate concerns. As Donald Emmerson (1994):12 observes: "Not all East Asian elites who worry about disorder are self-serving cynics looking for excuses to maintain the status quo. . . . [T]he greater incidence in Southeast Asia of spectacularly multicultural societies where the ever-present risk of ethnic and religious violence leads such officials as Lee and Mahathir to question the capacity of Western liberal democracy to ensure social discipline and order."

9. R. J. Vincent (1986):17–18.

10. Ban Gu (1962:1029).

11. Nishijima Sadao (1986):552.

12. Ambrose King (1985):58.

13. Dewey (1927):102.

14. The report was summarized in an English language Beijing newspaper, the *China Daily* 11 March 1996.

15. The titles of this body of literature are revealing: Liu Shengping and Xia Yong (ed), *Human Rights and the World* (1996); Song Huichang, *On Contemporary Human Rights* (1993); Liu Nanlai (ed), *Developing Nations and Human Rights* (1994).

16. Peerenboom (1998):251–52.

17. This illustration is from John Fairbank (1983):739.

18. Dewey (1973):152–53.

19. Dewey (1973):152.

20. Rorty (1993).

21. Rorty (1993):122.

22. Rorty (1993):122–23.

23. Rorty (1993):123.

24. Rorty (1993):116.

# WORKS CITED

Adkins, A. W. H. (1970). *From the Many to the One.* Ithaca, N.Y.: Cornell University Press.

Alitto, Guy S. (1979). *The Last Confucian: Liang Shu-ming and the Chinese Dilemma of Modernity.* Berkeley: University of California Press.

Allan, Sarah (1991). *The Shape of the Turtle: Myth, Art, and Cosmos in Early China.* Albany: State University of New York Press.

Ames, Roger T. (1991). "Reflections on the Confucian Self: A Response to Fingarette." In *Rules, Rituals, and Responsibility: Essays Dedicated to Herbrt Fingarette,* edited by Mary I. Bockover. La Salle, Ill.: Open Court.

——(1994). "The Focus-Field Self in Classical Confucianism." In *Self as Person in Asian Theory and Practice,* edited by R. Ames with W. Dissanayake and T. Kasulis. Albany: State University of New York Press.

—— (1997). "Continuing the Conversation on Chinese Human Rights." *Ethics and International Affairs* 11:177–205.

Ames, Roger T., and Henry Rosemont, Jr. (1998). *The Analects of Confucius: A Philosophical Translation.* New York: Ballantine.

Ban Gu 班固 (1962). *Hanshu* 漢書. Peking: Zhonghua shuju.

Baudelaire, Charles (1974). *Selected Writings on Art and Artists.* New York: Penguin.

Bauer, Joanne R. (1996). *Human Rights Dialogue.* New York: Bulletin of the Carnegie Council on Ethics and International Affairs. Vol 3.

Bell, Daniel (1996). *The Cultural Contradictions of Capitalism.* New York: Basic Books.

Bell, Daniel A. et al., eds. (1995). *Towards Illiberal Democracy in Pacific Asia.* New York: St. Martin's Press.

Berman, Marshall (1984). *All That is Solid Melts into Air—The Experience of Modernity.* New York: Penguin.

Berry, Thomas (1960). "Dewey's Influence in China." In *John Dewey: His Thought and Influence,* edited by John Blewett. New York: Fordham University Press.

Chang Hao (1987). *Chinese Intellectuals in Crisis.* Berkeley: University of California Press.

Chesterton, G. K. (1970). "The Ethics of Elfland." In *G. K. Chesterton: A Selection from his Non-fictional Prose,* edited by W. H. Auden. London: Faber and Faber.

Ching, Julia (1998). "Human Rights: A Valid Chinese Concept?" In *Confucianism and Human Rights,* edited by Wm. Theodore deBary and Tu Wei-ming. New York: Columbia University Press.

Cohen, Jerome Alan (1968). *The Criminal Process in the Peoples Republic of China, 1949–63: An Introduction.* Cambridge: Harvard University Press.

Cohen, Myron (1991). "Being Chinese: The Peripheralization of Traditional Identity." *Daedalus* 120, no. 2 (Spring):113–34.

Cohen, Paul A. (1984). *Discovering History in China: American Historical Writing on the Recent Chinese Past.* New York: Columbia University Press.

Croll, Elisabeth (1994). *From Heaven to Earth: Images and Experiences of Development in China.* New York: Routledge.

Cua, A. S. (1985). *Ethical Argumentation: A Study in Hsun Tzu's Moral Epistemology.* Honolulu: University of Hawaii Press.

Dewey, John (1927). *The Public and Its Problems.* Athens, Ohio: Ohio University Press.

—— (1934). *A Common Faith.* New Haven, Conn.: Yale University Press.

—— (1948). *Reconstruction in Philosophy.* Boston: Beacon Press.

—— (1957). *Human Nature and Conduct.* New York: The Modern Library.

—— (1958). *Art as Experience.* New York: Capricorn Books.

—— (1962). *Individualism Old and New.* New York: Capricorn Books.

—— (1963). *Freedom and Culture.* New York: Capricon Books.

—— (1969–72). *Early Works, 1892–98.* 5 vols. Edited by Jo Ann Boydston. Carbondale, Ill.: Southern Illinois University Press.

—— (1973). *Lectures in China.* Translated and edited by Robert Clopton and Tsuin-chen Ou. Honolulu: University of Hawaii Press.

—— (1976–83). *Middle Works, 1899–1924.* 15 vols. Edited by Jo Ann Boydston. Carbondale, Ill.: Southern Illinois University Press.

———— (1981–90). *Late Works, 1899–1924.* 17 vols. Edited by Jo Ann Boydston. Carbondale, Ill.: Southern Illinois University Press.

———— (1996). *Democracy and Education.* New York: Free Press.

Dirlik, Arif (1995). "Confucius in the Borderlands: Global Capitalism and the Reinvention of Confucianism." *Boundary* 2 (Fall):229–73.

Dodds, E. R. (1951). *The Greeks and The Irrational.* Berkeley: University of California Press.

Donnelly, Jack (1989). *Universal Human Rights in Theory and Practice.* Ithaca: Cornell University Press.

———— (1993). *International Human Rights.* Boulder: Westview Press.

———— (forthcoming, 1999). "Human Rights and Asian Values: A Defense of Western Universalism." In *The East Asian Challenge for Human Rights*, edited by J. Bauer and D. Bell. Cambridge: Cambridge University Press.

Eckert, Carter (1993). "The South Korean Bourgeoisie: A Class in Search of Hegemony." In *State and Society in Contemporary Korea*, edited by Hagen Koo. Ithaca, N.Y.: Cornell University Press.

Edwards, R. Randle (1986). "Civil and Social Rights: Theory and Practice in Chinese Law Today." In *Human Rights in Contemporary China*, edited by R. Randle Edwards, Louis Henkin, and Andrew J. Nathan. New York: Columbia University Press.

Emmerson, Donald (1994). *Japan Programs Occasional Papers* No. 5. New York: Carnegie Council on Ethics and International Affairs.

Fairbank, John (1983). Review of Eugene Lubot's *Liberalism in an Illiberal Age. China Quarterly* 96 (December):734–40.

———— (1987). *China Watch.* Cambridge, Mass.: Harvard University Press.

Friedman, Edward, ed. (1994). *The Politics of Democratization—Generalizing Asian Experiences.* Boulder: Westview Press.

Fukuyama, Francis (1992). *The End of History and the Last Man.* New York: The Free Press.

Ghai, Yash (1994). "Human Rights and Governance: The Asia Debate." In *Occasional Paper Series* 4 (November) by the Asia Foundation's Center for Asian Pacific Affairs.

Giradot, N. J.(1983). *Myth and Meaning in Early Taoism.* Berkeley: University of California Press.

Gladney, Dru (1994). "Representing Nationality in China: Relational Aspects of Majority/Minority Identities." *Journal of Asian Studies* 53, no. 1:92–123.

Gouldner, Alvin (1969). *The Hellenic World: A Sociological Analysis.* New York: Harper and Row.

Graham, A. C. (1986). Review of B. Schwartz's *The World of Thought in Ancient China. Times Literary Supplement* (July 18).

——— (1989). *Disputers of the Tao.* La Salle, Ill.: Open Court.

Greider, William (1997). *One World, Ready or Not: The Manic Logic of Global Capitalism.* New York: Simon and Schuster.

Hall, David L. (1978). "Process and Anarchy—A Taoist Vision of Creativity." *Philosophy East and West* 28, no. 3:271–85.

——— (1982). *The Uncertain Phoenix.* New York: Fordham University Press.

——— (1994). *Richard Rorty: Prophet and Poet of the New Pragmatism.* Albany: State University of New York Press.

——— (1997). "Cultural Encounters Between Asia and America: The New Confucianism and the New Pragmatism." In *Proceedings of the 32nd International Seminar.* American Studies Association of Korea. pp. 13–31.

——— (1997). "Dewey, China, and the Democracy of the Dead." in *Justice and Democracy: Crosscultural Perspectives,* edited by Ron Bontekoe and Marietta Stepaniants. Honolulu: University of Hawai'i Press. pp. 275–91.

——— (1998). "Love at Second Sight: The Reengagement of Confucianism and Pragmatism." In *Parallax.* Winter:(forthcoming).

Hall, David L., and Roger T. Ames (1987). *Thinking Through Confucius.* Albany: State University of New York.

——— (1995). *Anticipating China: Thinking Through the Narratives of Chinese and Western Culture.* Albany: State University of New York Press.

——— (1998). *Thinking From the Han: Self, Truth, and Transcendence in Chinese and Western Culture.* Albany: State University of New York.

Havel, Vaclav (1995). "The Politics of Responsibility." *World Policy Journal* 12, no. 3 (Fall):81–85.

Hu Shih (1962). "John Dewey in China." *Philosophy and Culture East and West,* edited by Charles A. Moore. Honolulu: University of Hawaii Press.

Huntington, Samuel (1987). "The Goals of Development." In *Understanding Political Development,* edited by Myron Weiner and Samuel Huntington. Boston: Little, Brown & Co.

——— (1991). *The Third Wave: Democratization in the Late Twentieth Century.* Norman: University of Oklahoma Press.

——— (1997). *The Coming Clash of Civilizations and the Remaking of the New World Order.* New York: Simon and Schuster.

Institute for American Values (1998). *A Call for Civil Society*. New York: Institute for American Values.

James, William (1950). *Principles of Psychology*, Vol. 1. New York: Dover Publications.

——— (1975). *Pragmatism*. Cambridge, Mass.: Harvard University Press.

Kent, Ann (1993). *Between Freedom and Subsistence: China and Human Rights*. Hong Kong: Oxford University Press.

Kim Dae Jung (1994). "Is Culture Destiny?" *Foreign Affairs* (November/December):189–94.

King, Ambrose (1985). "The Individual and Group in Confucianism: A Relational Perspective." In *Individualism and Holism: Studies in Confucian and Taoist Values*, edited by Donald Munro. Ann Arbor: University of Michigan Press.

Lee, Seung-hwan (1996). "Liberal Rights or/and Confucian Virtues?" *Philosophy East and West* 46, no. 3 (July):367–79.

Legge, James, trans. (1960 repr.). *The Chinese Classics*. 5 vols. Hong Kong: University of Hong Kong.

Levathes, Louise (1994). *When China Ruled the Seas: The Treasure Fleet of the Dragon Throne, 1405–1433*. New York: Oxford University Press.

Levenson, Joseph (1959). "The Suggestiveness of Vestiges: Confucianism and Monarchy at the Last." In *Confucianism in Action*. Stanford: Stanford University Press.

——— (1968). *Confucian China and Its Modern Fate: A Trilogy*. Berkeley: University of California Press.

——— (1977). *Confucian China and its Modern Fate*. Berkeley: University of California Press.

Li, Victor H. (1978). *Law Without Lawyers*. Boulder: Westview Press.

Li, Zehou 李澤厚 (1987). "Qin-Han sixiang jianyi 秦漢思想簡議." In *Li Zehou zhexue meixue wenxuan* 李澤厚哲學美學文選. Taipei: Gufeng Publishers.

Lin Tongqi, Henry Rosemont, Jr., and Roger T. Ames (1995). "Chinese Philosophy: An Essay on 'The State-of-the-Art'." *Journal of Asian Studies* 54, no. 3 (August):727–58.

Liu Nanlai, ed. (1994). *Fazhanzhong guojia yu renquan* 發展中國家與人權 [Developing nations and human rights]. Chengdu: Sichuan renmin chubanshe.

Liu Shengping 劉升平 and Xia Yong 夏勇, eds. (1996). *Renquan yu shijie* 人權與世界 [Human rights and the world]. Peking: Renmin fayuan chubanshe.

Major, John S. (1993). *Heaven and Earth in Early Han Thought: Chapters Three, Four, and Five of the Huainanzi.* Albany: State University of New York Press.

McMullen, David (1987). "Bureaucrats and Cosmology: The Ritual Code of the T'ang Dynasty." In *Rituals of Royalty*, edited by David Cannadine and Simon Price. Cambridge: Cambridge University Press.

Metzger, Thomas (1977). *Escape from Predicament: Neo-Confucianism and China's Evolving Political Culture.* New York: Columbia University Press.

Munro, Donald J. (1979). "The Shape of Chinese Values in the Eye of an American Philosopher." In *The China Difference*, edited by Ross Terrill. New York: Harper and Row.

———— (1985). "The Family Network, the Stream of Water, and the Plant." In *Individualism and Holism: Studies in Confucian and Taoist Values.* Ann Arbor: University of Michigan Press.

Nathan, Andrew (1986a). "Political Rights in the Chinese Constitutions." In *Human Rights in Contemporary China*, edited by R. Randle Edwards, Louis Henkin, and Andrew J. Nathan. New York: Columbia University Press.

———— (1986b). "Sources of Chinese Rights Thinking." In *Human Rights in Contemporary China*, edited by R. Randle Edwards, Louis Henkin, and Andrew J. Nathan. New York: Columbia University Press.

Nishijima Sadao (1986). "The Economic and Social History of Former Han." In *The Cambridge History of China.* Vol. 1, *The Ch'in and Han Empires 221 B.C.– A.D. 220.* Cambridge: Cambridge University Press.

Nussbaum, Martha C. (1986). *The Fragility of Goodness: Luck and Ethics in Greek Tragedy and Philosophy.* Cambridge: Cambridge University Press.

Peerenboom, Randell P. (1998). "Confucian Harmony and Freedom of Thought: The Right to Think Versus Right Thinking." In *Confucianism and Human Rights*, edited by Wm. T. de Bary and Tu Wei-ming. New York: Columbia University Press.

Porter, Deborah Lynn (1996). *From Deluge to Discourse: Myth, History, and the Generation of Chinese Fiction.* Albany: State University of New York Press.

Raphals, Lisa (1992). *Knowing Words: Wisdom and Cunning in the Classical Traditions of China and Greece.* Ithaca, N.Y.: Cornell University Press.

Rawls, John (1971). *A Theory of Justice.* Cambridge: Harvard University Press.

———— (1985). "Justice as Fairness—Political, not Metaphysical." *Philosophy and Public Affairs* 14:223–51.

———— (1993). *Political Liberalism.* New York: Columbia University Press.

Redding, Jean-Paul (1998). "Words for Atoms—Atoms for Words: Comparative Considerations on the Origin of Atomism in Ancient Greece and the Absence of Atomism in Ancient China." Unpublished paper presented to the "Thinking Through Comparisons: Ancient Greece and China" conference at the University of Oregon Humanities Center, May 28–30, 1998.

"River Elegy" (1991–92). Translated in *Chinese Sociology and Anthropology* 24, no. 2 (Winter):3–90.

Rockefeller, Steven (1991). *John Dewey: Religious Faith and Democratic Humanism.* New York: Columbia University Press.

Rorty, Richard (1979). *Philosophy and the Mirror of Nature.* Princeton: Princeton University Press.

——— (1982). *Consequences of Pragmatism.* Minneapolis: University of Minnesota Press.

——— (1989). *Contingency, Irony, Solidarity.* Cambridge: Cambridge University Press.

——— (1991). *Philosophical Papers.* Vol. 1, *Objectivity, Relativism, and Truth*; Vol. 2, *Essays on Heidegger and Others.* Cambridge: Cambridge University Press.

——— (1993). "Human Rights, Rationality, and Sentimentality." In *On Human Rights: The Oxford Amnesty Lectures,* edited by Stephen Shute and Susan Hurley. New York: HarperCollins.

——— (1998). *Philosophical Papers.* Vol. 3, *Truth and Progress.* Cambridge: Cambridge University Press.

Rosemont, Henry, Jr. (1991). *A Chinese Mirror.* La Salle, Ill.: Open Court.

——— (1991). "Right-Bearing Individuals and Role-Bearing Persons." *Rules, Rituals, and Responsibility,* edited by Mary I. Bockover. La Salle, Ill.: Open Court.

——— (1998). "Human Rights: A Bill of Worries." In *Confucianism and Human Rights,* edited by Wm. T. de Bary and Tu Wei-ming. New York: Columbia University Press.

——— (1999). "Whose Rights? Which Democracy?" In *A Confucian Alternative.* Honolulu: University of Hawaii Press.

Ryan, Alan (1995). *John Dewey and the High Tide of American Liberalism.* New York: W. W. Norton.

Sandel, Michael (1982). *Liberalism and the Limits of Justice.* Cambridge, Mass.: Harvard University Press.

——— (1996). *Democracy's Discontent: America in Search of a Public Philosophy.* Cambridge, Mass.: Harvard University Press.

Schoenhals, Michael (1992). *Doing Things with Words.* Berkeley: Institute of East Asian Studies.

Schwartz, Benjamin I. (1985). *The World of Thought in Ancient China.* Cambridge: Harvard University Press.

Smith, Adam (1952). *An Inquiry into the Nature and Causes of the Wealth of Nations.* Vol. 39 of *Great Books of the Western World.* Chicago: Encyclopedia Britannica, Inc.

Snell, Bruno (1960). *The Discovery of the Mind: The Greek Origins of European Thought.* New York: Harper and Row.

Solomon, Robert (1993). *The Bully Culture: Enlightenment, Romanticism, and the Transcendental Pretense 1750–1850.* Lanham, Md.: Rowman and Littlefield.

Song Huichang 宋惠昌 (1993). Xiandai renquan lun 現代人權論 [On contemporary human rights]. Peking: Renmin chubanshe.

Tu Wei-ming (1979). *Humanity and Self-Cultivation: Essays in Confucian Thought.* Berkeley: Asian Humanities Press.

——— (1985). *Confucian Thought: Selfhood as Creative Transformation.* Albany: State University of New York Press.

——— (1989). *Centrality and Commonality: An Essay on Confucian Religiousness.* Albany: State University of New York Press.

——— (1993). *Way, Learning, and Politics: Essays on the Confucian Intellectual.* Albany: State University of New York Press.

——— (1998). "Self-cultivation in Chinese Philosophy." In *Routledge Encyclopedia of Philosophy.* London: Routledge.

Unger, Robert Mangabeira (1987). *Social Theory: Its Situation and Its Task.* Vol. 1 of *Politics: A Work in Constructive Social Theory.* New York: Cambridge University Press.

Van Kemenade, Willem (1997). *China, Hong Kong, Taiwan, Inc.* New York: Knopf.

Vincent, R. J. (1986). *Human Rights and International Relations.* Cambridge: Cambridge University Press.

Walzer, Michael (1995). "The Communitarian Critique of Liberalism." In *New Communitarian Thinking: Persons, Virtues, Institutions, and Communities,* edited by Amitai Etzioni. Charlottesville: University of Virginia Press.

Westbrook, Robert B. (1991). *John Dewey and American Democracy.* Ithaca, N.Y.: Cornell University Press.

White, Donald (1998). *The American Century—The Rise and Decline of the United States as a World Power.* New Haven, Conn.: Yale University Press.

Whitehead, A. N. (1933). *Adventures of Ideas.* New York: Macmillan.

Wolf, Marjory (1994). "Beyond the Patrilineal Self: Constructing Gender in China." In *Self as Person in Asian Theory and Practice,* edited by R. T. Ames, T. P. Kasulis, and W. Dissanayake. Albany: State University of New York Press.

Yü Ying-shih (1993). "The Radicalization of China in the Twentieth Century." *Daedalus* 122, no. 2 (Spring):125–50.

—— (1994). "Changing Conceptions of National History in Twentieth-Century China." In *Proceedings of Nobel Symposium* 78. Berlin: Walter de Gruyter.

Zhou, Kate (1996). *How the Farmers Changed China: Power of the People.* Boulder: Westview Press.

# INDEX

literal view of the self - 105 - 108
agrippa's 108

EC 203, 207

3: "big tan" =
averbreh